D0897185

106

108   110   112   116   120   122

126   128   130   132   134   136

138   140   142   144   146   148

150   152   154   156   162   166

168   170   172   176   178   180

182   184   186   188   190   192

194   196   198   200   202   204

206   208   212   214   216   218

BUTTERFLIES *of* ILLINOIS

A FIELD GUIDE

Michael R. Jeffords
Susan L. Post
James R. Wiker

Designed by
Danielle M. Ruffatto

All photos, unless otherwise attributed, were taken by
Michael R. Jeffords and Susan L. Post.

The specimens presented in this field guide are from the
Wiker collection, the Illinois Natural History Survey (A Division of the Prairie
Research Institute) and University of Illinois at Urbana-Champaign collection,
the Illinois State Museum collection, the Southern Illinois University collection,
the Todd Wiley collection, and the William Frey collection.

Published by the Illinois Natural History Survey
Distributed by the University of Illinois Press

Illinois Natural History Survey
Manual 14

Prairie Research Institute
William Shilts, Executive Director

Illinois Natural History Survey
Brian Anderson, Director
1816 South Oak Street
Champaign, Illinois 61820

Editors: Charles E. Warwick, Jeff M. Levengood, Terry Harrison, Lisa A. Sheppard, and Danielle M. Ruffatto

ISBN 978-0-252-08446-1 (paperback)
ISBN 978-0-252-05147-0 (e-book)

P0785419-2.5M-06-2014

Library of Congress Control Number: 2014939778

Citation: Jeffords, M.R., S.L. Post, and J.R. Wiker. 2014. Butterflies of Illinois: A Field Guide. Manual 14. Illinois Natural History Survey, Champaign. 440 pp.

To Dr. James Sternburg (1919–2014),
a nearly lifelong mentor.
Hats off to you, Jim,
as a limitless source
of photographic
and entomological
knowledge.

- M. R. Jeffords

To John Bouseman (1936–2006)
John was the first person to hire me
at the Illinois Natural History Survey.
My job was to re-naphthalene the
Coleoptera (beetle) collection. (For at
least 10 years I did not need mothballs
for my sweaters!) John became my idol.
Not only did he introduce me to the INHS
library for my field botany class, where I
found a treasure trove of research material,
but he also seemed to know where every
organism was located in Illinois and something
about it. That became my goal—I am still
working on it, but thank you John for
sharing and seeing the potential.

- S. L. Post

To Roderick R. Irwin (1930–1994)
In the spirit of studying
the wonders of nature,
the quest for knowledge,
and the joy of following the
historical paths and words
of those before us,
I dedicate this book to
my colleague and friend.

- J. R. Wiker

ACKNOWLEDGMENTS

MRJ and SLP: As we have explored and roamed the state of Illinois for its lepidopteran treasures, many people have made the task easier. These include: Molie Oliver and Jim Waycuilis at the Cache River State Natural Area; Terry Esker, Karan Greuel, and Patty Gillespie at Ballard Nature Center and south-central Illinois; Liz Jones and Dave Shaffer, Cypress Creek National Wildlife Refuge and Frog Holler, respectively; Richard and Susan Day and their inspiring butterfly garden/refuge; Terry Moyer at Richardson Wildlife Center; Randy Nyboer in northwestern Illinois; Doug Taron in the Chicago area; and Shawnee Audubon's War Bluff Sanctuary in far southern Illinois. While all participants in the Illinois Wilds Institute for Nature (IWIN) butterfly workshops provided thought-provoking questions and identification challenges, several participants offered suggestions on how we could produce a better field guide—John and Cindy McKee, Bob and Alice Henry, and the Havana girls (Jo, Cindy, and Rhonda). John Wallace and Karen Frailey offered not only field guide insight, but southern Illinois butterfly locations as well. Bill and Diane Wasson were enthusiastic field companions and challengers for a "Butterfly Big Year" and introduced us to the Grand Prairie Butterfly Club. Phil Houser for the donation and use of the William Frey collection. Don Steinkraus, University of Arkansas, introduced us to the "magic" butterfly bush on his campus, while Rob and LuAnn Wiedenmann provided Arkansas hospitality.

Susan would like to thank her undergraduate entomology advisor, Stanley Friedman, for stressing the importance of learning plant taxonomy; her siblings Valerie, John, and Jenny who were always "happy" to carry a net or jar as they went on insect adventures; and her parents Richard and Mary Post who encouraged entomology as a 4-H project, built insect boxes and pinning blocks, and supported her life-long passion.

JRW would like to thank the following: Dave Baugher, Bob Hackman, Bob Croft, Bill Tobias,

Dave Lott, Susan Dees-Hargrove, Ray McCrite, Dan Wilson, Bob and Alice Henry, Jean Graber, Terry Harrison, Eric Quinter, Paul Goldstein, Ted Herig, Mo Nielsen, Russell Baugher, Kenny Cline, Stu Fliege, Bill McClain, Terry Esker, Dave Hess, Yale Sedman, Jack and Jean Greenlee, Rich Bray, Vern LaGesse, Angella Moorehouse, Don Laibly, Bob Pyle, Brian Russart, Todd Wiley, Dave Iftner, Tim Vogt, Henry Eilers, John and Cindy McKee, Frank Hitchel, Tony McBride, Ron Panzer, Paul Faber, Kathy Phelps, Bradd Sims, Clara Wiker, Sally Agnew, Ellis McLeod, Richard Heitzman, Irwin Leeuw, Richard Arnold, Ryan Yuzty, Josh Nelson, Dave Nance, Richard Funk, John Calhoun, Jackie Turner, Randy Nyboer, Liz Jones, and Dave Shaffer.

Tim Cashatt of the Illinois State Museum, Jim Boone of the Field Museum, Christine McAllister of Principia College, Terry Moyer and the Richardson Wildlife Foundation, J. E. McPherson of Southern Illinois University–Carbondale, Jason Williams of Southern Illinois University–Edwardsville, Don Miller, and the people of Severson Dells.

My parents Jim and Marlene Wiker encouraged my early ramblings in the field. My sister Mona; my brother Jeff; my wife Tammy; and scores of others have helped me along the way.

MRJ, SLP, and JRW: All three authors would like to thank their colleagues from the Illinois Natural History Survey who aided with locating butterfly populations and identifying plants. Those that went "above and beyond" include Jamie Ellis, Connie Carroll-Cunningham, Rick Phillippe, Greg Spyreas, Patty Dickerson, Joseph Spencer, and Jen Mui. We thank Sam Heads and M. Jared Thomas for assistance in photographing butterfly scales, Joseph Spencer for insight on Lepidoptera and Bt corn, the staff of the Prairie Research Institute library, Dmitry Dmitriev for unlimited access to the INHS Insect Collection, and, finally, Charlie Warwick, Jeff Levengood, and Lisa Sheppard for editing the manuscript.

Greg Neise and contributors to the *Dragonflies, Butterflies and Moths* link of the Illinois Birder's Forum and Paul Switzer and the Grand Prairie Butterfly Club. Photographers Bill Bouton, Mike Reese, Will Cook, Travis Mahan, Don Steinkraus, Jeffrey Pippen, James Sternburg, Joseph Spencer, David Riecks, and Paul Switzer for use of their photos. We thank our technical reviewers Robert Reber and Terry Harrison for reviewing the manuscript, and finally, Danielle Ruffatto, for her tireless design work and inspiration during the course of this project.

CONTENTS

ABOVE Trio of male
Tiger Swallowtails

ABOVE Coral Hairstreak nectaring on colic root

ABOVE Basking Painted Lady

FOREWORD

"Rare is the time when we can quiet our inquisitive minds sufficiently and enjoy the present tense. Rarer still is knowing which quick hours in a long life will be the kind of precious touchstones we will draw on in later life."

Stephen Lyons, *A View from the Inland Northwest*

My first memory of an insect was when I was six. Lying on our sidewalk was an elliptical creature no more than two inches long. It was black and white with two big, black spots that resembled eyes—the best part was, it could do tricks! When I touched the creature, it did a back flip! All I could think of was, "this is cool and I am going to have the best object ever for show-and-tell!" At school I found out my "trick" insect was an Eyed Elater, a beetle. Two years later, I was searching for a 4-H project. Prior to Title 9 in Illinois, there were clubs for girls (cooking and sewing projects) and clubs for boys (animal and gardening projects). Of course, I wanted to join

BELOW Eyed Elater

the boys' clubs; they had good snacks and you got to play co-ed Twister after each meeting. While I lived in the country, we did not have farm animals. I could garden, but I soon lost interest in that. My mother suggested entomology, and my first response was the expected, girly, "EEUW BUGS!" But my desire to join the boys' club outweighed the yuck factor, and soon every free space in our house was cluttered with jars; my mother's freezer held more bags with bugs than with produce. (I wonder if my mother ever regretted her suggestion!) With that 4-H project, my fascination with all things entomological began.

Michael's story began much like mine. While he has been a professional entomologist since 1973, he really began his insect career at age nine in the small town of Brookport in southern Illinois. While trekking home from school one day in May, he encountered the most wonderful creature. This must be a first—no one could ever have seen such an animal before! He coaxed the large moth onto his finger, put it in his lunch bag, and hurried home to find out what it was. He discovered it was a Cecropia Moth, newly emerged, and, as the book said, the most common giant silk moth in Illinois.

While he had not made a monumental discovery of a new species, that moth became the focal point for an early insect collection, a lifelong passion for insects, and ultimately led to his present career.

Michael and I met Jim Wiker, "the butterfly guy," in 1997—he was "an assignment" for an upcoming article I was to write for the *Illinois Steward Magazine*. Jim proved to be not only an avid collector of insects (especially Lepidoptera), but also a collector of entomological literature (especially on Lepidoptera); his library was probably the best we had ever encountered. Jim's story paralleled ours. He couldn't remember a time when he wasn't chasing insects. When he was five, a neighbor gave him an insect net. From then on Jim explored his small part of Illinois (near Athens) with an empty coffee can, and regularly filled it with entomological prizes. He soon realized that he couldn't collect everything. As a first grader, he discovered a caterpillar on the pawpaw tree in his yard. Curious, he reared it and was fascinated when it finally transformed into a Zebra Swallowtail. Butterflies, and later moths, became his focus. He has been collecting ever since and is a recognized authority on Illinois butterflies.

After I wrote the article about Jim, our paths seemed to cross more frequently, whether seeking butterflies in the field to photograph or participating at various insect events. Jim would eventually become a part of the Illinois Natural History Survey's IWIN (Illinois Wilds Institute for Nature) team with Michael and me. Together, we taught a series of field classes around Illinois. It was during the late evening hours after a long day in the field that we began to discuss what we would like to see in an Illinois butterfly field guide, and also hatched the idea of Michael and I doing an Illinois butterfly big year. A butterfly big year is simply a quest to see how many different butterfly species you can see in one year. We limited our big year to Illinois butterflies in superfamily Papilionoidea (no skippers for us!), and we tried our best to photograph each species that appeared on our year-long list. One reason for including the photographic caveat was that we (the authors) had just decided to redo the popular Illinois Natural History Survey manual:

Field Guide to Butterflies of Illinois. It was out of print and had not been created with digital technology, so a completely new version rather than an update seemed in order. Suddenly, all those late night conversations on how we would "improve" the Illinois butterfly field guide were pertinent, and 2011 became a butterfly year in more ways than one. We eventually amassed our list of 61 species, and acquired the daunting project of creating a new *Butterflies of Illinois: A Field Guide* from scratch.

The winter of 2010–11 proved to be cold and snowy. While there were a couple of "January thaws," we did not witness any overwintered Morning Cloaks or Question Marks flying about in the milder, yet snowy landscape. However, by mid-March it started to warm up and we saw our first butterfly—a Cabbage White. Seeing a Cabbage White as your first butterfly is like seeing an English Sparrow as your first bird of the New Year, but it was a start. Our butterfly big year was off and running.

During the spring, summer, and fall we kept in constant email contact with Jim about what we had seen and where we could find additional species.

BELOW Zebra Swallowtail

My field notes on June 17, 2011 state that, *"we meet our friend Jim Wiker at Sand Ridge and the search is on. The milkweed by the ranger's house is not as productive as in the past. Like the tide, by visiting Sand Ridge regularly, we watch the species ebb and flow. Today's trash (very common) species, American Copper and Gorgone Checkerspot, are dripping from the butterfly weed. We hit species #50 in the middle of a field of budding common milkweed, surrounded by courting Regals and calling Dickcissels from nearby stunted trees."*

What was it like relentlessly pursuing butterflies for an entire year? My notes from June 18, 2011 say, *"I am still picking cactus spines from my knee and ankles; the other knee supports a Lone Star Tick. Yesterday—what a day—hot, humid, wore a bandana around my head like a wounded solider—it soaked through twice. All day we drove, hopped out, found our target or an unexpected treasure, and then on to the next site."* Obviously, to a field biologist, great fun! We saw our final butterfly, a Sleepy Orange, on October 22. It was species number 61.

As for actually writing the field guide text, finding and photographing an increasingly uncommon Dogface was a far easier task (yet both eventually were

accomplished). We persevered by photographing specimens, creating maps and flight period graphs, and writing. Jim located Illinois collection records, so this field guide also contains historical records of pertinent species. We reviewed many other field guides to see how information was presented, incorporated the best ideas, and added a few of our own. With the addition of Danielle Ruffatto, a botanist and designer, to our team, any wild idea was suddenly within the realm of possibility. She was soon presenting layout and design ideas that far exceeded what we had initially envisioned as possible.

From the dedication page of this book, it should be obvious that we stand on the shoulders of present and past entomologists and lepidopterists who shared their knowledge and passion for insects with us, both personally, and through the literature. Thus, our goal for this book is not only to educate and create an awareness about butterflies, but also to inspire and challenge the next generation of butterfly enthusiasts to participate in subsequent "late night" talks about how they, too, can create the next permutation of *Butterflies of Illinois: A Field Guide*.

Susan Post, Champaign, IL December, 2013

PART I

INTRODUCTION

HOW TO USE THIS BOOK

Writing a field guide for any group of organisms—even one for a finite area (Illinois) and for a small group (butterflies), at least by insect standards—is a daunting task. While numerous butterfly field guides exist for areas of the U.S., one that is all-inclusive for a specific area makes the task of identification easier. An individual with little or no knowledge of insects and entomology should be able to pick up a field guide, thumb through the pages, and identify the insect in question. In *Butterflies of Illinois: A Field Guide*, we strive to make this book as user-friendly as possible. We have made every attempt to keep scientific jargon out of the species treatments, and have used only everyday terms to describe the location of diagnostic characters for Illinois' 100+ species of butterflies. Our introductory materials are meant to inform the reader about some of the interesting facts about butterflies, without being an encyclopedia of entomological knowledge.

LEFT Olive Hairstreak viewed through butterfly binoculars

BELOW Typical field view of a Dogface (notice that it is hard to see the dog face!)

We have loosely divided the characteristics needed to identify a butterfly into two categories—"collection characteristics" and "field characteristics." Collection characteristics are relevant when identifying a pinned, spread specimen with full collection data (e.g., date, collector, location). Traits such as shape of the sex patch (stigma) on the forewing of elfins and hairstreaks (usually not visible in the field as the butterflies sit with their wings closed) and the differing scale structure on the forewings of Spring and Summer Azures[1] (need a 20× lens to see them), fall into this category. Field characteristics are those that are readily visible with the naked eye or when viewed through butterfly binoculars. The different markings on the underside of the wings of various species fall into this category. As we have designed this book to be a true "in-the-field" type of guide, the field characteristics are emphasized in the species treatments. We encourage everyone to become a butterfly observer/photographer rather

BELOW Olive Hairstreak scales (Photo by M. Jared Thomas)

RIGHT Summer and Spring Azure scales, respectively (Photos by M. Jared Thomas)

50 μm

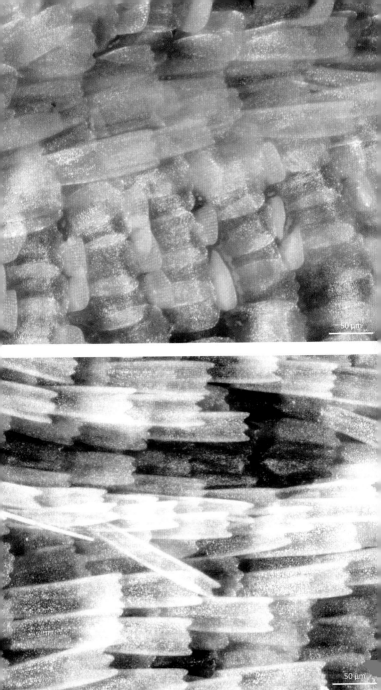

than a collector, so sharpen those observational skills, and perhaps even obtain a pair of close-focusing binoculars for your butterfly excursions.

FIELD GUIDE FEATURES AND ORGANIZATION A unique aspect of this field guide is an identification quick guide. The inside front pages have photos of all the Illinois butterfly species (top view) and the page number where their treatment can be found. The inside back pages depict the undersides of the same species. Thus, anyone who observes an Illinois butterfly can quickly go to the correct page and identify it.

The species treatments are organized by butterfly

family (there are only five in Illinois) and, where applicable, subfamily. With a little practice, and perhaps some tabs in the margins, a butterfly enthusiast should be able to observe an Illinois butterfly, assign it to its proper family, and determine its identity. In time, subfamilies will also become "second-nature" as your experience with the Illinois fauna grows. For especially difficult groups (e.g., the swallowtail mimicry complex, hairstreaks, Monarch/Viceroy, fritillaries, checkerspots, crescents, pearly-eyes, and eyed browns) we have included photos of the various species (pinned) as side-by-side comparisons in *Commonly Confused Illinois Butterflies* (see page 350).

ABOVE Tiger Swallowtail individual (intraspecific) variation

WHAT'S IN A SPECIES TREATMENT? The species treatments include short, non-technical written descriptions; field and pinned specimen photos; biological and distribution information; and handy field notes

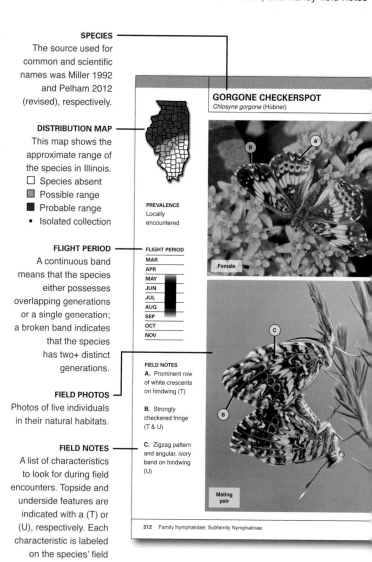

SPECIES
The source used for common and scientific names was Miller 1992 and Pelham 2012 (revised), respectively.

DISTRIBUTION MAP
This map shows the approximate range of the species in Illinois.
☐ Species absent
▨ Possible range
■ Probable range
• Isolated collection

FLIGHT PERIOD
A continuous band means that the species either possesses overlapping generations or a single generation; a broken band indicates that the species has two+ distinct generations.

FIELD PHOTOS
Photos of live individuals in their natural habitats.

FIELD NOTES
A list of characteristics to look for during field encounters. Topside and underside features are indicated with a (T) or (U), respectively. Each characteristic is labeled on the species' field photos.

GORGONE CHECKERSPOT
Chlosyne gorgone (Hübner)

Female

PREVALENCE
Locally encountered

FLIGHT PERIOD
MAR
APR
MAY
JUN
JUL
AUG
SEP
OCT
NOV

FIELD NOTES
A. Prominent row of white crescents on hindwing (T)

B. Strongly checkered fringe (T & U)

C. Zigzag pattern and angular, ivory band on hindwing (U)

Mating pair

312 Family Nymphalidae: Subfamily Nymphalinae

to aid in your identification endeavors. Below is an example of a species treatment included in this field guide. The major components are described for easy reference.

SPECIES TREATMENT
WRITTEN DESCRIPTION
"Description" is the technical characterization of the species' appearance (includes both field and collection characteristics).

"Could Be Confused With" includes a list of those species that look similiar to the one being described, as well as characters used to distinguish them.

"Habitat/Life History" discusses where the species can be found and other facts related to caterpillar and adult behavior. Any plants listed in this section follow the common names used in Mohlenbrock's 3rd edition *Vascular Flora of Illinois*.

"Status" discusses the current prevalence of the species in Illinois.

SPECIMEN PHOTOS
Featured specimen photos are shown life size (the minimum wingspan size). Maximum wingspan size is depicted as a gray shadow of the species.

SCRIPTION The Gorgone Checkerspot has a wing-[sp]an of 1.25–1.75 inches and similar sexes. The [up]perside is orange with complex black markings; [in f]resh specimens, the edge of the wing is strongly [ch]eckered with a black and white fringe. The up-[per]side of the hindwing has a row of black spots in [fro]m the margin and a row of white crescents in the [dar]k wing margin. The underside of the hindwing [ha]s a zigzag pattern of brown and white bands, [wit]h a row of black spots near the wing margin and [an] angular, ivory band near the center of the wing.

♂ T

♀ T

[CO]ULD BE CONFUSED WITH In flight and from above, [the] Gorgone Checkerspot may be confused with [an]y small, black-and-orange butterfly—especially [the] Pearl Crescent and Silvery Checkerspot (see [pa]ge 360). However, the pattern on the underside [of] the Gorgone Checkerspot's hindwing—a zigzag [pa]ttern of brown and white—is unique. Futher, it [is] intermediate in size between the smaller Pearl [Cr]escent and the larger Silvery Checkerspot.

[HA]BITAT/LIFE HISTORY The Gorgone Checkerspot is [fou]nd at dry, sunny sites—open areas, old fields, [pr]airies, town gardens, and old railroad grades. The [fe]male lays her eggs in clusters on various species [of s]unflowers and asters. The species overwinters [as] a partially grown caterpillar. The Gorgone [Ch]eckerspot has multiple generations each year in [Illi]nois and flies from early May to mid-September.

WINGSPAN
1.25–1.75 in

[STA]TUS The Gorgone Checkerspot is a butterfly [of] the Great Plains; the Great Plains Butterfly is [an]other of its common names. In Illinois, it is found [no]rth of Interstate 70. Work is underway to rein-[tro]duce this species to various Chicago remnant [ha]bitats. Populations of the Gorgone Checkerspot [inc]reased from the 1960s into the 1980s, especially [in c]entral Illinois. Since then numbers have mark-[ed]ly decreased. However, it can still be found in [the] sand and railroad prairies in the northern half [of I]llinois.

♂ U

♀ U

ABOVE The Gulf Fritillary, a rare visitor to Illinois

RIGHT The state-threatened Regal Fritillary, a denizen of sand prairies

WHAT ARE YOUR CHANCES?

Many people often ask, "Where do I go to see a... (particular species of butterfly)?" The answer is not always a simple one, as a number of factors enter into finding butterflies. For Illinois, we have divided the butterfly species into seven distinct categories. Species that are:

- a regular part of the Illinois fauna and overwinter (breed and overwinter in the state),
- a regular part of the Illinois fauna yet do not overwinter (breed here, don't survive the winter, and recolonize each year from the south),
- irregular visitors from adjacent areas,
- rare strays (e.g., species that enters Illinois on its own power),
- accidental visitors (e.g., species brought in by various means—on plants, by railroads, etc.),
- possible species that could occur here, but have not yet been recorded,
- and extirpated (eliminated from Illinois) species.

Obviously, your chances of seeing a particular butterfly species decrease as you head down the column of categories.

When we consider the above categories, the cyclic nature of butterfly populations (many times caused by regional and statewide weather conditions), and the impacts of global climate change, predicting the whereabouts of and finding a particular species can become extremely problematic. The authors have found that, overall, butterfly populations have declined in Illinois over the preceding decades, and even distribution patterns are changing. For those interested in such things, a diligent search of Illinois for an entire year (a.k.a., a Butterfly Big Year) can yield between 60–70 species, and on any given day, 20–30 species are possible. A few times, the authors have found all six species of Illinois' swallowtails (those in the first category), in a single location! The adventure and interest lie in the search, so become a butterfly enthusiast and explore the Illinois butterfly fauna.

LEFT The Great Purple Hairstreak, only collected once in Illinois

ABOVE The highly cyclic Red Admiral

NATURAL DIVISIONS OF ILLINOIS

Scientists have divided the terrestrial part of the earth into large, ecological regions called biomes. Examples of worldwide biomes include tropical rainforest, Asian steppes, African savanna, and a host of others. The North American continent also has biomes, such as Arctic tundra, Sonoran desert, and Appalachian forest. Illinois has had its landscape categorized into regions called Natural Divisions. The Natural Divisions of Illinois were first presented in 1973 in a technical report authored by state botanist John Schwegman and colleagues. They proposed that Illinois be divided into 14 Natural Divisions based on the characteristics of glacial history, soil type, topography, climate, and the distribution of native plants and animals. These 14 divisions were further subdivided into 33 subdivisions. Over the years, Illinois' Natural Divisions have proven very useful to the natural area preservation movement within the state. They help biologists categorize and prioritize Illinois' 90+ natural habitats for preservation and restoration efforts. While we have not used these Natural Divisions to characterize the distribution of Illinois' butterfly fauna, we do mention these divisions in certain species treatments and feel that individuals should be aware of these large Illinois regions.

BELOW/RIGHT The 14 Natural Divisions of Illinois

1	Wisconsin Driftless Division	**8**	Middle Mississippi River Border Division
2	Rock River Hill Country Division	**9**	Lower Mississippi River Bottomlands Division
3	Northeastern Morainal Division	**10**	Southern Till Plain Division
4	Grand Prairie Division	**11**	Wabash Border Division
5	Western Forest-Prairie Division	**12**	Ozark Division
6	Illinois River and Mississippi River Sand Areas Division	**13**	Shawnee Hills Division
7	Upper Mississippi River and Illinois River Bottomlands Division	**14**	Coastal Plain Division

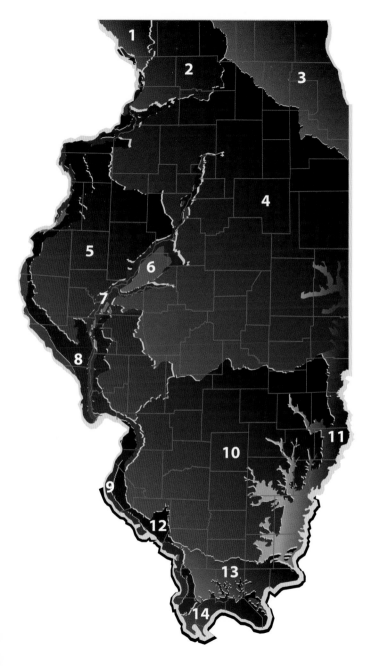

BUTTERFLY, MOTH, OR SKIPPER?

The only true taxonomic distinctions among butterflies, moths, and skippers are at the super-family level. Butterflies belong to the superfamily Papilionoidea (in Illinois these include the families Papilionidae, Pieridae, Riodinidae, Lycaenidae, and Nymphalidae), while skippers occupy the superfamily Hesperioidea. The moths occupy an astounding 40+ additional superfamilies! The distinctions among the three groups are based on a series of habits and physical characters, and a grouping of these characters will serve to differenti-ate the groups. Moreover, the differences are easy to observe. For example, butterflies have clubbed antennal tips, while skippers have hooked antennal tips (sometimes a half-moon shape). Alternatively, moth antennae are extremely variable and range from hairlike to feathery. In butterflies, the anten-nae arise from the head relatively close together, while in skippers the antennal bases are further apart. Wing position when at rest is also a useful characteristic. Nearly all butterflies (and skippers) rest with their wings held together over their backs. A few rest with the wings outspread or may bask with them open, but they never flex and fold them over the abdomen, as nearly all moths do. The size of the body compared to the wings also helps differ-entiate butterflies, moths, and skippers. Butterflies

BELOW Photographs depicting (a) butterfly, (b) skipper, and (c–d) moth antennae

RIGHT ABOVE Silver-spotted Skippers mating

RIGHT BELOW White-lined Sphinx Moth nectaring on thistle

have relatively slender bodies and large wings, while moths and skippers have stouter bodies and relatively short wings.

Butterflies and skippers are mostly diurnal (fly during the daylight hours); a few butterflies are crepuscular (fly during the early morning or late afternoon hours when the sun is low). Moths, with a few notable exceptions, are primarily nocturnal. A final character, less useful because it is not usually observable in the field, is the way the wings are coupled together in flight. Moths hold their wings together by means of a bristle (male) or bundle of bristles (female) called a frenulum. Butterflies have their fore- and hindwings overlapping. For those who have tried to spread butterflies for a collection, this characteristic is evident when the wings sometimes overlap in the wrong direction, making the specimen appear very odd. Thus, if an insect is diurnal, holds its wings together above the body, and has knobbed antennae, in all likelihood it is a butterfly.

LEFT Pair of Polyphemus Moths

ABOVE Corn Earworm Moth, a noctuid

ABOVE Monarch life cycle, (a) egg, (b) caterpillar, (c) chrysalis, (d) emerging butterfly, (e) butterfly expanding wings, and (f) adult butterfly ready to fly

RIGHT Spicebush Swallowtail caterpillar stages, (a) "bird-dropping mimic" and (b) "snake mimic"

BUTTERFLY LIFE CYCLE

BUTTERFLY LIFE CYCLE As every child is taught, usually beginning in early elementary school, the life cycle of a butterfly has four stages. Life begins with an egg, laid by a female on the correct host plant for the caterpillar. The egg is usually attached to a leaf or stem, and if it is not the overwintering stage, will soon hatch into a larva. In butterflies, we call this larval form a caterpillar. The caterpillar has one simple task—to consume enough food in its lifetime to provide nutrients for it to transform into an adult butterfly. Periodically it must shed its exoskeleton (the skeleton on the outside of its body) in a process called molting. The period between molts is called an instar. Most butterflies have five instars, with each instar larger than the last. Dramatic changes often occur in the appearance of a caterpillar across instars. For example, some swallowtails begin larval life as "bird-dropping mimics," while the last two instars are quite remarkable snake mimics. When the caterpillar is full grown, it molts once again into the pupal stage, called a chrysalis. Sometimes the adult emerges within a few weeks, but often the chrysalis serves as an overwintering stage for the butterfly. When the adult does emerge from its chrysalis, it expands its wings, and is soon flying about the landscape, feeding and searching for a mate.

BUTTERFLY CATERPILLARS Most people describe a butterfly caterpillar as soft and wormlike, and that

is true. However, the caterpillar of many species
has long spines and hairs that often mask its
wormlike appearance. A caterpillar's surface varies
greatly among the butterfly families. A Papilionidae
(swallowtails) caterpillar is typically bare, with an
early instar appearing as a fresh bird-dropping.
A later instar of some Papilionidae species either
mimics a small snake (complete with eyespots) or
centipede, or has transverse, colorful bands around
its body. Alternatively, a Pieridae (white and yellow butterflies) caterpillar has smooth to granular
skin, a Lycaenidae (gossamer-wing butterflies)

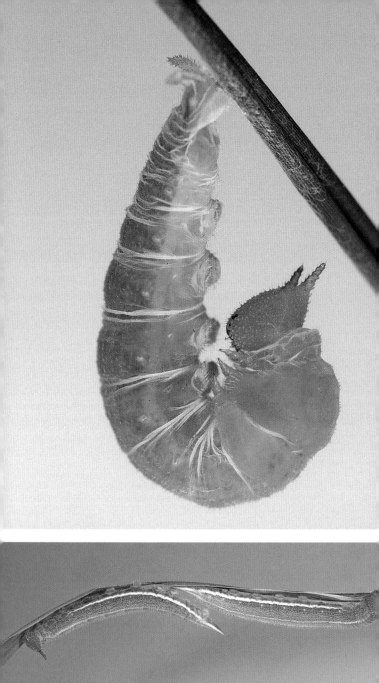

caterpillar is often small and sluglike, a Riodinidae (metalmark butterflies) caterpillar is very hairy, and a Nymphalidae (brush-footed butterflies) caterpillar is often very spiny or has a knobby, rough appearance. Identifying a butterfly by its caterpillar can be relatively easy (Papilionidae), to somewhat difficult (Nymphalidae), to downright challenging (Lycaenidae). This guide is not designed to allow you to identify butterfly caterpillars, but several good books exist that will help in your endeavor (see Wagner 2005).

BUTTERFLY CHRYSALIDS Whereas the pupa or chrysalis stage of a butterfly was once referred to as a "resting state," that is not the case. Massive

LEFT ABOVE Creole Pearly-eye pre-pupa (preparing to molt to a chrysalis)

LEFT BELOW Creole Pearly-eye caterpillars

BELOW TOP Regal Fritillary caterpillar on Bird's-foot Violet

BELOW BOTTOM Painted Lady caterpillar and eggs

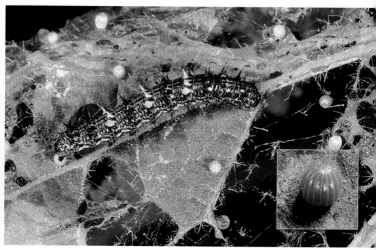

ABOVE Pipevine Swallowtail chrysalis with a cremaster and a silken girdle

RIGHT American Painted Lady (a Nymphalid) chrysalis suspended by a cremaster

changes occur within the chrysalis, both anatomical and physiological. After all, the last instar caterpillar bears little resemblance to the adult butterfly, so a more informative term for the chrysalis would be the stage of dramatic change.

All of the Illinois butterfly families except the Nymphalidae produce chrysalids with two features: a cremaster (a set of hooks on the rear end of the chrysalis that fastens it to the plant stem) and a silken girdle, which suspends the chrysalis at either a head-up or somewhat horizontal angle from the plant stem. Nymphalidae chrysalids lack the silken girdle, and are suspended head-down from a silk pad by the cremaster.

BUTTERFLY HABITATS

Whereas no single habitat type can cover all the various locations where butterflies are found, we typically associate their presence with open, sunny, flower-filled landscapes. Butterflies, however, are a diverse group and species occur in deep forests, open woodlands, wetlands, prairies and other grasslands, and even disturbed areas. In fact, in a state like Illinois, where over 99% of its natural landscapes have been altered in some fashion, the "disturbed" habitat is certainly one of the most important places to find butterflies.

What follows are brief descriptions of Illinois habitats where butterflies are likely to occur. Note: given their relatively great capacity for mobility, species can often be found far removed from their "typical" haunts, spending time searching for nectar or other sources of nutrition, or simply moving from one

location to another in Illinois' highly fragmented landscape.

ABOVE Oak-hickory forest in the spring

FORESTS Illinois currently has over 4 million acres of forested lands that include a number of different types. Most of the quality habitat that we typically associate with "wildlife" in Illinois occurs in forests. A forest is characterized by land where trees have a canopy coverage of 80% or greater.

OAK-HICKORY FOREST This is the major forest type in Illinois with 22 oak species and 16 hickory species. An oak-hickory forest is typically more open, with a less-dense canopy and an understory of small trees, shrubs, and forbs dispersed widely across the forest floor. Periodic fires, which keep the understory open without harming the thick-barked trees, are part of oak-hickory forest ecology.

BEECH-MAPLE FOREST Composed mostly of maples—

a group of trees that tolerates shade and reproduces well under a closed canopy—interspersed with scattered beech, this type of forest has increased dramatically over the last several decades. In fact, many oak-hickory forests are being taken over by maples due to the reduction in periodic fires.

ELM-ASH-SOFT MAPLE FOREST Found along bottomlands and in areas bordering streams, this forest type has been drastically reduced in Illinois and now mainly occurs in narrow, riparian corridors along Illinois streams and rivers. An elm-ash-soft maple forest is adapted to periodic flooding from nearby streams and rivers.

OAK-GUM-CYPRESS FOREST Confined to far southern Illinois along the bottomlands associated with the Lower Mississippi, Ohio, and Cache River drainages, this unique forest type is flooded for most or all of the year. It has an assemblage of species that are more southern in distribution, including bald cypress and water tupelo. Here, large cane

BELOW Beech-maple forest

RIGHT ABOVE Elm-ash-soft maple forest with phlox

RIGHT BELOW Oak-gum-cypress forest

ABOVE Cane thickets near oak-gum-cypress forest

RIGHT Woodland with an understory of sedges and shooting stars

thickets occur that support unique species of Illinois butterflies, moths, and skippers.

WOODLAND Distinguishing a woodland from a forest may seem like "splitting hairs," but the distinction is quite real. A woodland is a dry community dominated by trees, grasses, and forbs. Tree height seldom exceeds 50 feet and the trees, despite being the same species found in forests, have a very different growth form—the trunk is highly branched with spreading limbs. Some call them "wolf trees." The most prominent species are post and blackjack oak and black hickory. A woodland's canopy is very open and its shrub layer is sparse and dominated by farkleberry, while its herbaceous layer contains woodland sunflower, little bluestem, various asters, and often shooting star. Fire is extremely important in maintaining this community type.

BARRENS While the term "barrens" may give a distinct impression that a site is not worth visiting, nothing could be further from the truth. Barrens are a unique community type, rich in life and complex in structure. A barrens owes its existence to a

delicate balance of natural forces that prevent it from becoming a typical forest community. Unlike a forest where trees dominate, a barrens' herbaceous layer is equally as important as its trees. A barrens landscape has many vines, lichens, and mosses scattered about in patches of open ground, and surface rocks contribute to the unstable, often poor soil conditions. Barrens may be located on sandstone, limestone, or shale. However, the plant community remains very diverse with white, post, and blackjack oaks common (although all are scattered, stunted, and limby). The herbaceous layer includes farkleberry, little bluestem, Venus' looking glass, purple milkweed, Indian pink, New Jersey tea, and a host of other species. The Ozark Checkerspot is often found in this habitat type.

GLADES A glade differs from a barrens in that it has more exposed bedrock and a variety of mosses and lichens. It may be either sandstone or limestone. In areas of high visitation, a glade is often trampled, such that nothing but bare rock remains. Prickly

LEFT ABOVE Limestone barrens

LEFT BELOW Sandstone glade with blackjack oak

BELOW Limestone glade with purple coneflower

pear cactus is commonly found, as is *Sedum*. A limestone glade can be quite spectacular with displays of purple coneflower, wild hyacinth, and New Jersey tea. Eastern red cedar and blackjack oak may dominate. The Olive Hairstreak can be found here.

GRASSLANDS A prairie is a largely treeless grassland dominated by warm-season grasses and forbs. Trees cover less than 10% of the land. Six types of prairie are recognized in Illinois—typical tallgrass prairie on silt-loam soils, sand prairie, gravel prairie, dolomite prairie, hill prairie, and shrub prairie. A savanna habitat is mostly composed of grasses and flowers, but also has widely spaced trees (mostly oaks) creating a very park-like setting.

Prairies and savannas were once widespread in Illinois (nearly 22 million acres at European settlement), but are now relegated to only a few thou-

LEFT ABOVE Mesic tallgrass prairie

LEFT BELOW Sand prairie

ABOVE Hill prairie

BELOW TOP Shrub
prairie

BELOW BOTTOM Oak
savanna

RIGHT Sand savanna
with bird's-foot violets

sand acres scattered across the state. Even though vanishingly rare, prairie is often very diverse with upwards of 500 species of plants. Prairie and savanna represent the ultimate, sunny, open, flower-filled landscape that we associate with butterflies.

WETLANDS While we don't often associate butterflies with a wetland, some species are associated with

the habitat and occur in very localized populations, often closely associated with their food plants. A wetland occurs where the water table is at or near the surface, and thus is occupied by plant species adapted to life in water or saturated soils. Wetland types in Illinois include marsh, swamp, bog, fen, sedge meadow, panne, shrub swamp, seep, and spring.

DISTURBED AREAS Nearly all the natural landscapes that once occurred in Illinois have been converted to agriculture. In the early stages of succession, grasses and forbs dominate the recovering land after forests have been cut or prairies plowed. Disturbed areas now represent a very important component for many of Illinois' species, especially butterflies. Much of Illinois' checkerboard landscape is now connected only by narrow strips along roadsides, drainage ditches, powerline cuts, and railroad tracks. These neglected areas, often rife with blooming plants, are an important refuge for numerous species of Illinois butterflies. In recent years, excessive roadside and field edge mowing has reduced these important butterfly feeding and breeding corridors.

LEFT ABOVE Fen with a marl flat

LEFT BELOW Woodland seep

BELOW Former agricultural landscape

BUTTERFLY BEHAVIOR

PUDDLE-CLUBBING BY BUTTERFLIES A puddle club is a gathering, often quite large in size, of mostly bachelor male butterflies. Occuring in any region of the state, a puddle club is generally on a moist spot on the soil that contains salts, minerals, or some other compound (e.g., nitrogen, urea) the butterflies find attractive. A puddle club can consist of a single species or a mixture of species congregating on the moisture source, even "elbowing" each other out of the way for the prime imbibing locations. Scientists speculate that a puddle club serves two purposes: it provides needed micronutrients not found in nectar, and it creates leks. A lek is a gathering of males of certain animal species, for the purpose of creating a competitive mating display. While most often associated with mammals, this phenomenon has been noted in butterflies for centuries by observant naturalists. The authors have personally observed many puddle clubs, especially of male swallowtails

LEFT Large puddle club of male swallowtails

BELOW Puddle club of sulphurs

ABOVE A multi-species puddle club (i.e., Question Mark, Red-spotted Purple, Tiger Swallowtail, and Pearl Crescent)

RIGHT ABOVE Puddle club of Silvery Checkerspots

RIGHT BELOW Basking Baltimore

that are judiciously feeding on the ground until a female happens by. This creates chaos in the otherwise single-minded males as they all flutter up and take note of the passing female. While not documented experimentally, empirical evidence suggests that this may be true lekking behavior. A puddle club may form when a single male lands on an appropriate site, but he is not alone for long as he is soon joined by several of his cohorts. Collectors have long known that the best place to find pristine butterfly specimens is at a puddle club. These large groups of colorful butterflies (members of all of Illinois' butterfly families engage in this behavior) can be quite striking, especially when an unsuspecting hiker disturbs them—the butterflies take wing, swirl around in an erratic flight, but soon settle back to continue their feast. This brief, colorful shrouding of a person by butterflies is certainly one of the great experiences of butterfly watching.

TERRITORIALITY, PATROLLING, AND HILL-TOPPING A male butterfly uses three types of behaviors to find a mate and increase his chances of mating success: territoriality, patrolling, and hill-topping. In territoriality, a male butterfly perches on a branch, leaf, or other exposed surface to survey the surrounding landscape. He will chase away any intruders in his perceived "territory," and then return to his perch.

Intruders are usually males of the same species, but other butterflies of similar size may also elicit a response from the male. When a female of the correct species happens by, the male will sally forth and begin his courting behavior. If the female is receptive, she will respond appropriately and mating will take place. Thus, territoriality is strictly a reproductive type of behavior. Nymphalidae males are notoriously territorial.

Patrolling behavior is somewhat self-explanatory; a male purposely flies through a habitat (often along a corridor such as a trail or along a wood's edge) in search of a receptive female. The male's slow, often languid flight can quickly change should an appropriate female enter his field of vision. Papilionidae males endlessly patrol wooded corridors in search of females.

While hill-topping behavior is often observed in butterflies that live in mountainous regions, it also occurs in Illinois. An Illinois hill prairie is a prime location for this behavior as males often perch on the exposed, open land and await the arrival of potential mates. Certain members of the Illinois

LEFT "Jousting" Checkered White males

ABOVE Perched Edwards' Hairstreak guarding his territory

ABOVE Courting Falcate Orangetips

RIGHT ABOVE Mating Buckeyes

RIGHT BELOW Mating Gorgone Checkerspots

Pieridae exhibit hill-topping behavior. A Pierid male may spend most of his fleeting adult life perched and waiting, only occasionally flying out for a brief sip of nectar from nearby flowers.

COURTSHIP AND MATING BEHAVIOR Butterflies use sight as an initial way to begin courtship. When a male butterfly recognizes a female of his own species, he will actively pursue her and begin the courtship ritual. A male will approach the female from above and behind. Once close to her, he may release chemicals (called pheromones) from sex patches on his wings (called either stigma or androconia), which will stimulate the female. A male butterfly may also conduct a species-specific courtship dance to attract the attention of the female. A receptive female, one that has not already mated, will actively participate in the courtship dance to signal her availability. Mating occurs when the two join abdomens end-to-end by means of claspers, and the male passes either sperm or a sperm packet to the female. She uses the sperm later to fertilize her eggs as they pass through the egg-laying tube.

BUTTERFLY MOVEMENT An adult butterfly traverses its environment by flying about. Unlike a bird, a butterfly is more susceptible to the capricious nature of various climates (e.g., temperature, wind, rain), because it is cold-blooded and is not an extremely powerful flier. However, given its perceived frailty, a butterfly gets around quite well and may even undertake epic, continent-spanning migrations. Therefore, long distances are often not a barrier to butterfly movement. Certainly the best-known butterfly migrant is the Monarch, and the *Models, Migration, and Mimicry* section included in this book provides many details on this unique phenomenon (see page 63). Other species—such as the Painted Lady—can move hundreds of miles, but

ABOVE Monarch in flight

this phenomenon is not considered a true migration, only movement away from a given location. Other types of movement simply involve dispersal flights, as many Illinois butterfly species move into the state from far southern or southwestern climates where they can survive the winters. Others colonize from adjacent areas. Illinois seems to have a unique location within the continental United States and occurs on the edge of the ranges of many species; consequently, vagrants or strays often end up in Illinois during any given year. We have included these butterflies in our species treatments, although they are never predictable in their visits to Illinois.

ADULT BUTTERFLY FEEDING BEHAVIOR

NECTARING We most often associate butterflies with nectar feeding on a great variety of flowers. A butterfly is uniquely adapted for imbibing the carbohydrate-rich nectar of flowers as it has a long, coiled proboscis—hollow in the center—that it uses to obtain its liquid diet. Because flowers are of different sizes and sequester their nectar in various parts, the butterfly's proboscis has evolved to exploit these resources. Usually, the proboscis is in proportion to the butterfly's size, allowing nectar feeding on a given range of flower sizes—a large butterfly with a long proboscis can exploit almost any flower for nectar, whereas a smaller species may be confined to visiting flowers where the nectar is in a more accessible location. Many flowers advertise their nectaries by converging lines on the petals or other landmarks that direct a butterfly (or

LEFT Gray Copper nectaring on a brown-eyed susan

ABOVE Olive Hairstreak nectaring on a dandelion

ABOVE Pearl Crescents and a Hackberry Butterfly feeding on raccoon dung (environmental fluids)

other insect) to the correct location. These lines or landmarks can be either visible in the normal light seen by the human eye, or can be in the ultraviolet range, only detectable by insect eyes. In any case, flowers and butterflies have co-evolved in a give-and-take genetic dance over the millennia to ensure that both benefit from their interaction. Namely, butterflies receive a nutritious food source, while flowers are pollinated by the actions of butterflies.

FEEDING ON "OTHER" FLUIDS IN THE ENVIRONMENT While nectar is a great source of energy for flight, most nectar lacks needed elements for certain butterfly activities—producing eggs and sperm and main-

taining various body tissues. Therefore, a butterfly
that specializes on nectar does not pass up the
opportunity to imbibe other fluids that contain these
necessary nutrients. These fluids include urine, animal dung, decaying carcasses, tree sap, and even
the sugary effluent from various colonies of aphids,
mealy bugs, and other members of the insect Order
Homoptera. Thus, a large or small aggregation of
butterflies can often be found on piles of raccoon
dung, or simply at a moist spot along a stream bank
or roadside that has had some micronutrient depos-
ited by a passing animal. Some groups of butterflies
rarely or never visit flowers, but rather specialize on
the nutrient sources described above—dung, car-

rion, urine, tree sap, etc. These specialists include many of the Nymphalidae. Seldom will anyone find a Hackberry Butterfly on a flower, but a large aggregation of Hackberry individuals will sometimes occur, especially on the dung of omnivores such as raccoons. If the aggregation occurs on a busy road, the smashed bodies of Hackberry Butterflies accumulate and can lead to quite an impressive crowd of butterflies. Trees that exude sap, usually rich in various nutrients, are also prime feeding locations for the groups that specialize in non-nectar feeding behavior. A tree struck by lightning that is exuding copious quantities of sap can become a magnet for butterflies—entomologists call these "butterfly trees." The trees remain attractive as long as the sap is fresh and flowing, and can have several species feeding collectively, including the Hackberry Butterfly, Tawny Emperor, Red-spotted Purple, and Red Admiral. Rotting fruit also produces consider-

BELOW Red Admirals feeding on sap from a "butterfly tree"

RIGHT Large aggregation of Hackberry Butterflies

able amounts of liquids that are attractive to butterflies—these nutrient-rich liquids, often fermented,
can host sizable feeding aggregations of butterflies.
The authors have seen various swallowtails imbibe
too much of the alcohol-laced treat, actually "stag-
ger" away from the feast, and be unable to fly for a
given time period.

LEFT/ABOVE Ozark
Checkerspot feeding on
fluids from a decaying
box turtle

ABOVE Olympia Marble nectaring on a bird's-foot violet

RIGHT Hoary Elfin perched on bearberry at Lake Michigan dunes

SPRING EPHEMERALS

The term "spring ephemeral" evokes trips to the woods to see an ever-changing palette of favorite spring wildflowers. But have you ever thought of butterflies as ephemerals? While we are used to seeing swallowtails, Mourning Cloaks, Cabbage Butterflies, and the first Monarch of spring, we know we will continue to see them throughout the spring, summer, and even into fall. But what about those butterflies that are out for only a few short weeks each spring? Illinois has 10 species that appear and disappear like the blooms of the bloodroot. And like the petals of a bloodroot blossom, inevitably carried away by spring winds, these butterflies only make brief appearances each Illinois spring.

Two species, the Falcate Orangetip and the Olympia Marble, are related to the ever-present Cabbage Butterfly. Four species—Hoary, Frosted, Henry's, and Eastern Pine—are tiny, brown elfins. The term elfin is defined as, "small, delicate and graceful, a mysterious creature." The elfin butterflies certainly fall into this category. The final four—Spring Azure, Dusky Azure, Silvery Blue, and Northern Hairstreak—belong to the Lycaenidae. The species occur in shades of blue and gray, but when they settle they show their undersides, a mix of "crescents and dashes—a language in code."

MODELS, MIGRATION, AND MIMICRY

Long before states had official flowers, trees, grasses, or insects, the Monarch butterfly—the state insect of Illinois—had already piqued human curiosity. Charles V. Riley, an early entomologist, noted as early as 1878 that midwestern populations of the Monarch underwent birdlike migrations each autumn. Professor F.A. Urquhart, a Monarch researcher for over 40 years, later devised a butterfly tagging system that involved thousands of collaborators. He was able to confirm that the Monarch generally moves in a southwesterly direction each autumn. However, the question of where they went remained a mystery until January 2, 1975, when two of Urquhart's associates discovered that Monarchs from eastern North America overwinter south of the Tropic of Cancer in the mountains of central Mexico; they located millions of nonreproducing Monarchs at high altitudes resting on Oyamel fir trees, also called sacred firs. The Monarchs were so dense that the branches literally sagged under their weight. Fir trunks were so densely clad with bright orange Monarchs that they mimicked the shingle-like scaling found on each Monarch's

LEFT/BELOW Cluster of Monarchs in Mexico on Oyamel fir

ABOVE Monarch caterpillar feeding on swamp milkweed

wings. The migration of these many millions of Monarchs is perhaps the best-known feature of this remarkable creature, but it is not the entire story. The life of the Monarch is a fascinating tale!

A MONARCH'S LIFE   This story, like all good stories about insect life cycles, begins with an egg. A female Monarch is an excellent, if somewhat narrowly focused, botanist and chooses only milkweeds as a home for her young. These common plants of Illinois roadsides, fields, and prairies are not so common chemically, as most are laced with toxic compounds called cardenolides (heart poisons). If eaten, these chemicals can cause irregular heartbeats and emesis (vomiting) in unsuspecting ingesters. A Monarch caterpillar doesn't seem to mind the poisons though, and incorporates these chemicals into its body as a potent defense against predators. An adult that emerges after five caterpillar instars and pupation retains the toxins. As any predator would tell you, the Monarch caterpillar and adult simply don't taste good, and they advertise their vile taste to the world. The caterpillar is colorfully adorned with alternating white, yellow, and black bands, while the adult's bright orange and black coloration is worthy of any highway traffic warning sign! Entomologists have a name for this: aposematic coloration. Does this warning system work? Judge for yourself. In one study, a young Blue Jay that consumed a single Monarch vomited nine times in less than 30 minutes. The next Monarch it encounters—or anything remotely resembling one—will likely be strictly off its menu. Other jays that were fed a Monarch actually retched at the sight of the butterfly!

THE SAGA CONTINUES Read virtually any popular article or book about butterflies and you will find butterfly wings described as gossamer-like, fragile, delicate, lacy, or ethereal. Such adjectives are singularly inappropriate when applied to the Monarch. This butterfly is a tough little beast. A personal experience will illustrate: One fall, Jeffords was returning from a field trip and whacked into a Monarch at nearly 40 miles per hour. It lodged under the car's windshield wiper. As the specimen still seemed to be in good shape, it was extricated from the wiper, to be placed in the Illinois Natural History Survey's collection. The butterfly, though, was not dead, only stunned. In a few minutes, it had recovered and

BELOW Worn male Monarch at Mexico overwintering site

was again winging its way south. Toughness is a highly appropriate characteristic for an insect that may travel as far as 3,600 kilometers (2,160 miles) to winter in Mexico, and return the following spring to the southern United States.

The story of migration really begins with the last Monarch generation produced in the Midwest. In most Illinois summers we have three generations, or broods, of the Monarch. The last generation is unique because it delays reproduction by entering a phase called reproductive diapause. When the cool days of September and October approach, Monarchs begin to congregate and head in a southwesterly direction. As far as scientists know, they stop their flights as dusk approaches and form temporary clusters on trees or shrubs. These groups may break up the next morning or last for a few days, depending on the weather.

BELOW/RIGHT
Congregation of Monarchs in a wet meadow in the Sierra Madre, Mexico

Although most people are familiar with the Monarch (the Monarch is the first, and often only, butterfly that children know by name), few have witnessed its true migratory behavior. The migratory scenario for the eastern Monarch goes something like this.

ABOVE Group of Monarchs waiting for a puddle of frozen water to thaw

When wind and weather conditions are favorable, an eastern Monarch glides up on rising air currents and soars skyward. Glider pilots have observed the Monarch as high as 1,250 meters (0.78 miles) above the ground. The journey can take 75 days, and an individual may average at least 50 kilometers (31 miles) per day to reach the high-altitude forests of the Sierra Madre where it will spend the winter. The journey gives new meaning to the words "genetic memory," for this migrant is three to five generations removed from the spring migrants that came north the previous year. This inherited behavior can be summarized quite simply. First, migration is activated each autumn and spring; second, migration is repressed in winter and summer; and, third, migration switches 180 degrees in orientation between autumn and spring (south in autumn, north in spring).

The midwestern Monarch is adapted to the Mexican alpine forests. The cold temperatures allow the Monarch to lower its metabolic rate and activity from mid-November to mid-March while it rests quietly in the familiar, densely clustered firs. The Monarch must conserve its fat reserves if it is to make the return flight. Occasionally, large numbers of Monarchs fly off to drink water or fly about to cool off if direct sunlight hits them for extended periods. As the winter proceeds, mating frequency increases in preparation for the return trip. After the spring equinox, the Monarch returns to the Gulf Coast states and lays eggs on southern milkweeds to produce the first generation of new adults. This generation migrates northward (as far as southern Canada) laying eggs as it goes. Up to three generations are produced in the upper Midwest. The final, reproductive diapause generation—often the great-great-great-grandchildren of the spring migrants—must then make the long return flight.

WHY ARE MONARCHS IMPORTANT? While the species is in little danger of extinction—western populations overwinter in protected coastal California areas, while a resident population also occurs in Florida—the biological phenomenon of eastern migration may be endangered. The story is the same as it is for most species, and habitat destruction by humans is the culprit. Progressive deforestation is opening up the montane forests and affording the overwintering Monarch less than ideal conditions for survival (e.g., a changing microclimate). Increased ecotourism, while a boon to the local economies, may also be disturbing the Monarch and causing depletion of fat reserves. Ultimately

BELOW Monarchs on Oyamel Fir

though, ecotourism may provide the revenue to preserve endangered Monarch habitat.

Several years ago, a natural factor entered the picture: a rare snowstorm in the Sierra Madre that may have killed as many as 15% to 35% of the Monarchs. Both *The New York Times* and the *Chicago Tribune* noted the event with feature stories. They quoted Professor Lincoln Brower, a world authority on the Monarch: *"I think this was probably a bad freeze, but not the worst. Storms have been occurring for the last 10,000 years, and Monarchs have adapted to them at those high altitudes."* He continued, *"The problem is that the Mexicans are thinning the forest… It's like camping outside with a hole in your blanket that lets in the cold."*

BELOW/RIGHT Monarchs waiting for the migration back to the eastern United States

What does all this mean to Illinois' Monarchs? Most scientists think the odd weather will have little impact on Monarch populations in the long term. While data from annual 4th of July Butterfly Counts (the butterfly equivalent of the Christmas Bird Count) from 1977 to the present have shown year-to-year fluctuations in Monarch numbers, often coinciding with unusual weather events, Monarch numbers once appeared to be relatively stable. However, a lengthy drought in the Midwest during the early part of the 21st Century has caused a decline of both nectar plants and milkweeds; the former is necessary to replenish food reserves during the long migration to Mexico, and the latter to keep Monarch populations large and viable. The increased drought has also allowed more extensive mowing of roadside and other "waste place" landscapes—prime habitat for both nectar plants and milkweeds. In any year Monarch numbers may decrease somewhat, but the species will hopefully rebound as conditions improve. Only time will tell. Currently, national awareness of the Monarch and the importance of milkweed to the species is increasing. The Monarch often receives special attention from The Nature Conservancy's butterfly monitoring program and from volunteers who collect data during the July 4th count. With a little help from its friends (all of us), this most beloved of butterflies will continue to grace the Midwestern landscape and make its annual epic journey from the backyards of Illinois to the boughs of ancient firs in the Mexican highlands and back again each succeeding spring.

BATESIAN AND MÜLLERIAN MIMICRY   The Monarch allows us to discuss the widespread phenomenon, especially noted in butterflies, of mimicy. Mimicry is simply the similarity of one species to another, which helps protect one, or both, from predation. The similarity can be in appearance, behavior, or sound, but for our purposes, we will concentrate on appearance. When an insect with a particular color pattern feeds on a toxic plant that makes it unpalatable or has some other defensive mechanism (like a sting) that protects it from predation, through time and by the process of natural selection, other insects may come to mimic that pattern. This convergence of color patterns, noted first by tropical biologist Henry Bates in the nineteenth century, is called Batesian Mimicry. The toxic species is called the model, while the palatable species that derives protection from its resemblance to the toxic species is called the mimic. Research undertaken by Jeffords and J. G. Sternburg at the University of Illinois in the 1970s noted that these mimicry complexes (a model and several mimicking species) actually convey a significant survival advantage to the mimics. A related phenomenon, noted by a tropical naturalist Fritz Müller, has various unpalatable species sharing similar color patterns. This was particularly noted in the Heliconiidae (longwing butterflies) of tropical America. Why should this be? As it turns out, visually orienting predators soon learn what is edible and what it not, and the fewer patterns they have to learn to avoid, the greater the protection afforded to those toxic species; in other words, fewer "mistakes" are made by predators. Thus, the classic toxic model and the palatable mimic of Batesian Mimicry is replaced by a group of toxic butterflies that share a common pattern (Müllerian Mimicry). Both types of mimicry form quite an elegant evolutionary scenario.

Let's look for an Illinois example to illustrate just

how complex mimicry can actually become. Certain insects take advantage of the Monarch's lack of appeal to hungry predators by mimicking its color pattern. The Viceroy, an assumed palatable, orange butterfly with a pattern remarkably similar to the Monarch's, achieves some measure of protection from predation by birds that have nibbled on its near twin. This phenomenon, as noted above, is called Batesian Mimicry. Even though this story appears in numerous textbooks and is "common knowledge for most people," the story is not quite so simple. Studies in Florida have shown that the Viceroy is almost as unappetizing as the Monarch. While the Viceroy caterpillar feeds on supposedly nontoxic willows, it somehow manages to secure its own chemical defenses. Thus, the Monarch (the original toxic model) and its supposed mimic (the Viceroy) are both toxic and are actually exhibiting the other type of mimicry—Müllerian Mimicry. To further complicate this story, some of the milkweeds that the Monarch eats do not contain heart poisons (cardiac glycosides) and thus some individuals are palatable. This means that some Monarchs may actually be Batesian mimics of Viceroys!

BELOW Viceroy basking—note the dark line across the hindwing

ATAVISM AND MIMICRY Atavism is the tendency to revert to an ancestral type. In biology, an atavism is an evolutionary throwback, such as traits reappearing that existed generations before. Relative to mimicry complexes, atavism often reveals the ancestry of a particular mimetic color pattern.

PIPEVINE SWALLOWTAIL MIMICRY COMPLEX Another interesting Batesian Mimicry complex exists in Illinois (and much of the eastern U.S.), and has as its model the unpalatable Pipevine Swallowtail. The Pipevine Swallowtail caterpillar feeds on pipevine, dutchman's pipe, and other members of *Aristolochia*, making both the adult and caterpillar toxic and emetic (cause predators to retch and vomit upon ingestion). This large, black butterfly (with a steel blue sheen and large orange spots) is very distinctive in its woodland habitats.

BELOW Viceroy and Red-spotted Purple courting

Several species of butterflies (and the male of a day-flying, giant silkmoth) have evolved patterns that closely resemble the Pipevine Swallowtail.

LEFT A likely example of atavism: top and underside of a Viceroy/Red-spotted Purple ancestral type.[2] Specimens are actual size

Members of this mimicry complex include the Black Swallowtail female, Spicebush Swallowtail female, and Tiger Swallowtail dark form female. Note that only the females of these species are mimics; the males retain their ancestral color patterns. This is thought to be because the females respond only to the ancestral male color patterns during courtship. Other members of the mimicry complex include both sexes of the Red-spotted Purple, Diana females (males retain orange and black pattern), and the most unlikely of all, males of the Promethea Silk Moth. In this latter species, the female releases a pheromone into the wind for the male to follow and locate her. Thus, the male is on the wing trying to find a receptive, yet stationary, female. In the vast majority of the Family Saturniidae, this behavior happens under the cover of darkness. However,

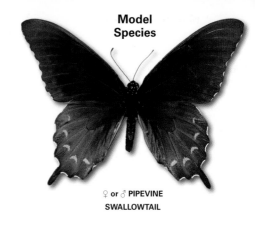

Model Species

♀ or ♂ **PIPEVINE SWALLOWTAIL**

RIGHT Species included in the Pipevine Swallowtail mimicry complex. Specimens are half their normal size

the Promethea Moth female releases her pheromone in mid-afternoon. Thus, the male is active during the day, exposing him to visually orienting predators—this explains why the male Promethea Moth has diverged from the ancestral, cryptic color pattern and is very dark-colored, resembling the Pipevine Swallowtail in flight.

The mimicry story does not end here though! It also involves the distribution of the Pipevine Swallowtail and two of its mimicking species—the Tiger Swallowtail and the Red-spotted Purple/White Admiral (*Limenitis*) subspecies. Where the ranges of the Pipevine Swallowtail and the Tiger Swallowtail overlap (generally south of Wisconsin/Michigan), the majority of female Tiger Swallowtails are the dark form mimic—yellow females are predominant in the north. The same phenomenon occurs with *Limenitis*. Where Pipevine and *Limenitis* distributions overlap, the Red-spotted Purple subspecies is present; where the Pipevine does not occur in the northern states, the White Admiral becomes the common subspecies. A somewhat narrow transition zone occurs in the northern U.S. where intergrades between the Red-spotted Purple and the White Admiral regularly occur. It appears the benefit of mimicking a toxic species ceases to be adaptive when the model is no longer present.

Mimicking Species

♀ DIANA

♀ TIGER
SWALLOWTAIL
(DARK FORM)

♀ SPICEBUSH
SWALLOWTAIL

♀ or ♂ RED-SPOTTED PURPLE

♂ PROMETHEA
MOTH

♀ BLACK
SWALLOWTAIL

BINOCULARS FOR BUTTERFLY OBSERVATION

The days are mostly gone when a butterfly enthusiast heads out "to the field" armed only with a favorite net and a killing jar. While certain enthusiasts, and some scientists, still never leave home without a net, many individuals today explore the butterfly world only with notebooks, cameras, and a pair of "butterfly binoculars." Just like "regular" binoculars for bird watching, a good pair of butterfly binoculars will improve your ability to see the subtle features of color, wing shape, and behavior, and will allow an easier study of skittish species such as the Gemmed or Carolina Satyrs, species that never seem to land.

The most important feature of a pair of butterfly binoculars is its ability to focus close. Look for binoculars that focus ten feet or closer—those that focus as close as six feet are ideal. Most standard bird watching binoculars do not allow for close focus, so you will be constantly backing up to view an ever-smaller subject. The ability to focus your binoculars on a subject only a short distance away will enhance your field identification skills.

BELOW A Tawny Emperor helping with its identification

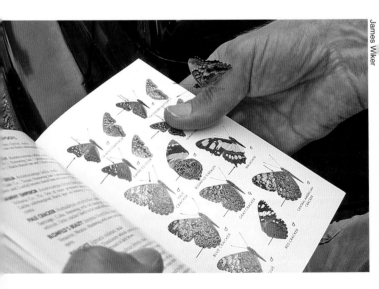

James Wiker

James Wiker

ABOVE Butterfly guru Robert Michael Pyle using close-focusing binoculars for butterfly observation

Magnification and light gathering should also be taken into consideration. Six to 8× magnification works well, as the butterflies are being observed at close range. While light gathering ability is very important for birds in forests or in dark shadows, remember that butterflies are usually active in bright or dappled sunlight, so quick focusing may be more important than light-gathering capabilities. Unlike birders who must arise at the crack of dawn, butterfly watching is usually confined to the civilized hours between 10 am and 5 pm, when there is plenty of light. So if the cost of really "fast binoculars" does not fit your budget, a less expensive pair will work very well for butterfly watching. Before you make a purchase, attend a local butterfly field outing and observe what others are using. Don't be afraid to inquire of others, "Mind if I take a look?" (This is how we happened to find the type we use.)

Using your close-focusing binoculars, you will notice that that butterfly you thought was a Gemmed Satyr bouncing around the woods edge actually has several eyespots, and is really a Carolina Satyr. Soon you will not leave home without your butterfly binoculars!

DOCUMENTATION OF ILLINOIS BUTTERFLIES

The historical norm for scientific purposes has always been, and will likely continue to be, the making of collections of well-curated specimens (pinned, spread, and labeled with appropriate collection data). The collecting of common insects by children for 4-H and school projects has led to many entomological careers. However, given the advanced state of human development on the landscape, we can no longer say with assurance that "collecting butterflies has little or no impact

on populations." Thus, unless you are a serious amateur who plans to donate the collection to an appropriate scientific institution or a scientist doing systematic studies, we encourage you to engage in butterfly watching and photography rather than collecting. Digital photography has advanced to the point that almost anyone, with a little practice and a decent quality point-and-shoot camera, can obtain good photos of butterflies that are easily identifiable. When coupled with locality, date, and other information, these photos can become important data points for Illinois butterfly documentation.

ABOVE Illinois Natural History Survey (University of Illinois at Urbana-Champaign) insect collection (Photo by David Riecks, NRES)

ABOVE Note-keeping, an important component of observing butterflies

RIGHT ABOVE Photography, the preferred method for documenting butterfly records in today's world

RIGHT BELOW Collections such as the Todd Wiley collection (1975–2000) are valuable for scientific studies; however, due to potential declines in butterfly populations, routine collection is no longer encouraged

Over the years, we have noted that the public is relatively observant and notices Illinois' butterflies. During the spring of 2012, an influx of the Red Admiral was noted by both the print and electronic media, and the authors fielded many questions about this seemingly curious and "unusual" phenomenon. During late summer of 2013, a flurry of media attention on the Monarch and its seeming absence from the Illinois landscape led to a series of newspaper articles and National Public Radio spots on the subject. It was both gratifying and somewhat alarming to the authors. Gratifying in the fact that individuals noticed the large number of Red Admirals, and alarming in that so few Monarchs graced the Illinois landscape as to attract widespread attention.

Do not hesitate to keep a notebook on your butterfly observations. Remember, one entry is an observation, two observations are a trend, and three observations are the start of data!

BUTTERFLY GARDENING AND CONSERVATION

"Butterflies add another dimension to the garden, for they are like dream flowers—childhood dreams—which have broken loose from their stalks and escaped into the sunshine."

Miriam Rothschild, 1983
British entomologist and avid gardener

A butterfly garden can be a colorful window to the local environment. It will let you know what butterflies are in your area and provide habitat and food for these colorful "flowers." All you need to become a butterfly gardener is a sunny space, good soil, a little bit of hard work, and an assortment of nectar-producing flowering plants. If those plants happen to be native to Illinois prairies, wetlands, or woodlands, so much the better; the butterfly garden can become a personal biological preserve. For those of you who are not merely content to watch the daily feeding rituals of adult butterflies, but instead desire a more intimate experience, caterpillar food plants

can be interspersed with the adult nectar plants. One can then watch a diminutive "bird dropping" caterpillar slowly change into a rough, green snake mimic (the caterpillar of the Spicebush Swallowtail), or observe the tiger-striped Monarch caterpillar as it transforms into a jeweled chrysalis.

Butterflies add an additional dimension to the garden—carefree flight. While we cannot confine them to one garden, we can lure them to our flowers with careful planning. Unfortunately, they don't stay in one spot or where we would like them to; instead, they "charge through the garden like a wild roller coaster—up to a tree top, over a roof, and down the block." But we can lure them again and again! It is best to locate your garden in a sunny area—butterflies are cold-blooded and need sunlight to warm their flight muscles. When not feeding, a butterfly likes to relax in the sun. Flat stones or boards placed in and around the garden will provide ideal resting sites. Wind and predators are two serious threats to a butterfly. Although not much can be done about predators, planting your garden in a protected spot next to a vine-covered

fence, a wall, or a windbreak of shrubs or trees will protect butterflies from summer winds. To provide a cool drink for a thirsty butterfly, add a mud puddle, made from an old container without drainage holes that is sunk into the ground. A mud puddle provides important sources of moisture, and is as irresistible to a butterfly as it is to a child. A final step before designing a garden is to become familiar with the native butterfly fauna of your area, including their life cycles and food preferences.

To get started with your butterfly garden, plant carrots or dill in an area of your vegetable garden and allow the inevitable Black Swallowtail caterpillars that will appear to thrive here. Move any caterpillars from the "vegetable garden" to this area, "designated just for wildlife," and enjoy watching them develop. If your butterfly garden is to be a success, remember to refrain from using any pesticides in that area. Also, several of the other swallowtail caterpillars feed on such common small trees as cherry, pawpaw, sassafras, wafer ash, and prickly ash. These often grow in little noticed areas at the edges or corners of property and are very important to the survival of most of the swallowtail species.

LEFT Black Swallowtail caterpillars feeding on dill

BELOW Alfalfa Butterfly on Mexican sunflower, a common butterfly garden plant

ABOVE Overwintered Mourning Cloak

RIGHT Bark flaps, good overwintering sites for butterflies

Before deciding on a strategy of "clean gardening," consider the wildlife (in this case butterflies) that may call it home. The aforementioned plants do not require a large area to thrive and provide food for caterpillars and shelter for birds and small mammals. Another good idea is to provide shelter and overwintering sites for butterflies—these are not the butterfly houses now prominent in most garden centers (butterflies simply don't use them). However, a log or brush pile can provide prime overwintering refuges for those species that spend the winter as adults. Also, leave plant debris in your butterfly garden for those species that overwinter as chrysalids or as partially grown caterpillars. Remember: a clean garden is often a butterfly-free garden!

Whether your garden encompasses several acres or resides in a few containers on the back deck, butterflies will be attracted if their basic needs are satisfied. If everyone employed these simple gardening strategies and left a small area of the yard "wild" and wildlife friendly, our Illinois landscape would be much more inviting to its birds, bees, and butterflies. Just as your garden grows, so will your knowledge and enjoyment of Illinois butterflies.

THREATS TO ILLINOIS BUTTERFLIES

We live in constantly changing times, and the human influence on the earth's landscape continues to grow. While continual progress and economic growth are always considered as "good outcomes" by most citizens, they usually come with a price. That price is most often paid in decreased natural habitats and landscapes, areas necessary for preservation of the earth's biodiversity, butterflies included. A simple analogy here will perhaps describe the state and fate of Illinois' butterflies. For the last decade or so, honey bee populations have been decreasing at an alarming rate. We take note of this because the honey bee is an economically important insect. The phenomenon has been given a specific name—Colony Collapse Disorder—for a generalized and difficult-to-pinpoint cause. Scientists today have concluded that Colony Collapse Disorder has no single cause, but is the cumulative effect of many factors including pesticides, disease, loss of habitat, parasites, and even possibly global climate change. Perhaps butterflies are undergoing a similar fate caused by a set of factors similar to those adversely affecting honey bees. It may be too soon to tell, but it is well known that butterfly populations are declining in Illinois, in the Midwest, in the United States, and certainly on a world-wide scale. It is not too late to reverse this trend; however, the solutions are not easy and will not come without some sacrifice. It's up to all citizens to become in-

BELOW Mowed roadside

RIGHT Roadside containing weedy flowering plants and roadside with a scattering of native species, respectively. Both of these roadside types are necessary for the overall health of Illinois butterfly populations

ABOVE Roadkill Monarch illustrating that automobiles take their share of butterflies

RIGHT Corn field from above (Photo by Joseph Spencer)

formed and to develop a conservation ethic toward all organisms of the earth. After all, we appear at this time to be the only planet in the immensity of the universe that supports the amazing diversity of organisms that call earth home. Let's begin the campaign by learning about, appreciating, and conserving a representative group of that diversity, the butterflies of Illinois.

Lepidoptera and Bt Corn

JOSEPH L. SPENCER—ILLINOIS NATURAL HISTORY SURVEY, PRAIRIE RESEARCH INSTITUTE, UNIVERSITY OF ILLINOIS

Certain members of the Order Lepidoptera (butterflies and moths) are among the most damaging pests of corn; many spend the majority of their time feeding within the plant tissues, making them difficult to manage with insecticides alone. One of the most widespread and damaging of those pests is the European Corn Borer (ECB, *Ostrinia nubilalis* (Hübner)), which is responsible for $1 billion in losses annually. In 1996, the first corn plants genetically engineered to kill harmful insects were sold in the USA. Those corn hybrids produced toxins derived from the soil microbe *Bacillus thuringiensis* (Bt) that had been found to specifically kill the larvae of lepidopteran pests. The Bt microbes end up in

ABOVE Crop plane spraying pesticides

the caterpillar's gut and then escape into the body where they infect and kill it.

Bt crops with resistance to insect pests offered many advantages over the use of traditional chemical insecticides. Use of Bt hybrids reduced harm to beneficial insects (predators, pollinators, and parasites), reduced grower exposure to insecticides, and was as effective at eliminating pests as traditional insecticides. Following their introduction, Bt corn hybrids were rapidly adopted and dramatic reductions in the impact of ECB and other lepidopteran pests were observed.

The relative safety of Bt corn to beneficial insects came into question following publication of a laboratory study by Losey et al. (1999) in the journal *Nature*. It suggested that the Monarch caterpillar (*Danaus plexippus* (L.)) was vulnerable to mortality caused by consumption of pollen from Bt corn. The implication of this article was that the Monarch, and perhaps other nontarget organisms, was threatened by the cultivation of Bt corn. However, the brief publication did not adequately provide evidence that Bt corn presented a true ecological risk to Monarch populations.

Soon after the publication of Losey, controversy surrounding the purported Bt corn risk to the Monarch caterpillar led to research and publication of multiple papers addressing Bt corn pollen toxicity. A prominent series of six papers appearing in the *Proceedings of the National Academy of Science*, USA (PNAS) yielded a definitive risk assessment of the impact of Bt corn on Monarch butterfly populations. The final paper of the PNAS series concluded that: "This two-year study suggests that the impact of Bt corn pollen from commercial hybrids on Monarch butterfly populations is negligible." An additional worst-case assessment suggests that 2.4% of the Monarch butterfly breeding population in the Corn Belt could be at risk from Bt corn pollen. However, even under the worst-case scenario, the conclusion was: "…it is likely that Bt corn will not affect the sustainability of Monarch butterfly populations in North America."

The potential for Bt corn pollen to impact the biology of several other nontarget Lepidopteran species has also been studied. These studies clearly indicate that Bt corn constitutes a potential hazard to nontargets, but a comprehensive assessment of the risks requires more data.

BELOW Sand prairie with no buffer zone between it and adjacent corn field

NATURAL HAZARDS

Anyone who has spent time in nature is familiar with the food chain—organisms eat other organisms in a never-ending struggle for survival. Because of insects' location in the food chain (they occupy mostly the second and third trophic levels), they are not only important, but vital, components of energy flow through ecosystems. An insect in the second trophic level is an herbivore, while an insect in the third trophic level is a carnivore and feeds on other organisms. A butterfly, despite its beauty and charisma, is certainly not immune to predation and its "place" in nature is often easily observed. A butterfly sitting on a flower behaving somewhat erratically may, upon closer inspection, actually be the captive of a crab spider that is slowly dissolving its internal structures for its upcoming

LEFT Crab spider eating an Alfalfa Butterfly

BELOW Diagram of an energy pyramid depicting the four major trophic levels

4 — TOP CARNIVORES

3 — CARNIVORES

2 — HERBIVORES

1 — PRODUCERS

ABOVE Spicebush Swallowtail being eaten by a wasp

RIGHT ABOVE *Argiope*, an orb web spider, with *Colias* prey

RIGHT BELOW Carolina Mantis nymph eating a Cabbage Butterfly

meal. An orb web spider takes its share of unwary butterflies. A mantis is also a conspicuous predator of butterflies. More subtle, but no less lethal, hazards to a butterfly include predation by ants on its caterpillar, and attacks by parasitoid wasps and flies. A parasitoid is an insect that lays its eggs in or on a host; each egg hatches into a larvae that feeds on the host's internal (sometimes also external) structures, ultimately resulting in the host's death. Most everyone has seen a lepidopteran caterpillar (especially a Tomato Hornworm in your garden) that has an array of fuzzy, egg-shaped structures on its body. These structures are actually the cocoons of a tiny wasp that laid eggs in the younger caterpillar's body. As the parasitoid larvae grow, the caterpillar continues to feed, but will ultimately die. A butterfly, like a moth, has a vast array of parasitic insects that regularly prey on it. A look at a Black Swallowtail caterpillar seemingly thriving in your home garden may reveal a tiny, white egg or two affixed just behind its head. The eggs were placed there by a Tachinid Fly, the location chosen carefully so the caterpillar cannot turn around and bite off the eggs! The maggots that hatch burrow into

the caterpillar's body, ultimately producing more Tachinid Flies, rather than a beautiful swallowtail. Like a human, a butterfly has a variety of diseases that can affect it, including various bacteria, viruses, fungal infections, and even a unique group of pathogens called Microsporidia. Lastly, a butterfly falls relatively easy prey to many species of birds, especially the very active flycatchers and Blue Jay. As the season progresses, an observer will often see wedge-shaped sections missing from butterfly wings—graphic evidence of a close encounter with a usually lethal predator. Keep in mind that all these predator-parasite-prey interactions are natural parts of our living world, and should become part of our observations on butterflies and their role in various ecosystems.

BELOW Zebra Swallowtail with a beak mark

RIGHT Flight-worn Tiger Swallowtail

PART II

SPECIES TREATMENTS

- Family Papilionidae
- Family Pieridae
- Family Lycaenidae
- Family Riodinidae
- Family Nymphalidae

Pipevine Swallowtail

Zebra Swallowtail

FAMILY PAPILIONIDAE
Swallowtail Butterflies

The Family Papilionidae contains Illinois' largest butterflies, the swallowtails. This group is showy and unmistakable, and includes the largest butterflies on earth. The Indonesian Birdwings have females with a wingspan of nearly a foot. Illinois Papilionids are smaller than these tropical giants, and our representatives are all distinctively "tailed"—they have a projection on each hindwing that extends beyond the bottom edge. The tails, reminiscent of the forked tails of swallows, give these butterflies their common name. Another Papilionid characteristic is that spring adults are considerably smaller (and often more brightly colored) than later generations—a summer form may be nearly twice the size of its spring counterpart.

Any large butterfly found in Illinois with tailed hindwings should immediately be identified as one of the swallowtails. Six species breed here, each overwintering as a cryptic (camouflaged to look like a dead leaf or plant stem) pupa (called a chrysalis) either on or near the host plant. Another species may occur here, but has not yet been found (Joan's Swallowtail[3]). A final species occasionally enters as a rare stray (Palamedes Swallowtail).

Swallowtail caterpillars are quite distinctive. With the exception of the Pipevine, which lays its eggs in groups, Illinois' swallowtails lay their eggs singly. The caterpillars have various ways of defending themselves, including mimicry, crypsis, and resemblance to snakes, centipedes, and bird droppings. A unique structure—the osmeterium—is found behind the head of a swallowtail caterpillar. It is a tubular, V-shaped gland (resembling a brightly colored forked tongue) that is normally hidden. If the caterpillar is disturbed or threatened, this structure is everted and emits smelly secretions. Male swallowtails have a tendency to puddle at wet sites on the ground or along stream banks. Swallowtails are drawn to flowers. With their large size and bright colors, they are welcome visitors to flower gardens and are adept pollinators for a number of herbs, shrubs, and trees.

SPECIES

- Pipevine Swallowtail
- Zebra Swallowtail
- Black Swallowtail
- Giant Swallowtail
- Tiger Swallowtail
- Spicebush Swallowtail
- Palamedes Swallowtail

PIPEVINE SWALLOWTAIL

Battus philenor (Linnaeus)

DESCRIPTION Velvety-black, iridescent, and blue-green are all descriptors for the Pipevine Swallowtail. The Pipevine

Male

Male

PREVALENCE
Widely
encountered

FLIGHT PERIOD

MAR
APR
MAY
JUN
JUL
AUG
SEP
OCT
NOV

FIELD NOTES

A. Reflective, blue to bluish-green scales on outer two-thirds of hindwing (♂ T)

B. Single row of seven large, orange spots (U)

has a wingspan of 3.5–4.5 inches. The upperside is a deep, soft black; pale spots occur along the lower half of the forewing and on the outer margins of the hindwing. The outer two-thirds of the upper- and underside of the hindwing are covered with reflective, blue-green scales that flash in the sun. While more prevalent on the male, both sexes are iridescent and otherwise similar. The underside has a single row of seven large, circular, orange spots that follow the curve of the hindwing.

COULD BE CONFUSED WITH Though the Pipevine Swallowtail is the model for a Batesian mimicry complex, it is relatively easily identified. Due to mimicry, any of the dark-colored swallowtails, the Red-spotted Purple, and the Diana female could be mistaken for the Pipevine (see page 352). The Pipevine Swallowtail is Illinois' only dark swallowtail with no red or orange spot (sometimes part of an eye spot) near the tail on the upperside of the hindwing. The Red-spotted Purple and Diana female do not have tails or seven large, orange spots on the underside of their hindwings.

HABITAT/LIFE HISTORY Though often found in flower gardens, the Pipevine Swallowtail is typically a forest butterfly and is seldom far from the woods. The caterpillar feeds on pipevine, dutchman's pipe, and other members of the plant genus *Aristolochia*. The toxins in the caterpillar host plant carry over into the adult, making it unpalatable or noxious to most predators. The Pipevine Swallowtail has multiple generations a year, with the adult present from April into October. The species over-winters as a chrysalis.

STATUS The Pipevine Swallowtail can be found in most of Illinois; however, it is scarce north of Peoria's latitude and is absent from the northwest corner of the state due to the lack of host plants. The species is rather common in the southern half of Illinois, though never as abundant as the other swallowtails.

♂ T

WINGSPAN
3.5–4.5 in

♂ U

ZEBRA SWALLOWTAIL
Eurytides marcellus (Cramer)

PREVALENCE
Widely
encountered

FLIGHT PERIOD

MAR	
APR	
MAY	
JUN	
JUL	
AUG	
SEP	
OCT	
NOV	

FIELD NOTES

A. Long, thin tails

B. Black-and-white striped wings (T & U)

C. Red stripe (U)

Male: spring form

Female: summer form

DESCRIPTION The Zebra Swallowtail has a wingspan of 2.5–4.0 inches, with the spring individual smaller. The upper- and underside are both black-and-white striped, with a red spot and a dash of blue on the hindwing. The underside of the hindwing also has a black-bordered, red stripe. With its long, thin tails, the Zebra Swallowtail's appearance is showy and distinctive.

COULD BE CONFUSED WITH Nothing in Illinois.

HABITAT/LIFE HISTORY The Zebra Swallowtail inhabits moist, shaded, deciduous woods where pawpaw, its caterpillar food plant, occurs. A Zebra Swallowtail's black-and-white stripes blend in remarkably well in sun-dappled woods, and the red spot at the base of its long tails gives predators a false head to aim at. These features increase an adult's chances of surviving a bird attack, though it is often observed with one or both tails missing. The adult flits about on woodland flowers or in flower-filled meadows. A spring generation female appears in the forest two to three weeks before pawpaw trees leaf out. Once the leaves open, the female lays her eggs on the upper surface. The species overwinters as a chrysalis. The adult appears by early April in the south and late April farther north, making it one of the first large butterflies to emerge each spring. The Zebra Swallowtail has multiple generations per year in most of Illinois. It has a long emergence period—a few individuals are always present from spring to late summer. An adult observed between generations may be battle-worn, with no tails and shredded wings.

STATUS The Zebra Swallowtail is found throughout the state, but is far more common south of Peoria's latitude. If pawpaw is absent, the butterfly will usually not be found.

♂ T

WINGSPAN
2.5–4.0 in

♂ U

BLACK SWALLOWTAIL
Papilio polyxenes asterius (Stoll)

PREVALENCE
Widely
encountered

FLIGHT PERIOD

MAR
APR
MAY
JUN
JUL
AUG
SEP
OCT
NOV

FIELD NOTES

A. Rows of
yellow (T) and
orangish-yellow
spots (U)

B. Reddish-
orange patches
with centered
black spots (T
& U)

Female

Male

DESCRIPTION The sexually dimorphic Black Swallowtail has a 2.75–4.0 inch wingspan, with the female larger and the spring individual smaller. The upperside of both sexes is black with rows of yellow spots. At the trailing edge of the hindwing note a reddish patch with a centered black spot (an eye spot). The male upperside has irregular yellow spots in two rows with a blue band on each hindwing. The female upperside has less yellow and more sky blue scaling than the male upperside. The underside pattern of both sexes is similar to the upperside, but with a hint of greenish scaling on the outer edge of the blue. Also, most of the yellow is replaced by orange on the underside.

COULD BE CONFUSED WITH The Pipevine Swallowtail, which the Black Swallowtail female mimics, has little or no yellow on it (see page 352). The Spicebush Swallowtail female has blue-green chevrons on the outer margin of her hindwing, whereas the Black Swallowtail has bright yellow spots. The Pipevine and Spicebush lack the Black Swallowtails's hindwing eyespot.

HABITAT/LIFE HISTORY The Black Swallowtail is the state's most widespread Papilionid. It is equally at home in the suburbs as it is in rural settings. The species occurs along roadways, old fields, vacant lots, and city gardens—anywhere nectar sources and caterpillar host plants (members of the carrot family) grow. To gardeners, the caterpillar is better known than the adult, as it favors carrot, parsley, and dill. Few people realize this "obnoxious worm" turns into an adult Black Swallowtail. The adult male is known for "hill-topping," and often perches on the highest point he can find to await a passing female. Multiple generations occur each year, and the adult can be found from April through October. The species overwinters as a chrysalis.

STATUS The Black Swallowtail is found throughout the state, likely occurring in every county.

♂ T

♀ T

WINGSPAN
2.75–4.0 in

♂ U

GIANT SWALLOWTAIL
Papilio cresphontes Cramer

PREVALENCE
Widely
encountered

FLIGHT PERIOD

MAR
APR
MAY
JUN
JUL
AUG
SEP
OCT
NOV

FIELD NOTES

A. Yellow bands
across the wings
(T)

B. Tail with a
yellow center (T)

Male

Female

DESCRIPTION The Giant Swallowtail, the largest butterfly in the U.S., has a wingspan of 5.0–6.0 inches, with the spring individual smaller. The upperside is dark brown with various yellow markings that form yellow bands. The underside is predominantly yellow with a small amount of blue and orange in the middle of the hindwing. The hindwing tail is dark brown with a yellow center, and is wider than those on other Illinois swallowtails.

COULD BE CONFUSED WITH The only butterfly that could be confused with the Giant Swallowtail is the Palamedes Swallowtail. Although the upperside of both species is similar in appearance, the underside of the Palamedes is brown, whereas the underside of the Giant is predominantly yellow. Note that the Palamedes is a rare stray in Illinois.

HABITAT/LIFE HISTORY The Giant Swallowtail can be found along the edges of woods, especially those containing the caterpillar host plants, wafer ash and prickly ash. The caterpillar is an excellent bird-dropping mimic—when half-grown, it is brown and white and appears shiny or wet, giving it a "fresh" bird-dropping appearance. The caterpillar often rests in plain sight on the upper surface of a leaf. The adult is an avid flower visitor with a slow, languid flight, intent on visiting every bloom available. It is fond of thistles, cultivated clover, and ironweed, but visits a wide variety of flowers in various habitats. While sipping nectar, it continually flutters its wings. There are two overlapping generations a year, and the adult is on the wing from April through October. The species overwinters as a chrysalis.

♂ T

WINGSPAN
5.0–6.0 in

**FIELD NOTES
(CONTD)**

B. Tail with a yellow center (U)

C. Shades of yellow with a small amount of blue and orange on the hindwing (U)

Female

Female

The Giant Swallowtail occurs throughout Illinois; however, it is most common in a band across the state that runs from Effingham north to Peoria, and less common at the northern and southern extremes of Illinois. The Giant Swallowtail is secure in Illinois, but is never as abundant as its fellow swallowtails.

WINGSPAN
5.0–6.0 in

♂ **U**

TIGER SWALLOWTAIL
Papilio glaucus Linnaeus

PREVALENCE
Widely
encountered

FLIGHT PERIOD

MAR	
APR	
MAY	
JUN	
JUL	
AUG	
SEP	
OCT	
NOV	

FIELD NOTES
A. Bright yellow
with black stripes
(♂ T & Yellow form
♀ T)

Female

Male

DESCRIPTION The Tiger Swallowtail has a wing-span of about 5 inches, with the spring individual smaller. The male is bright yellow with black stripes on the upperside, and is similarly colored underneath with the addition of small, orange-and-blue areas.

The female has two different color forms. One form resembles the male, except that it has extensive blue scaling on the upperside of the hindwing. This form is much more common in the northern third of the state. The second form is black; the "black tiger stripes" that are prominent in the yellow form are subdued, but distinguishable, on the underside. The blue hindwing coloring occurs on the dark form as well. The dark form is more common in the southern two-thirds of the state, where the Pipevine Swallowtail (which it mimics) is common. This trend (the dark form female common and the yellow form female rare) continues throughout the southern United States. A "mosaic"—an aberrant, intermediate individual that has both yellow and black coloration—occurs, but is uncommon (see page 7).

♂ T

WINGSPAN
~ 5.0 inches

COULD BE CONFUSED WITH The Tiger Swallowtail male and yellow female should not be confused with any other butterfly in Illinois. The dark form female is similar to the other dark swallowtails and the Red-spotted Purple; however, the faint but noticeable "tiger stripes" on the underside should identify this species (see page 352).

HABITAT/LIFE HISTORY The striking Tiger Swallowtail is one of the most familiar large butterflies in the state. It is at home in woodland areas, but can frequently be seen in city landscapes. In Illinois, the caterpillar feeds on a variety of plants, including cherry, tulip

TIGER SWALLOWTAIL (CONTD)
Papilio glaucus Linnaeus

FIELD NOTES (CONTD)

B. Faint, black stripes on dark form (♀ U)

Female: yellow form

Female: dark form

poplar, and wafer ash. A young caterpillar looks like a bird-dropping, but as it grows older it resembles a green snake, complete with eyespots. The adult male will often congregate with a large number of other males at a damp spot along roads, streams or rivers, forming a large puddle club. There are multiple generations each season, and the adult is on the wing from late March to early November. The species overwinters as a chrysalis.

STATUS The Tiger Swallowtail is common and found statewide; it no doubt occurs in every county.

WINGSPAN
~ 5.0 inches

♀ **U**
dark form

SPICEBUSH SWALLOWTAIL
Papilio troilus Linnaeus

DESCRIPTION The sexually dimorphic Spicebush Swallowtail has a wingspan of 3.0–5.0 inches, with the spring individual smaller. The upperside of the forewing is black in both sexes, with one row (sometimes a very weak, second inner row) of pale yellow spots along the outer

PREVALENCE
Widely
encountered

FLIGHT PERIOD

MAR	
APR	
MAY	
JUN	
JUL	
AUG	
SEP	
OCT	
NOV	

FIELD NOTES

A. Pale greenish-blue chevrons (T)

B. Blue-green scales (♂ T)

C. Iridescent blue scales (♀ T) [refer to ♀ T specimen on next page]

D. Two rows of orange spots (U)

E. Break in row of orange spots (U)

Male

Male

margin. These spots become larger toward the inner wing margin. The male upperside has a predominantly green (with a hint of blue) area of scales across the middle of the hindwing; on the female upperside, this area is iridescent blue. Both sexes have spoon-shaped tails and pale blue-green chevrons along the outer margin of the upperside of the hindwing, with the uppermost marking a large, orange spot (this spot can be absent in the male on rare occasions). The underside of both sexes is similar; the hindwing has two rows of orange spots with blue, iridescent scales in between. Also, the blue, iridescent scaling interrupts the inner row after the fourth orange spot.

COULD BE CONFUSED WITH The Pipevine Swallowtail, Black Swallowtail female, and Tiger Swallowtail dark form female are all similar, but lack the green chevrons found on the Spicebush Swallowtail (see page 352). They also lack the interrupted inner row of orange spots on the underside of the Spicebush hindwing.

HABITAT/LIFE HISTORY The Spicebush Swallowtail is a denizen of open woods with adjacent fields and suburban parks with forested areas; it is also commonly seen in flower gardens. The caterpillar feeds on spicebush and sassafras. The young caterpillar is a convincing bird-dropping mimic. As it grows, this disguise is replaced by a resemblance to the head of a green snake. Look for the caterpillar in a leaf folded over into a silk-lined shelter. As the caterpillar grows, its leaf shelter gets larger—a small sassafras tree can have several graduated leaf shelters, each vacated as the caterpillar grows. The adult often flies rapidly from flower to flower during springtime in woods, appearing to be in a hurry. The Spicebush Swallowtail has two generations per year in Illinois, and is on the wing from late March to early November. The species overwinters as a chrysalis.

WINGSPAN
3.0–5.0 in

STATUS The Spicebush Swallowtail is common in the southern two-thirds of Illinois. It becomes sporadic north of Interstate-80, and is likely absent from the northwestern corner of Illinois.

PALAMEDES SWALLOWTAIL
Papilio palamedes Drury

PREVALENCE
Rare stray

FLIGHT PERIOD

MAR	
APR	
MAY	
JUN	
JUL	
AUG	
SEP	
OCT	
NOV	

FIELD NOTES
A. Brown base
color (U)

Will Cook

Female

Will Cook

A

Male

DESCRIPTION   The Palamedes Swallowtail has a wingspan of 4.5–6.0 inches. It is dark brown when it first emerges, but quickly fades to a lighter shade of brown. The upperside of all wings has two rows of yellow spots. On the forewing the spots in the outer row are round; the inner spots are chevron-shaped. On the hindwing, the outer row is made up of crescent-shaped spots, while the inner area is nearly a solid band. The underside of the forewing has the same pattern as the top. The underside of the hindwing has a middle region of yellow-orange and blue, chevron-shaped markings.

COULD BE CONFUSED WITH The Giant Swallowtail is the only species that could be confused with the Palamedes Swallowtail in Illinois. Although the uppersides are similar (the Palamedes has a somewhat more complex pattern), the Palamedes is almost completely brown on the underside, with a thin, hindwing tail. The Giant is mostly yellow on the underside with a wide tail on the hindwing.

HABITAT/LIFE HISTORY In its native range in the southern U.S., the Palamedes Swallowtail favors swampy woodlands. Sassafras, a common plant species in Illinois, is among the caterpillar hosts. The Palamedes Swallowtail could possibly breed in the southern tip of Illinois, but winter conditions will likely be the deciding factor whether it can persist beyond a single season. The adult could be found anytime between late March and mid-October, with mid to late-summer more likely.

STATUS The Palamedes Swallowtail is a rare stray from the southern U.S., and not a regular part of the Illinois fauna.[4]

♂ T

WINGSPAN
4.5–6.0 in

♂ U

Checkered White

Alfalfa Butterfly

FAMILY PIERIDAE
Whites and Sulphurs

The Family Pieridae (whites and sulphurs) includes Illinois' most common butterflies. Drive down any country road from April to October and members of this family—Cabbage Butterfly, Alfalfa Butterfly, and Clouded Sulphur—may be seen flying across or nectaring at the side of the road. These three species have an extensive flight period, and once on the wing, are continuously encountered from March into November. Pierids have a tendency to puddle at moist spots, usually along roads. Also, many species rest with their wings closed, making field identification difficult.

Pierids lay their eggs on the caterpillar's food plant—mustards for the whites, and predominantly legumes for the sulphurs. The eggs soon turn red or orange. This coloration is thought to be a warning to other female Pierids, as they will reject the plant if previously laid eggs are found on it. Even though the caterpillars feed on leaves, buds, and flowers of their host plants, many Pierid caterpillars are also cannibalistic. Eating a sibling or another Pierid species is just a convenient meal. Each species pupates and forms a chrysalis on or near its food plant. Pierids have seasonal, adult forms. In spring and fall, the butterflies have an underside that is redder or darker, thought to be triggered by differing day lengths.

Sixteen species have been recorded from Illinois, with some species quite common (Cabbage Butterfly, Alfalfa Butterfly, and Clouded Sulphur); others have only been documented once or twice (Great Southern White, Orange-barred Sulphur, and Large Orange Sulphur). Two species, Olympia Marble and Falcate Orangetip, are on the wing less than a month each spring. Populations of the other species—Little Yellow, Dogface, Cloudless Sulphur, Sleepy Orange, and Dainty Sulphur—build throughout the summer. Populations of the resident Checkered White are quite local and variable. The Mustard White, unfortunately, appears to have been extirpated from the state.

SPECIES
- Dainty Sulphur
- Mexican Yellow
- Little Yellow
- Sleepy Orange
- Clouded Sulphur
- Alfalfa Butterfly
- Dogface
- Cloudless Sulphur
- Orange-barred Sulphur
- Large Orange Sulphur
- Falcate Orangetip
- Olympia Marble
- Mustard White
- Cabbage Butterfly
- Checkered White
- Great Southern White

DAINTY SULPHUR
Nathalis iole Boisduval

**Male:
fall form**

Female

PREVALENCE
Locally
encountered
migrant

FLIGHT PERIOD

MAR
APR
MAY
JUN
JUL
AUG
SEP
OCT
NOV

FIELD NOTES

A. Elongated
forewing

B. One to two
black dots visible
on forewing (U)

DESCRIPTION The Dainty Sulphur is Illinois' smallest Pierid, with a wingspan of 0.75–1.25 inches. Both sexes are yellow with elongated forewings. The tip of the forewing is black on the upperside. The upperside also has a black bar that extends along both the trailing edge of the forewing and the leading edge of the hindwing; this bar is wider in the female, giving her hindwing a diffuse, black border. The underside of the hindwing is yellow to grayish (gray in the fall form) in both sexes. The underside of the forewing has three black dots; however, this species spends most of its time with its wings closed, so only one or two of the dots may be visible. The male has an oval scent patch (androconial spot) near his body high on the upperside of the hindwing—it is only visible in pinned specimens.

COULD BE CONFUSED WITH The Little Yellow is larger and does not have elongated forewings or black dots on its underside.

HABITAT/LIFE HISTORY The Dainty Sulphur favors open, dry places, such as old fields, prairies, meadows, sandbars along rivers, and roadsides. Unlike most of the state's Pierids whose caterpillar hosts are mustard or legumes, the Dainty Sulphur caterpillar feeds on low-growing members of the daisy family. The adult flies low to the ground and rests with its wings closed. Once the species arrives from the south, several generations are produced in Illinois each year. Historically, the earliest date on record was July, and the latest November, with the majority of sightings observed from mid-August through mid-October. However, in recent years individuals have been observed in Illinois as early as late April.

STATUS The Dainty Sulphur cannot survive an Illinois winter (although the exceedingly mild winter of 2011–2012 may be the exception), so each year it must recolonize the state. The population size varies from season to season. According to Irwin and Downey (1973), it is found throughout the state, but is rare in Cook County.

♂ T

♀ T

WINGSPAN
0.75–1.25 in

♂ U

♀ U
gray
form

MEXICAN YELLOW
Eurema mexicana (Boisduval)

Male

A

PREVALENCE
Rare stray

FLIGHT PERIOD

MAR	
APR	
MAY	
JUN	
JUL	
AUG	
SEP	
OCT	
NOV	

FIELD NOTES
A. Short tail on hindwing

DESCRIPTION The Mexican Yellow has a wingspan of 1.75–2.5 inches. The sexes are dimorphic, with the male more heavily marked than the female. The upper- and underside is pale yellow to creamy white. The upperside of the forewing has a black border with a stylized "dog face" marking. The character that separates it from all other similar butterflies in the state is a short, but very noticeable, tail on its hindwing margin.

COULD BE CONFUSED WITH The Little Yellow and Sleepy Orange are somewhat similar, but the "tailed" hindwing of the Mexican Yellow will separate it from these two species. The Mexican Yellow is an extremely rare stray in Illinois.

HABITAT/LIFE HISTORY In its normal range, the Mexican Yellow thrives in dry prairies and desert-type habitats. In Illinois, hill prairies and sandy areas are the most likely habitats for this butterfly to occur in. The caterpillar feeds on *Chamaechrista* (formerly *Cassia*), a common group of plants in Illinois. Heitzman (1987) reported that it has bred in Missouri. The Mexican Yellow would likely fly in Illinois from late summer to fall.

STATUS The Mexican Yellow is a rare, but historically consistent, visitor to Illinois, colonizing from the southwest. The oldest record known is from 1904, Cook County; the most recent is from the fall of 1981 in Randolph County.[5]

♂ T

♀ T

WINGSPAN
1.75–2.5 in

♀ U

LITTLE YELLOW
Pyrisitia lisa (Boisduval & Le Conte)

PREVALENCE
Widely
encountered
migrant

FLIGHT PERIOD

MAR	
APR	
MAY	
JUN	
JUL	
AUG	
SEP	
OCT	
NOV	

FIELD NOTES
A. Scattered
smudges on
hindwing (U)

Male

Female
(worn)

Male

DESCRIPTION The sexually dimorphic Little Yellow has a wingspan of 1.0–1.75 inches. The male upperside is yellow, with a wide, black tip on the forewing and a black border along the hindwing. The female upperside may be cream or yellow, and both color forms have an incomplete black border on both wings. Both sexes have a small, dark dot on the upperside of the forewing; however, like other Pierids, the Little Yellow rests with its wings closed, making the dot difficult to see. Following the species' low flight pattern provides the observer with the best chance of seeing the upperside pattern. The underside of both sexes is yellow (or cream in the cream form female) with scattered smudges and a marginal red-orange dot on the hindwing.

♂ T

COULD BE CONFUSED WITH When first viewing a Little Yellow, the initial impression might be "an odd-looking, miniature Clouded Sulphur"; however, the Clouded Sulphur is larger and has a different underside pattern. The Sleepy Orange is orange, not yellow. The Dainty Sulphur is smaller, has black spots on the underside of the forewing, and an elongated wing shape.

♀ T
yellow
form

HABITAT/LIFE HISTORY The Little Yellow is a butterfly of dry, open areas—roadsides, old fields, and forest edges. The female lays single eggs on *Chamaechrista* (formerly *Cassia*) and other legumes. These plants have finely compound leaves, which camouflage the slender, green caterpillar. The chrysalis is also green and cryptic. The Little Yellow flies from April to October, with the greatest number occurring from July through the end of September. It is a migrant that recolonizes Illinois each year, and several generations may be produced in the state once the species arrives.

♀ T
cream
form

WINGSPAN
1.0–1.75 in

STATUS The Little Yellow is found throughout Illinois. The species usually cannot survive an Illinois winter, so it must recolonize the state from the South (Mississippi to Arizona). By late summer populations have increased and it can be common.

♂ U

SLEEPY ORANGE
Abaeis nicippe (Cramer)

PREVALENCE
Locally
encountered
migrant

FLIGHT PERIOD

MAR
APR
MAY
JUN
JUL
AUG
SEP
OCT
NOV

FIELD NOTES

A. Small, black crescent on forewing (T) [refer to ♂T specimen on next page]

B. Indistinct line on hindwing (U)

C. Notably orange-colored when flying (T) [refer to ♂T specimen on next page]

Female

Female

DESCRIPTION The Sleepy Orange has a wingspan of 1.25–2.25 inches. The upperside of both sexes is orange-yellow with a small, black crescent on the forewing. The butterfly's common name is from its upperside wing pattern—it was thought that the forewing's black crescent resembled a sleeping or closed eye. Unfortunately, the species very seldom rests with its wings open to see this "sleepy" pattern. A black border is also found on the upperside of both wings; however, the male's border is complete while the female's is incomplete. The underside of the hindwing is yellow, with a scattering of mauve spots and slashes that form an indistinct line.

The underside of the fall form is orange-red. In a form called *flava*, the upperside is totally yellow rather than orange. The *flava* form is extremely rare, and has only been found once in Illinois.

COULD BE CONFUSED WITH The Clouded Sulphur and Alfalfa Butterfly have a silver spot encircled with red on the underside of their hindwing; the Sleepy Orange does not.

HABITAT/LIFE HISTORY The Sleepy Orange is found in old fields, roadsides, prairies, sandy areas, and along the edges of forests. The adult male patrols ditches and flat areas seeking a female. When disturbed, its flight is quite rapid. While a female may lay her eggs on several legume species, the main host is *Chamaechrista* (formerly *Cassia*). The adult is on the wing from early April through early November. In Illinois, the Sleepy Orange has several generations. It is thought that Illinois winters are too cold for the species to survive; thus, it must recolonize the state each year from the south.

STATUS Although Irwin and Downey (1973) once saw and captured thousands of the Sleepy Orange, this species is no longer common. Today, seeing one or two would be a very good year for an Illinois butterfly enthusiast. However, on occasion the Sleepy Orange can be locally common, and may be found throughout the state as its populations build over the summer months. The exception is the northwest corner of Illinois, where the species has not been found.

♂ T

♀ T

WINGSPAN
1.25–2.25 in

♂ U

♀ U

CLOUDED SULPHUR

Colias philodice Godart

PREVALENCE
Widely
encountered

FLIGHT PERIOD

MAR	
APR	
MAY	
JUN	
JUL	
AUG	
SEP	
OCT	
NOV	

FIELD NOTES

A. Greenish-yellow base color (T & U)

B. Silver spot encircled with red on hindwing (U)

Male

Female:
cream form

DESCRIPTION The Clouded Sulphur has a wingspan of 1.6–2.4 inches. The male upperside is yellow to greenish-yellow with a solid, black border on both the wings. The female upperside can be yellow or cream (less common form), and its black border contains spots the same color as the wings. The underside of both sexes is yellow or cream, the same as each individual's upperside color. The underside of the hindwing has a silver spot with a red ring around it. The Clouded Sulphur never sits with its wings open.

COULD BE CONFUSED WITH The Dogface is larger, with a pointed forewing. The Cloudless Sulphur is almost twice the size of the Clouded Sulphur, and is a brighter yellow. The Alfalfa Butterfly is orange (even the pale, early-season specimens will still have a tint of orange); however, the cream-colored females of the Alfalfa Butterfly and Clouded Sulphur are virtually indistinguishable.

HABITAT/LIFE HISTORY The Clouded Sulphur is a sun-seeking, habitat generalist that flutters through open areas, fields, parks, roadsides, farms, and gardens, sipping from various flowers. The adult is an avid puddler and sometimes forms large clouds on country roads. The female lays her eggs singly on a legume host, with clover preferred. The Clouded Sulphur is on the wing from March to November. In Illinois, there are several generations a year, with the species overwintering as a chrysalis.

STATUS The Clouded Sulphur is so ubiquitous in the Illinois landscape that its absence is noted more often than its presence. The species likely occurs in every Illinois county.

♂ T

♀ T
yellow
form

♀ T
cream
form

WINGSPAN
1.6–2.4 in

♂ U

ALFALFA BUTTERFLY
Colias eurytheme Boisduval

Female

FLIGHT PERIOD

MAR
APR
MAY
JUN
JUL
AUG
SEP
OCT
NOV

FIELD NOTES

A. Yellowish-
orange base color
(T & U)

B. Silver spot
encircled with red
on hindwing (U)

Female

DESCRIPTION The sexually dimorphic Alfalfa Butterfly is one of the state's more familiar species, with a wingspan of 1.8–2.5 inches. The male upperside is yellow-orange with a hint of iridescence, and has a solid black border. The female upperside can be yellow-orange or cream-colored, and the black border contains spots the same color as the wings. The underside of both sexes is yellow-orange or cream (female form), depending on the color of the upperside. There is seasonal variation in size and color, with the spring individual smaller and paler. To make field identification even more troublesome, the Alfalfa Butterfly usually sits with its wings closed.

COULD BE CONFUSED WITH The Sleepy Orange has an indistinct line on the underside of the hindwing, while the Alfalfa Butterfly has a row of dots. The Clouded Sulphur is somewhat smaller and much yellower. The cream-colored females of the Alfalfa Butterfly and Clouded Sulphur are virtually indistinguishable.

HABITAT/LIFE HISTORY The Alfalfa Butterfly is a sun-seeking, habitat generalist; it frequents fields, meadows, roadsides, farms, and gardens, sipping nectar from a variety of blooms. The adult is also an avid puddler. The male reflects ultraviolet (UV) light; unfortunately, human eyes are not sensitive to UV light. The female lays a single egg on a legume host, with alfalfa preferred. The Alfalfa Butterfly is on the wing from March to November. In Illinois, there are several continuous generations a year, with the species overwintering as a chrysalis.

STATUS It is no longer common to see a large cloud of Alfalfa Butterflies dancing above alfalfa and clover fields; however, the species is likely found in every county in Illinois.

♂ T

♀ T
yellow
form

♀ T
cream
form

WINGSPAN
1.8–2.5 in

♂ U

DOGFACE
Zerene cesonia (Stoll)

Female

Male

Female *rosa* form

PREVALENCE
Locally
encountered
migrant

FLIGHT PERIOD

MAR
APR
MAY
JUN
JUL
AUG
SEP
OCT
NOV

FIELD NOTES

A. Falcate
(hooked) forewing

B. "Dog face"
pattern (T & U)

DESCRIPTION The Dogface has a 2.0–3.0 inch wingspan. The upperside is bright, lemon-yellow with a thick, black border. The outer tip of the forewing is falcate (pointed) in both sexes; this is diagnostic for the species, but is difficult to see in the field. The male is brighter yellow, with a darker border and a wider, sharper edge on the hindwing than the female. The marking on the upperside of the forewing resembles a dog's head (e.g., the profile of a poodle). The underside is yellow, with a white-centered, black dot on the forewing and two small, white spots on the hindwing. A *rosa* form, usually seen later in the season, has extensive pink shading on the underside.[6]

COULD BE CONFUSED WITH In flight, the Dogface could be confused with the other yellow sulphurs, but the size, brightness of the yellow base color, contrasting black edges, and falcate wing tips will separate it from other species.

HABITAT/LIFE HISTORY The Dogface occurs in open fields, forest margins, clover/alfalfa fields, and sandy areas along rivers and lakes. Prairies with false indigo and hill prairies with leadplant (both caterpillar host plants in Illinois) are likely places to search. The caterpillar is green with black-and-yellow or orange bands—it is cryptic on its host plants. The adult's hurried flight, with brief stops at flowers before quickly flying away, is distinctive. The Dogface flies from early April to late October. The species likely does not survive the winter in Illinois and recolonizes the state from the south each year. It is a regularly occurring migrant that establishes breeding populations during most years.

STATUS Only on rare occasions is the Dogface locally common.[7] In most areas of the state, seeing one or two during any given season is normal. While the species can occur anywhere in Illinois, it is more often seen in the southern half of the state.

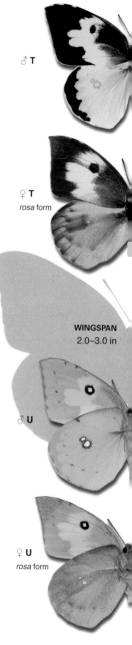

♂ T

♀ T
rosa form

WINGSPAN
2.0–3.0 in

♂ U

♀ U
rosa form

CLOUDLESS SULPHUR
Phoebis senna (Linnaeus)

PREVALENCE
Locally
encountered
migrant

FLIGHT PERIOD

MAR	
APR	
MAY	
JUN	
JUL	
AUG	
SEP	
OCT	
NOV	

FIELD NOTES

A. Bright lemon-yellow base color
(♂ T & U)

B. Reddish-brown marks (♀ U)

Male

Female

DESCRIPTION The wingspan of the sexually dimorphic Cloudless Sulphur is around 2.5 inches. The male upperside is pure lemon-yellow. The very thin, black trim on the outer margin of the forewing appears as tiny, dark dots at the end of the veins. The male underside can be either pure yellow or yellow with reddish-brown mottling. The female upperside can be yellow to white; the forewing has varying amounts of black spotting along the outer margin, and has a large, black spot just above the center of the wing. The female underside is more heavily marked with irregular patterns of reddish-brown. The underside of both sexes has spots just above the center of all four wings.

COULD BE CONFUSED WITH The Large Orange Sulphur female has forewing markings (upper- and underside) in a straight line from the tip to the middle of the inner wing margin. The Orange-barred Sulphur is larger and more strongly marked. Both of these species are extremely rare in Illinois, so confusion with them should not be an issue.

HABITAT/LIFE HISTORY While the Cloudless Sulphur is a frequent visitor to flower gardens, it is most often seen in open fields, along power line cuts, forest edges, sandy areas along rivers and roadsides, or railroad rights-of-way—it seems to follow habitat edges. The caterpillar feeds on *Chamaechrista* (formerly *Cassia*). The Cloudless Sulphur adult, described as a "lightning bolt passing through the countryside," is a strong, rapid flier. It is often seen flying above patches of its host plant, nectaring on the flowers, and laying eggs on the leaves. The adult flies from April to November, with most sightings from July through September. The Cloudless Sulphur migrates into Illinois each year and breeds continuously once it arrives. It can have as many as three generations in the southern part of the state.

STATUS The Cloudless Sulphur is a migrant that recolonizes Illinois annually, and varies in abundance from common to nearly absent. The species has been recorded from all regions of the state, but is usually more common in the southern half of Illinois.

♂ T

♀ T

WINGSPAN
~2.5 in

♀ U

ORANGE-BARRED SULPHUR
Phoebis philea (Linnaeus)

DESCRIPTION With a wingspan of over 3.0 inches, the sexually dimorphic Orange-barred Sulphur is the largest,

MAR	
APR	
MAY	
JUN	
JUL	
AUG	
SEP	
OCT	
NOV	

FIELD NOTES
A. Mottling of red-to-pinkish spots along wing margin (U)

Female

Female

regularly-occurring sulphur in North America. The male upperside is bright yellow with an orange bar in the middle of the forewing. The upperside of the male hindwing is yellow with the outer edge orange. The female has several forms, with the upperside ranging from yellow, with variable orange shading, to mostly dirty white; all forms have brown to black marginal borders, with a second, inner, irregular row of smaller, blackish spots. The male underside is mostly yellow, while the female underside is more orange-yellow, with variable red shading. The underside of the forewing of both sexes has an irregular, broken row of red-to-pinkish spots that terminates at the tip of the wing.

COULD BE CONFUSED WITH The Cloudless Sulphur and Large Orange Sulphur are similar, but much smaller. The orange bar on the male forewing is unique, and should immediately identify the Orange-barred Sulphur. The female is more strongly marked, with brownish black on the wing margins, and an irregular row of inner spots on the forewing.

HABITAT/LIFE HISTORY While possibly occurring anywhere in Illinois—flower gardens, along rivers, in open fields and margins of forests—it is unlikely to be encountered. In the southern U.S., the caterpillar feeds on various species of *Chamaechrista* (formerly *Cassia*). Its food plants do occur in Illinois, making a seasonal breeding colony possible. The species' fast and direct flight, with infrequent stops at flowers, makes it difficult to observe and positively identify. The adult could be found anytime between May and October.

STATUS This far-ranging, migratory butterfly has entered the borders of Illinois on rare occasions. The authors are aware of three recorded specimens from Illinois, all from the northern two-thirds of the state (Cook and Coles counties).[8] It may be overlooked in years with explosive numbers of the Cloudless Sulphur. The Orange-barred Sulphur is a rare stray in Illinois.

♂ T

♀ T

WINGSPAN
>3.0 in

♂ U

LARGE ORANGE SULPHUR
Phoebis agarithe (Boisduval)

PREVALENCE
Rare stray

FLIGHT PERIOD

MAR	
APR	
MAY	
JUN	
JUL	
AUG	
SEP	
OCT	
NOV	

FIELD NOTES
A. Straight, diagonal line across wings (U)

Male

Male

DESCRIPTION The Large Orange Sulphur has a wingspan of 2.5–3.0 inches. The male upperside is entirely orange; the outer wing margin has a hint of tiny dots located at the end of the veins. The female upperside is variable and can range from orange to off-white—sometimes with a pinkish tinge—with dark brown markings on the outer margins. A straight, diagonal line occurs from her forewing tip, across the wing, toward the middle of the inner margin. This line is brown on the female upperside and reddish-brown on the female underside. The same line is present on the underside of the male forewing, but it is much less prominent.

COULD BE CONFUSED WITH The Cloudless Sulphur male is bright yellow, with no orange. The Cloudless Sulphur female is similar, but does not have the straight, diagonal line on the upper- and underside of her forewing. The Orange-barred Sulphur is larger, and the male is more yellow than orange. The Orange-barred Sulphur female is similarly marked, but with irregular spots. She also lacks a straight, diagonal line on the upper- and underside of her forewing.

HABITAT/LIFE HISTORY While the Large Orange Sulphur inhabits subtropical brushy areas and open woodlands, its wide-ranging tendencies mean it may be seen anywhere. It might pass through Illinois, perhaps following the migration of its close relative, the Cloudless Sulphur. The Large Orange Sulphur is most likely to be found flying along forest edges or sand areas near rivers. The adult could be found anytime between May and October.

STATUS Irwin and Downey (1973) listed this species as one of the "Butterflies of Possible Occurrence in Illinois," and were aware it was mentioned by Klots (1951) as "strays n. to Illinois." Although individuals undoubtedly pass through Illinois in wandering dispersal flights (two records occur), it is not a regular part of our fauna and can only be considered a rare stray.[9]

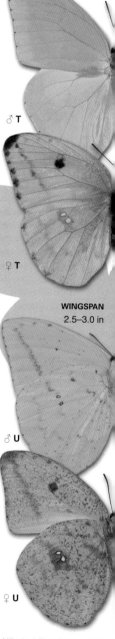

♂ T

♀ T

WINGSPAN
2.5–3.0 in

♂ U

♀ U

FALCATE ORANGETIP
Anthocharis midea (Hübner)

Male

Male

Female

PREVALENCE
Locally
encountered

FLIGHT PERIOD

MAR	
APR	
MAY	
JUN	
JUL	
AUG	
SEP	
OCT	
NOV	

FIELD NOTES

A. Falcate wings

B. Orange-tipped
wings (♂ T)

C. Mottled
underside (U)

DESCRIPTION The sexually dimorphic Falcate Orangetip has a wingspan of 1.5–1.8 inches. The male gives the species its common name; he has bold, orange tips on the upper- and underside of his sickle-shaped (falcate) forewings. Otherwise, the upper- and underside of both sexes are cream-colored to white, with a black spot on each forewing (the female's spot is larger). The underside of the hindwing is mottled black and white—a salt and pepper effect—mixed with green marbling.

COULD BE CONFUSED WITH The marbling on the underside of the Olympia Marble hindwing is not as dense, and the likelihood of encountering these two species in the same habitat is almost nonexistent.

HABITAT/LIFE HISTORY The Falcate Orangetip prefers moist, open, deciduous forests, especially those with young trees and plenty of small, open areas. The species is one of the true harbingers of spring in southern Illinois, as it visits the blooms of spring ephemerals. It flies through the woodlands only a few feet above the ground, and seemingly never pauses. However, once a Falcate Orangetip alights it is very approachable and can be studied at length. An adult male will establish a territory and patrol for females during the late morning and early afternoon. The female lays only one red-orange egg per plant on a developing leaf or flower bud. Caterpillar host plants include rock and winter cresses as well as other mustards. The green-patterned caterpillar feeds on the buds, flowers, and seedpods and will form a chrysalis on sticks and branches near the dying (senescing) host plants. The brown, overwintering chrysalis has a hook at the end that resembles a thorn on a plant stem. The species flies from mid-March to mid-May, and has one generation per year.

STATUS The Falcate Orangetip is rarely found north of Interstate 72 and is most common in southern Illinois. During 1961, a Chicago collector observed over 1,000 individuals in Union County (Irwin and Downey, 1973); however, seeing half a dozen now qualifies as a good day.

♂ T

♀ T

WINGSPAN
1.5–1.8 in

♂ U

♀ U

OLYMPIA MARBLE
Euchloe olympia (W.H. Edwards)

Female

Female

Male

PREVALENCE
Locally
encountered

FLIGHT PERIOD

MAR	
APR	
MAY	
JUN	
JUL	
AUG	
SEP	
OCT	
NOV	

FIELD NOTES

A. Black smudge
on forewing tip (T)

B. Marbleized
pattern with rosy
blush (U)

DESCRIPTION The Olympia Marble has a wingspan of 1.2–1.8 inches. The upperside of the wings is white. The upperside of the forewing has black dots and a black smudge at the tip. The underside has a yellow-green, marbleized pattern with a rosy blush—the common name comes from this marble-like underside.

COULD BE CONFUSED WITH The underside of a Cabbage Butterfly is pale cream with no marbling. Also, the Olympia Marble is two-thirds the size of a Cabbage Butterfly. The flight pattern also differs between the two species: the Olympia Marble's flight is purposeful and direct and it seldom lands.

HABITAT/LIFE HISTORY The Olympia Marble occurs in dry, sandy, prairie remnants; oak savannas; and sand dunes. Each spring when the cleft phlox blooms and the oaks begin to leaf out in the sandy areas of Illinois, it's time to search for the Olympia Marble. The green-patterned caterpillar feeds on the flowering parts and seedpods of various rock cresses. The male stakes out a hilltop location or an elevated site and patrols just a few feet above the ground. The flight of the Olympia Marble is low, rapid, and direct—it seems to dance through the air, seldom landing, and is always one step ahead of the observer. When the species does land, it is usually into the wind. The female deposits her eggs (orange-yellow) singly on young flower buds of the caterpillar host plants. The species overwinters as a chrysalis that resembles a thorn. The Olympia Marble flies from April until May, and its short flight season (less than 30 days) makes it a true spring ephemeral. It has one generation per year.

STATUS In Illinois, the Olympia Marble is locally encountered in sandy areas and dry hill prairies along the Mississippi and Illinois rivers.

♂ T

♀ T

WINGSPAN
1.2–1.8 in

♂ U

♀ U

MUSTARD WHITE
Pieris oleracea (T. Harris)

PREVALENCE
Extirpated

Mike Reese

FLIGHT PERIOD

MAR	
APR	
MAY	
JUN	
JUL	
AUG	
SEP	
OCT	
NOV	

summer form

spring form

FIELD NOTES

A. White to cream base color with no markings (T)

B. Gray-green scales along the vein margins on the hindwing (U)

summer form

DESCRIPTION The Mustard White has a wingspan of 1.5–2.5 inches. The sexes are nearly identical, but two seasonal forms occur in the Midwest. The upper- and underside of the spring form is white; however, the underside of the hindwing has grayish-green scales along the veins. The summer form is generally unmarked—the upper- and underside are both pure white.

COULD BE CONFUSED WITH The upperside of the Cabbage Butterfly forewing has one or two black spots and is black tipped. Even in the lightest individual, these markings are visible. The upperside of the Mustard White forewing is usually pure white.

HABITAT/LIFE HISTORY Habitats for the Mustard White include open wooded areas, floodplain forests, and shrubby wetlands. This butterfly was probably extirpated from Illinois by deforestation, and, to a lesser degree, by competition with the introduced Cabbage Butterfly. Early reports of the Illinois State Entomologist by C. Thomas (1878,1880, and 1881) note the caterpillar feeding and being a pest on cabbage and turnip leaves. In the wild, the caterpillar is reported to feed on water cress and other plants in the mustard family. Just outside of Illinois the Mustard White flies from April through September.

STATUS The Mustard White is presumed extirpated from Illinois, and was probably the first butterfly that disappeared after European settlement. To our knowledge, there are no known historic Illinois specimens. Its occurrence in Illinois was always marginal, and northern Illinois likely represented the very southern edge of its range.[10] However, the northern tier of Illinois counties still lies within the range of this species—the territory from Winnebago County east to Lake County is the most likely place for it to reoccur. The species sometimes wanders into southeast Wisconsin and breeds in northern Indiana; however, it has never been recorded from Iowa.

♂ T
spring
form

♀ T
summer
form

WINGSPAN
1.5–2.5 in

♂ U
spring
form

♀ U
summer
form

CABBAGE BUTTERFLY
Pieris rapae (Linnaeus)

Female

Courting Pair

Mating Pair

PREVALENCE
Widely encountered

FLIGHT PERIOD

MAR	
APR	
MAY	
JUN	
JUL	
AUG	
SEP	
OCT	
NOV	

FIELD NOTES

A. Black forewing tip (T & U)

B. Pure cream base color with no pattern (U)

DESCRIPTION The Cabbage Butterfly has a wingspan of 1.75–2.25 inches. The upperside of both sexes is white, with a black forewing tip. The male upperside has one black dot in the middle of the forewing; the female upperside has two dots. The underside of both sexes is a cream color. Like the upperside, the male has one black dot on the underside of the forewing and the female has two. An early spring generation individual is smaller, and the underside of its hindwing is often darker.

COULD BE CONFUSED WITH Unlike the Checkered White, Olympia Marble, and Falcate Orangetip, the Cabbage Butterfly has no distinct underside wing pattern. Also, the Cabbage Butterfly's flight is slower and more undulating, while the other species' flight is more direct and purposeful.

HABITAT/LIFE HISTORY The Cabbage Butterfly is one of the state's most familiar butterflies and is found in any open space—fields, gardens, and roadsides—from town to country. The caterpillar host plants are both wild and cultivated crucifers—even the invasive weed garlic mustard can serve as a host. The caterpillar is the bane of many home gardeners, and can cause economic damage to commercial producers of crucifers. The female lays her eggs singly on the foliage of the caterpillar host plants. The Cabbage Butterfly is on the wing from March to November. With a life cycle of less than a month, several generations occur and the species appears continuously throughout the growing season. The last generation overwinters as a chrysalis.

STATUS The Cabbage Butterfly is a North African and Eurasian agricultural pest. It was introduced into Quebec around 1860, and the first definitive collection in Illinois was September, 1875, in Kane County (Scudder 1889). It is found in every county in Illinois.

♂ T

♀ T

WINGSPAN
1.75–2.25 in

♂ U

♀ U

CHECKERED WHITE
Pontia protodice (Boisduval & Le Conte)

Female

PREVALENCE
Locally
encountered

FLIGHT PERIOD

MAR	
APR	
MAY	
JUN	
JUL	
AUG	
SEP	
OCT	
NOV	

FIELD NOTES

A. Spotted (♂ T) or checkered (♀ T) forewing tip

B. Checkered brown pattern (♀ T)

C. Zigzag pattern (♀ U)

D. Veins lined with light brown (♀ U)

E. Scattered marks (♂ U)

Female

Male

154   Family Pieridae

DESCRIPTION The sexually dimorphic Checkered White has a wingspan of 1.75–2.25 inches. The upperside of both sexes is white, but has different, gender-specific patterns. The male upperside pattern is limited to dark spots on the forewing, while the female upperside has an extensive charcoal-to-brown checkered pattern on both wings. The underside of the male hindwing is plain white or may be faintly marked. The underside of the female hindwing is marked with a lighter-colored, zigzag pattern near the outer margin, while the veins are lined with light brown.

COULD BE CONFUSED WITH The Cabbage Butterfly has the forewing tip solid black and one or two black spots on the forewing. The Olympia Marble is smaller and has a marbled underside.

HABITAT/LIFE HISTORY The Checkered White is found in old fields, prairies, pastures, and along road-sides—anywhere there is dry, open habitat. Its flight is rapid and direct, and the adult nectars on a wide variety of plants. In Illinois, the caterpillar is known to feed on common pepper-grass, and the species overwinters as a chrysalis. The Checkered White is on the wing from March through October.

STATUS In Illinois, the Checkered White can be uncommon; however, it may outnumber Cabbage Butterflies in certain local habitats.[11] It can be found throughout the state, but its occurrence is hard to predict, as the species is an opportunistic nomad—always on the move.

♂ T

♀ T

WINGSPAN
1.75–2.25 in

♂ U

♀ U

GREAT SOUTHERN WHITE
Ascia monuste (Linnaeus)

PREVALENCE
Rare stray

FLIGHT PERIOD

MAR	
APR	
MAY	
JUN	
JUL	
AUG	
SEP	
OCT	
NOV	

FIELD NOTES
A. Turquoise antennal tips

B. Border of black triangles that follow veins (T)

Male

Female

Male

Bill Bouton

DESCRIPTION The Great Southern White has a wingspan of approximately 2.0 inches. The male upperside is pure white, with a black border along the outer margin of the forewing. The border forms a series of triangles that follow the veins inward. The upperside of the male hindwing is unmarked. The female upperside is either white like the male, or can be ash gray, with a prominent black dot on the forewing. The underside of both sexes varies from white, to pale tan, to a mottled gray. Both sexes have bright, turquoise antennal tips.

COULD BE CONFUSED WITH In flight, the Great Southern White could possibly be mistaken for a Checkered White or Cabbage Butterfly, but its larger size and forewing border pattern should readily separate it. Its turquoise antennal tips are unique in Illinois.

HABITAT/LIFE HISTORY In its range, the Great Southern White favors coastal dunes and marshes. Various crucifers are used as caterpillar hosts in the southern U.S. These host plants occur in Illinois and could support short-lived, late-summer colonies. If the Great Southern White did stray into Illinois, it would be found mid to late summer.

STATUS The Great Southern White can only be considered a rare vagrant, straying into Illinois from the southern U.S.[12] Although it undoubtedly enters our borders upon occasion, it cannot be considered a regular part of the state's fauna. It could be found anywhere in Illinois, though it is most likely to be encountered in the southern tip of the state. It flies all year in southern Florida, the Gulf Coast, and southern Texas.

♂ T

♀ T

WINGSPAN
~2.0 in

♂ U

♀ U

Eastern Tailed Blue

Gray Hairstreak

FAMILY LYCAENIDAE
Gossamer-Winged Butterflies

The Family Lycaenidae, called the gossamer-winged butterflies due to their "delicate" appearance, is one of the largest families, with approximately 6,000 species worldwide. The family, which constitutes about 40% of all butterfly species, is further divided into subfamilies, four of which occur in Illinois—Miletinae (Harvester), Lycaeninae (Coppers), Theclinae (Hairstreaks), and Polyommatinae (Blues).

The adults are diminutive and brightly colored. The males' forelegs are slightly reduced in size, but, unlike the brush-footed butterflies, the males still use them. Females have three pairs of normal legs. Lycaenids will rest with their wings closed, but often bask with them open or partially so. Females lay eggs singly on the leaves or flower buds of their host plants. The caterpillars are short, broad, and oval in appearance, which many field guides describe as "sluglike." David Wagner notes in *Caterpillars of Eastern North America*, "While adult lycaenids are surely among the planet's most beautiful animals, their caterpillars are a mundane lot—to my eyes, the larvae of the hairstreaks, blues, and coppers are among the most structurally monotonous large groups of externally feeding Lepidoptera."

At least half of the world's Lycaenid caterpillars are tended by ants. The caterpillars produce honeydew that attract the ants and they, in turn, guard the caterpillars. Most Lycaenids overwinter as an egg or a chrysalis. Lycaenid butterflies are one of the more challenging groups to identify.

SUBFAMILIES
- Miletinae (Harvester)
- Lycaeninae (Coppers)
- Theclinae (Hairstreaks)
- Polyommatinae (Blues)

Harvester

SUBFAMILY MILETINAE
Harvesters

The majority of the subfamily Miletinae lives in Africa and Asia. Only one species occurs in North America—the Harvester. This diminutive, brown-and-orange butterfly does not visit flowers (its proboscis is too short); rather, it imbibes honeydew (secretions from aphids) or nutrients from dung, carrion, or wet spots on the ground. The caterpillar is carnivorous—instead of being adapted for chewing leaves, it has piercing-sucking mouthparts and feeds on various species of wooly aphid. In fact, a female lays her eggs in the middle of wooly aphid colonies. The Harvester overwinters as a chrysalis.

SPECIES
• Harvester

HARVESTER
Feniseca tarquinius (Fabricius)

PREVALENCE
Locally
encountered

FLIGHT PERIOD

MAR
APR
MAY
JUN
JUL
AUG
SEP
OCT
NOV

FIELD NOTES
A. Spots ringed
with white (U)

Female

Male

DESCRIPTION The "Halloween-hued" Harvester is the only carnivorous butterfly (i.e., its caterpillar) in North America. The adult has a wingspan of 1.0–1.3 inches. The upperside of the wings has blotches of orange and brown. The underside is orange to reddish-brown with darker spots edged with white circles. Areas of the hindwing underside look as if they are dusted with powdered sugar. Unlike the hairstreaks, the Harvester does not rub its hindwings together while at rest.

♂ T

COULD BE CONFUSED WITH The Harvester could be confused with the American Copper, but the underside of the latter does not have spots edged with white.

♀ T

HABITAT/LIFE HISTORY The Harvester prefers woodland habitats, often near streams or ponds, where alder, ash, or beech harbor the caterpillar's prey—wooly aphids. The adult never strays far from the plant host; when disturbed, it flies erratically in a small area, before landing again in almost the same spot.

The female lays her eggs singly on or near wooly aphid colonies. In a few days the egg hatches and the caterpillar lives among the aphids. Instead of the chewing, plant-eating mouthparts that most caterpillars have, the Harvester caterpillar has piercing-sucking mouthparts which it uses to pierce aphids and suck their juices. The caterpillar has moderately long hairs, and many times it will incorporate the empty, wooly skins of its victims onto its body to camouflage its presence. Due to its protein-rich diet, the caterpillar is able to complete development and form a chrysalis within 11 to 12 days. The adult Harvester does not nectar at flowers—it prefers the honeydew secretions of aphids, liquids from carrion, animal droppings, and damp soil. In Illinois, it overwinters as a chrysalis. The Harvester is on the wing from April to November, and has at least two generations a year in Illinois.

WINGSPAN
1.0–1.3 in

♂ U

STATUS The Harvester is found statewide, but is easily missed, as only one or two adults may be found flying at a time.

♀ U

Gray Copper

American Copper

Bronze Copper

SUBFAMILY LYCAENINAE
Coppers

The subfamily Lycaeninae are small butterflies that range in color from orange-red to brown. The male of most species has a coppery iridescence on the upper surface of his wings. This background color and iridescence are responsible for their common name—coppers. Coppers are found in open habitats and most live in local colonies near their caterpillar food plants. They are strong fliers and often bask with their wings open. Coppers overwinter as partially grown caterpillars or as chrysalids.

SPECIES
- American Copper
- Gray Copper
- Bronze Copper
- Purplish Copper

AMERICAN COPPER
Lycaena phlaeas (Linnaeus)

PREVALENCE
Widely
encountered

FLIGHT PERIOD

MAR	
APR	
MAY	
JUN	
JUL	
AUG	
SEP	
OCT	
NOV	

FIELD NOTES

A. Vibrant, red-orange base color (T)

B. Distinctive two-tone base color (U)

C. Narrow, red-orange, jagged line (U)

Female

Female

Mating Pair

DESCRIPTION The American Copper has a wingspan of about 1.0 inch, and similar sexes. The upperside of the forewing is shiny, copper-penny red with spots and an outer brownish-black border. The upperside of the hindwing is brownish-black with an orange border and small, black chevrons along the outer edge. Some individuals have a row of tiny blue spots on the hindwing, just above the orange band. The underside of the forewing is orange with black spots and a gray border. The underside of the hindwing is gray, with a few black spots and a jagged, red-orange line along the outer margin. An aberrant form of this butterfly occasionally shows up in Illinois—the black spots on the upperside of its forewing are greatly exaggerated, sometimes causing the wing to be almost half black. This is known as the form *fasciata*, named by Herman Strecker in 1878.

♂ T

♀ T

COULD BE CONFUSED WITH The Bronze Copper is larger and has a different pattern. The Purplish Copper female is similar, but the upperside of her forewing is orange, and she has additional black spotting on the upperside of both her wings.

WINGSPAN
~1.0 in

HABITAT/LIFE HISTORY The American Copper occurs in any open area with low vegetation. It is usually found in direct association with its caterpillar host plants, sheep sorrel and curly dock. Although known to be native in the mountainous areas of the western U.S., the eastern populations seem to be more closely related to those in Europe, and it is likely they were introduced with imported hay in colonial America. The adult flies from April through October, with multiple generations over the season. This species likely overwinters as a partially grown caterpillar or as a chrysalis. It is the earliest copper species on the wing in Illinois.

♂ U

STATUS The American Copper is likely to occur in every county in Illinois, but perhaps not during the same year. It can be common or rather scarce, but appears secure in the state.

♀ U

GRAY COPPER
Lycaena dione (Scudder)

Male

FLIGHT PERIOD

MAR
APR
MAY
JUN
JUL
AUG
SEP
OCT
NOV

FIELD NOTES

A. Gray base color (T)

B. Light gray base color (U)

C. Broad, orange, jagged line (U)

Female

DESCRIPTION With a wingspan of 1.25–1.75 inches, the Gray Copper is the largest of the North American coppers. The sexes are similar. The upperside has a gray base color with black spots and an orange band on the outer margin of the hindwing. The orange band is more pronounced on the female than the male; the female's orange band even crosses over to the lower, outer margin of her forewing. The underside is grayish-white with black spots and a jagged, orange band.

COULD BE CONFUSED WITH The two-toned underside of the American and Bronze Coppers should separate them from the Gray Copper.

HABITAT/LIFE HISTORY The Gray Copper prefers low, open, damp areas along back roads and railroads where its host plants grow. The caterpillar hosts include curly dock and probably other *Rumex*. An avid flower visitor, the male often perches for long periods on tall plants waiting for a female; occasionally he darts out to chase away intruders. The Gray Copper is seldom seen outside of its breeding area. It is usually flying by the second week of June, and is mostly gone by the middle of July. The species has one generation a year and overwinters as a partially grown caterpillar or a chrysalis.

STATUS This early-summer butterfly is found in local colonies, scattered north of St. Louis' latitude. It is one of the few species that seems to be expanding its range and could possibly occur in open areas in southern Illinois. The species can be relatively common, but is generally confined to colonies existing in close proximity to the caterpillar host plants.

♂ T

♀ T

WINGSPAN
1.25–1.75 in

♂ U

♀ U

BRONZE COPPER
Lycaena hyllus (Cramer)

Female

Female

PREVALENCE
Locally
encountered

FLIGHT PERIOD

MAR	
APR	
MAY	
JUN	
JUL	
AUG	
SEP	
OCT	
NOV	

FIELD NOTES

A. Muted orange
base color (♀ T)

B. Wide, orange
band (U)

DESCRIPTION The wingspan of the sexually dimorphic Bronze Copper is about 1.5 inches, making it the largest of the three orange coppers. The upperside of the male forewing is brown with a purple sheen and a few small, black spots. The upperside of his hindwing is similar, with an orange border along the outer margin. The upperside of the female forewing is orange with black spots and a dark brown border; her hindwing is the same as the male's. The sexes are alike on the underside—the forewing is orange with many black spots and a light outer margin, and the hindwing is gray-white with many black spots and an orange outer margin.

COULD BE CONFUSED WITH The American and Purplish Coppers are similar, but the Bronze Copper's size and underside markings will immediately separate it from these two species.

HABITAT/LIFE HISTORY The Bronze Copper is associated with damp areas—wet prairies, meadows, marshes, pond/lake margins, and roadsides—and may even appear in urban flower gardens. This species seems to wander about and does not need quality habitat. The Bronze Copper will find recently made ponds and lakes if its caterpillar host plant (curly dock) is present. The male often perches in tall vegetation in search of a passing female. The species has two generations in Illinois and is mostly seen in May/June and August/September, although it may appear anytime from May through October. The species overwinters in the egg stage.

STATUS The Bronze Copper has been recorded from most counties in the state. It varies in abundance and can be common in small areas. At this time, the species appears secure in Illinois.

♂ T

♀ T

WINGSPAN
~1.5 in

♂ U

♀ U

PURPLISH COPPER

Lycaena helloides (Boisduval)

PREVALENCE
Rare

FLIGHT PERIOD

MAR
APR
MAY
JUN
JUL
AUG
SEP
OCT
NOV

FIELD NOTES

A. Purplish sheen (♂T)

B. Zigzag orange band (T & U)

C. Pale orange base color (U)

Courting Pair

Mating Pair

DESCRIPTION The sexually dimorphic Purplish Copper has a wingspan of 1.25 inches. The striking male upperside is brown with iridescent purple when viewed in sunlight. While the amount of reflective purple varies, it is always evident. The male forewing border is black, while his hindwing border is a zigzag pattern of orange and black. The female upperside is orange and brown, with no iridescence. Both sexes have varying numbers of black spots on the upperside of both wings. The underside of both sexes is similar—the forewing is light orange with a faint gray border and black spots, and the hindwing is gray with a zigzag orange band.

COULD BE CONFUSED WITH The Purplish Copper is superficially similar to the American Copper, but the American is generally smaller, iridescent red, and has a different number and pattern of black spots on its underside. The Bronze Copper is somewhat similar on the upperside, but is larger and dissimilar on the underside.

HABITAT/LIFE HISTORY The Purplish Copper is usually found near damp areas—wet meadows and along pond/lake edges—where docks and knotweeds, the caterpillar hosts, abound. The adult frequently visits flowers and is fairly easy to observe while feeding. The species has two or more generations each year. It appears in May and often seems to fly continuously until October. The Purplish Copper probably overwinters as a small caterpillar.

STATUS The Purplish Copper is the least common of Illinois' four copper butterflies, and is found in local colonies scattered through the northern half (mostly northern quarter) of Illinois. It is generally confined to small areas in close proximity to its caterpillar host plants. Over the last several years this butterfly has experienced a noticeable decline in numbers in Illinois and Iowa (Dennis Schlicht, pers. comm., 2011). The cause of the decline is uncertain; whether it is a natural population fluctuation, the result of climate change, or some other factor remains to be determined.

♂ T

♀ T

WINGSPAN
1.25 in

♂ U

♀ U

Coral Hairstreak

Olive Hairstreak

SUBFAMILY THECLINAE

Hairstreaks and Elfins

The subfamily Theclinae contains the hairstreaks and elfins. Most hairstreaks have tails on their hindwings with bright spots that resemble eyes. This combination gives the illusion that the back end is really the head, thereby increasing the butterflies' chance for survival by fooling potential predators. The elfins either have stunted (nubbinlike) tails or lack tails. In Asia and Europe, the elfins are commonly known as green hairstreaks. Along with the tails, another visible characteristic is the sex patch (called stigma) on male forewings of many species; it is used to stimulate the female for mating. The stigma is difficult to see in the field as most hairstreaks sit with their wings closed.

The flight in both groups is swift and erratic. These butterflies usually cover no more than several yards before landing. In Illinois, elfins and some hairstreaks have a single generation, flying only in the spring and early summer. Great Purple, Olive, Gray, White-M, and Red-banded hairstreaks have more than one generation. Many of the hairstreaks spend considerable time in the canopy of the forest. This makes observing them problematic, and chance encounters for some species are the rule.

SPECIES

- Atala
- Great Purple Hairstreak
- Acadian Hairstreak
- Coral Hairstreak
- Edwards' Hairstreak
- Banded Hairstreak
- Hickory Hairstreak
- Striped Hairstreak
- Northern Hairstreak
- Olive Hairstreak
- Hoary Elfin
- Frosted Elfin
- Henry's Elfin
- Eastern Pine Elfin
- Gray Hairstreak
- White-M Hairstreak
- Red-banded Hairstreak

ATALA
Eumaeus atala Poey

PREVALENCE
Accidental
occurrence

FLIGHT PERIOD
Not applicable

FIELD NOTES
A. Distinctive
red-orange
abdomen

B. Row of
metallic, green
spots (U)

C. Deep orange
spot (U)

Will Cook

Female

Donald Steinkraus

Female

DESCRIPTION The wingspan of the Atala is about 1.5 inches. The upperside of the male forewing is iridescent blue-green with a black border. The upperside of his hindwing is velvety black with varying amounts of iridescent green and blue-green spots along the outer margin. The upperside of the female forewing is velvety black with varying amounts of iridescent blue-green. The upperside of her hindwing is velvety black with blue-green, iridescent spots along the outer margin. The underside of both sexes is the same—velvety black with an unmarked forewing, and three rows of blue-green spots on the outer half of the hindwing. A conspicuous, deep-orange spot occurs along the bottom edge of the hindwing. The abdomen of both sexes is orange.

COULD BE CONFUSED WITH The Atala is unmistakable.

HABITAT/LIFE HISTORY The Atala is a butterfly of the Caribbean—Cuba, Bahamas, and southern Florida. According to Cech and Tudor (2005), it was once "abundant where downtown Miami now stands." The caterpillar host plants include coontie (a fossil gymnosperm of the Paleozoic) as well as cultivated cycads.

STATUS A single record, likely introduced by accident, indicates this species is not a normal part of our fauna.[13]

♂ T

♀ T

WINGSPAN
~1.5 in

♂ U

♀ U

GREAT PURPLE HAIRSTREAK

Atlides halesus (Cramer)

DESCRIPTION The wingspan of the sexually dimorphic Great Purple Hairstreak is 1.5–2.0 inches, with the female

PREVALENCE
Rare

FLIGHT PERIOD

MAR
APR
MAY
JUN
JUL
AUG
SEP
OCT
NOV

FIELD NOTES

A. Orange abdomen

B. Metallic marks near very long tails (U)

C. Three red-orange spots at base of wings (U)

Female

Female

larger than the male. The male upperside is a brilliant, metallic blue-green—depending on the angle of light—with dark gray to black borders. The male has a large stigma (sex patch) on the upperside of his forewing and two tails on each hindwing, with marks of iridescent light blue above them. The female upperside is similar, except that she lacks a stigma, and her dark wing borders extend at least halfway across the wings, towards the thorax. The underside of both sexes is dark, with three small patches of bright, red-orange near the body. The outer wing angle above the tail has short bands of metallic blue and gold. The abdomen is blue on top and bright orange below.

COULD BE CONFUSED WITH The only species that approaches the Great Purple Hairstreak's upperside color is the White-M Hairstreak. However, the White-M Hairstreak is smaller, a brighter shade of blue, and has a prominent, white "M" on the underside of its hindwing.

HABITAT/LIFE HISTORY A butterfly of moist hardwood and bottomland forests, the Great Purple Hairstreak will likely be found in the lowlands around the convergence of the Ohio and Mississippi rivers where its caterpillar host, mistletoe, grows. Mistletoe occurs in several counties in southern Illinois, mostly south of Route 13. The Great Purple Hairstreak stays high in the trees, but will come down on occasion to nectar at flowers. There are likely two generations, but most records from nearby western Kentucky are from September. The species overwinters as a chrysalis.

STATUS The only record for this species in Illinois is a single sweep net capture on September 17, 1966, at Pine Hills in Union County. While rare in nearby Kentucky, Bill Black—a Paducah, Kentucky resident—has noted a breeding population just across the Ohio River from Illinois in Paducah. The authors see no reason the Great Purple Hairstreak shouldn't occur, at least sporatically, in southernmost Illinois, especially along the Ohio River. Southern Illinois is at the extreme northern edge of this butterfly's range and that of its caterpillar food plant.

♂ T

♀ T

WINGSPAN
1.5–2.0 in

♂ U

ACADIAN HAIRSTREAK
Satyrium acadica (W.H. Edwards)

Mike Reese

Female

B

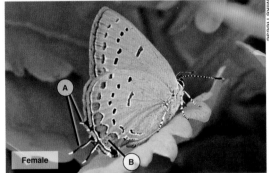

Mike Reese

Female

A

B

Mike Reese

Nectaring Group

PREVALENCE
Locally
encountered

FLIGHT PERIOD

MAR	
APR	
MAY	
JUN	▮
JUL	▮
AUG	
SEP	
OCT	
NOV	

FIELD NOTES

A. Two tails on hindwing

B. Blue tail spot surrounded by orange (U)

DESCRIPTION The Acadian Hairstreak has a wingspan of 1.25–1.5 inches. The sexes are similar, but the male has a stigma (sex patch) on the upperside of his forewing. The upperside of both sexes is brown, usually with an orange spot on the outer hindwing margin between the two tails. The underside is light gray with a row of white-ringed, black spots near the middle of both wings. The outer margin of the hindwing has a row of white-and-black-capped, orange spots that sometimes continue on the lower part of the forewing. Below the second, longer tail, note a conspicuous blue spot surrounded on three sides by deep orange.

COULD BE CONFUSED WITH The Coral Hairstreak is similar, but is darker and lacks hindwing tails. Edwards' Hairstreak is similar in pattern, but the underside of its hindwing is darker and its blue tail spot is not surrounded by orange.

HABITAT/LIFE HISTORY The Acadian Hairstreak is found around wetlands, marshes, and along streams with stands of willow, its caterpillar host. The adult visits flowers, such as milkweeds and dogbane, near its wetland haunts. It tends to stay low and often rests on wetland vegetation. If alarmed, the adult rapidly darts off, but often returns to the spot just vacated. The Acadian Hairstreak has a single, early-summer generation. It appears in mid-June and by the end of July most individuals are gone, with a few stragglers lasting into August. The species overwinters in the egg stage.

STATUS The Acadian Hairstreak is limited to the northern quarter of the state, mostly found in wetlands south of Lake Michigan. It could occur in the northwestern quarter of the state, since there are records from southeastern Iowa. The Acadian Hairstreak can be fairly common locally, and appears secure in the region.

♂ T

♀ T

WINGSPAN
1.25–1.5 in

♂ U

♀ U

CORAL HAIRSTREAK
Satyrium titus (Fabricius)

PREVALENCE
Widely
encountered

FLIGHT PERIOD

MAR	
APR	
MAY	
JUN	
JUL	
AUG	
SEP	
OCT	
NOV	

FIELD NOTES

A. No tails

B. Row of bright
coral-red spots (U)

Male

Female

DESCRIPTION The Coral Hairstreak has a wingspan of 1.0–1.5 inches. The sexes are similar in color, but differ in wing shape—male wings are sleek and pointed, while female wings are broader and more rounded. Also, the male has a stigma (sex patch). The species is tailless and the upperside of both sexes is dull brown. Some specimens have a hint of orange on the outer margin of the hindwing. The underside is a lighter brown than the upperside and has a row of white-ringed black spots just past the middle of the wings. The outer margin of the hindwing has a row of conspicuous, coral-red spots that are capped with black and white crescents.

COULD BE CONFUSED WITH The Acadian Hairstreak is similar, but has two tails on each hindwing and a lighter-colored underside. In the event that a predator has clipped the tails off, remember the Acadian Hairstreak is a wetland-loving, willow-feeding species that does not stray far from its habitat.

HABITAT/LIFE HISTORY Shrubby open fields, pastures, prairies, woodland margins, savannas, and gardens—all with many flowering plants—are likely places to find the Coral Hairstreak. Caterpillar hosts include wild cherry and other *Prunus* species. The adult is territorial and combative toward other butterflies. A single generation occurs, with the adult on the wing from late May into August. The majority of the population occurs in late June, coinciding with the blooming of most milkweed species. The Coral Hairstreak overwinters in the egg stage.

STATUS Although it occurs in localized colonies, the Coral Hairstreak is found statewide and is not difficult to locate. Sometimes it can be seen in large numbers on various milkweeds in the sand prairies of central Illinois.

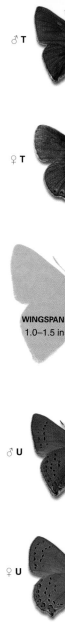

♂ T

♀ T

WINGSPAN
1.0–1.5 in

♂ U

♀ U

EDWARDS' HAIRSTREAK
Satyrium edwardsii (Grote & Robinson)

PREVALENCE
Locally
encountered

FLIGHT PERIOD

MAR	
APR	
MAY	
JUN	■
JUL	■
AUG	
SEP	
OCT	
NOV	

FIELD NOTES
A. Blue spot not surrounded by orange (U)

B. Inner row of spots on hindwing prominently ringed with white (U)

Female

Male

DESCRIPTION The Edwards' Hairstreak wingspan is 1.0–1.25 inches. The sexes are similar, but the male has a thin stigma (sex patch) on his forewing that is wider towards the apex and tapers towards his body. The upperside of both sexes is plain brown. The underside is a shade lighter, with two tails on each hindwing. In from the wing margins are prominent bands formed with separate, white-bordered, dark brown spots. On the forewing, these spots are edged with white towards the outer margin only; conversely, as the spots descend on the hindwing they become totally encircled with white. The outer margin of the hindwing also has a row of white-and-black-capped, orange crescents. The large, blue spot at the outer angle of the hindwing is topped with a thin, white-over-black crescent (no orange).

COULD BE CONFUSED WITH The two hairstreaks most likely to be confused with the Edwards' Hairstreak are the Acadian and Banded (see page 356). The Acadian Hairstreak has a lighter base color and black underside spots. The Banded Hairstreak has underside bars rather than spots.

HABITAT/LIFE HISTORY In Illinois, Edwards' Hairstreak commonly occurs in scrub oak–sand prairie savannas and woodland openings in association with milkweeds, New Jersey tea, and leadplant. It is an avid flower visitor and often sits on the same flower head with other "banded" *Satyrium* species. The caterpillar is a nocturnal feeder and eats oak buds early in the season and oak leaves later in the season. The caterpillar is often tended by ants and is sometimes found in ant nests during the day. A single generation occurs and the adult flies from early June to late July, with most records from late June. The species overwinters in the egg stage.

STATUS The Edwards' Hairstreak can be locally common. It is mainly found in the Illinois River basin, the counties around southern Lake Michigan, and the remnant savannas of the Grand Kankakee Marsh. A few scattered records occur from the southern half of Illinois. Edwards' Hairstreak numbers vary widely from year to year.

♂ T

♀ T

WINGSPAN
1.0–1.25 in

♂ U

♀ U

BANDED HAIRSTREAK
Satyrium calanus falacer (Godart)

DESCRIPTION The Banded Hairstreak has a wingspan of 1.0–1.25 inches. The sexes are similar, but the male has a large, oval-shaped stigma (sex patch) on his forewing—

PREVALENCE
Widely
encountered

FLIGHT PERIOD

MAR	
APR	
MAY	
JUN	
JUL	
AUG	
SEP	
OCT	
NOV	

FIELD NOTES

A. Blue spot and adjacent orange crescent are approximately the same height (U)

B. White crescents above the blue spot and orange crescent touch, forming a line (U)

Male

Male: variant specimen

the largest of the *Satyrium* group. For both sexes, the upperside is brown, the underside is medium to dark brown, and the hindwing has two tails. The row of bands, located in from the underside border, varies in shape and width. They are straight-sided and edged with white, more prominently on the outer edge, and weak to nonexistent on the inner edge. The band located on the underside of the hindwing near the center of the upper wing margin has straight, white-edged sides. The orange crescent located between the hindwing tails is approximately the same height as the large, blue spot adjacent to it. The orange crescent and the blue spot are both capped with thin, white-on-black crescents that meet at the same point.

COULD BE CONFUSED WITH The other "banded" hairstreaks are similar (see page 356), especially the Hickory Hairstreak. On the Banded, the uppermost band on the underside of the hindwing is thinner, straight, and nearer the outer wing margin; conversely, on the Hickory it is wider, shaped like parentheses, and centered along the wing margin. The large, blue spot and adjacent orange crescent are about the same height on the Banded, while the blue spot is twice the height of the orange crescent on the Hickory. Lastly, the white crescents that top the orange crescent and blue spot meet at the same point on the Banded, but are offset on the Hickory.

HABITAT/LIFE HISTORY The Banded Hairstreak inhabits forests, woodland openings, savannas, and urban areas near woods. Oak is the preferred caterpillar host in Illinois. The adult is an avid flower visitor. The male is territorial and engages in aerial battles, swirling and jousting for a perch to scan for females. The species has a single generation, with the adult present from late May to early August. Population size peaks in mid-June to early July. The species overwinters in the egg stage.

STATUS The Banded Hairstreak is the most common of the "banded" hairstreaks in Illinois, and likely occurs in most oak stands statewide. Population sizes vary.

♂ T

♀ T

WINGSPAN
1.0–1.25 in

♂ U

♀ U

FLIGHT PERIOD

MAR	
APR	
MAY	
JUN	■
JUL	
AUG	
SEP	
OCT	
NOV	

FIELD NOTES

A. Blue spot taller than adjacent orange crescent (U)

B. White crescents above the blue spot and orange crescent do not touch (U)

C. Uppermost spot enclosed with white parentheses (U)

HICKORY HAIRSTREAK
Satyrium caryaevorus (McDunnough)

DESCRIPTION The Hickory Hairstreak has a wingspan of 1.0–1.25 inches. The sexes are similar, but the male has a slender stigma (sex patch) that tapers at each end. The upperside of both sexes is brown and the hindwing has two tails. The underside base color is a little lighter than that of the upperside. The band located inward from the wing margins is composed of wide, connected (yet offset) bars. These bars have dark centers—sometimes with a hint of orange—and white edges. The uppermost band on the underside of the hindwing is wide, centered along the leading margin, and sometimes enclosed in white parentheses. The blue spot at the outer angle is usually twice the height of the white-and-black-capped orange crescent adjacent to it. The white crescents over the blue spot and orange crescent are offset.

Will Cook

Female

COULD BE CONFUSED WITH[14] The other "banded" hairstreaks are similar (see page 356), especially the Banded Hairstreak. On the Hickory, the uppermost band on the underside of the hindwing is wider, shaped like parentheses, and centered along the wing margin; conversely, on the Banded it is thinner, straight, and nearer the outer wing margin. The large, blue spot is twice the height of the orange crescent adjacent to it on the Hickory, while the blue spot and adjacent orange crescent are about the same height on the Banded. Lastly, the white crescents that top the orange crescent and blue spot are offset on the Hickory, but meet at the same point on the Banded.

♂ T

♀ T

HABITAT/LIFE HISTORY The Hickory Hairstreak frequents forest openings, savannas, and barrens, always occurring near hickories, the caterpillar hosts. Little is known about the life history of this obscure species. It visits flowers, especially New Jersey tea, and occurs with the other *Satyrium* species. The species overwinters in the egg stage.

WINGSPAN
1.0–1.25 in

STATUS The Hickory Hairstreak is uncommon to rare and very localized—it is the least encountered *Satyrium* species in the state. Scattered records indicate that it occurs mainly in the northern half of Illinois, roughly north of I-72. A Jackson county record suggests that it may be overlooked in much of the state.

♂ U

♀ U

STRIPED HAIRSTREAK
Satyrium liparops strigosa (T. Harris)

Male

Female

PREVALENCE
Rare

FLIGHT PERIOD

MAR	
APR	
MAY	
JUN	
JUL	
AUG	
SEP	
OCT	
NOV	

FIELD NOTES

A. Large, blue spot capped with white, black, and orange (U)

B. Wide, broken, darker-brown bands edged in white (U)

DESCRIPTION The Striped Hairstreak has a wingspan of 1.0–1.25 inches. The sexes are similar, but the male has an oval-shaped (widest in the middle) stigma (sex patch) on his forewing. The species has two tails on each hindwing, and usually the upperside is plain brown. Some specimens have an orange patch in the central area of the forewing—this patch occurs more frequently in the Striped Hairstreak than in other "banded" hairstreaks. The underside is a lighter shade of brown than the upperside. The bands on the underside are wide, dark in the center, and occasionally tinged with orange; they have white trim on each side. The bands are not aligned, and appear random. The underside of the hindwing has a scattering of black-capped, orange spots along its outer margin. A white-black-and-orange-capped black spot is located between the tails. Below the tails is a large, blue spot capped with white, black, and orange crescents.

COULD BE CONFUSED WITH Of the four "banded" hairstreaks in Illinois, the Striped Hairstreak is the most easily distinguished (see page 356). The Hickory, Banded, and Edwards' Hairstreaks all have a much tighter banding pattern on their underside.

HABITAT/LIFE HISTORY The Striped Hairstreak is never far from woodlands. Forest margins, savannas, prairie openings, and wet, shrubby meadows are haunts of this butterfly. In Illinois, the caterpillar feeds on plums, hawthorns, willows, oaks, and many other species. The adult is an avid flower visitor and often occurs with other *Satyrium* hairstreaks. One generation occurs with the adult flying from late May into early August. Peak flight is from late June to mid-July. The species overwinters in the egg stage.

STATUS While an uncommon breeding resident, the Striped Hairstreak is found throughout the state. It is most often found singly. Without a close look, the species can blend in with the other "banded" hairstreaks.

♂ T

♀ T

WINGSPAN
1.0–1.25 in

♂ U

♀ U

NORTHERN HAIRSTREAK
Satyrium favonius ontario (W.H. Edwards)

Male

PREVALENCE
Rare

FLIGHT PERIOD

MAR	
APR	
MAY	■
JUN	
JUL	
AUG	
SEP	
OCT	
NOV	

FIELD NOTES

A. Brown base color (U)

B. Broken, black-and-white line across hindwing (U)

Male

DESCRIPTION The wingspan of the Northern Hairstreak is 1.25 inches. The sexes are similar, but the male has a stigma (sex patch) on his forewing. The upperside of both sexes is brown, with small amounts of orange scaling in the middle of the forewing; this may be quite noticeable or completely absent. The underside is brownish-gray with a white and black line located in from the wing margin and a row of orange crescents on the outer wing margin. Between the tails note a large, black-and-white-capped, orange crescent adjacent to a large, blue spot. The blue spot is capped with thin white, black, and orange crescents.

COULD BE CONFUSED WITH The Gray Hairstreak is very similar (see page 356); however, its wings are more rounded and lighter in color, its upperside is brownish-gray, and its underside is a pale gray. Further, the Gray Hairstreak has a tricolored line (orange, black, and white) on its underside—the Northern Hairstreak has a two-colored line (it lacks the orange).

HABITAT/LIFE HISTORY The Northern Hairstreak is a canopy-dwelling butterfly of oak forests that seldom reveals itself. Look for it along woodland edges or forest trails. It uses white oak, as well as other oaks, as caterpillar hosts. A single generation occurs each year and all Illinois records are from the last two weeks of May; the one exception is a single specimen captured in Hancock County on June 21. The species overwinters in the egg stage.

STATUS The Northern Hairstreak is a rare, breeding resident and one of the least encountered species in Illinois. It appears sporadically and could be found anywhere in the state where oaks abound, but few records exist.[15] This is likely due to the butterfly's habits, more than its actual rarity, as it undoubtedly spends most of its life in the oak canopy.

♂ T

♀ T

WINGSPAN
1.25 in

♂ U

♀ U

OLIVE HAIRSTREAK
Callophrys gryneus (Hübner)

FLIGHT PERIOD

MAR	
APR	
MAY	
JUN	
JUL	
AUG	
SEP	
OCT	
NOV	

FIELD NOTES

A. Unique green
base color (U)

Female:
spring
form

Female:
summer
form

DESCRIPTION Illinois' only green butterfly, the seasonally dimorphic Olive Hairstreak has a 1.0 inch wingspan. The sexes are similar, but the male has a prominent stigma (sex patch) on his forewing. The spring generation upperside is orange-brown with brown borders. The summer generation upperside is dark brown with very little or no orange coloring. The underside of both generations is olive green with a jagged band that is bright-white on the outer side and reddish-brown toward the inside. Each hindwing has two hairlike tails.

COULD BE CONFUSED WITH No butterfly is similar in Illinois.

HABITAT/LIFE HISTORY The Olive Hairstreak resides on hill prairies, sandy areas, rolling forests, glades, and river valleys where its caterpillar host, red cedar, grows. The species' fast, erratic flight makes it difficult to follow with the eye, but the moment it lands its identity is obvious. Tapping red cedar with a net handle or stick will often send the adult twirling into the air, but it will usually settle back quickly on nearly the same perch. Two distinct generations occur in Illinois: the first from April into May, and the second in July. The species overwinters as a chrysalis.

STATUS The Olive Hairstreak can be locally common along the Illinois, Mississippi, and Ohio River valleys, and is probably more widespread than in the past. Fire suppression has affected most hill prairies and open river valleys and allowed woody invasion. Red cedar has become more prevalent and widespread, creating a favorable situation for the Olive Hairstreak. The species has been scarce to absent in much of east-central and south-central Illinois, but as red cedar spreads, it may become established in that region as well.

♂ **T**
summer
form

♀ **T**
spring
form

WINGSPAN
1.0 in

♂ **U**
summer
form

♀ **U**
spring
form

HOARY ELFIN
Callophrys polios (Cook & F. Watson)

PREVALENCE
Locally
encountered

FLIGHT PERIOD

MAR	
APR	■
MAY	■
JUN	
JUL	
AUG	
SEP	
OCT	
NOV	

FIELD NOTES

A. Silvery gray
margin (U)

B. No tails

Female

Male

DESCRIPTION The wingspan of the Hoary Elfin is 1.0 inch. The sexes are similar, but the male has a stigma (sex patch) on his forewing. The upperside of both sexes is dark brown. The underside is dark brown towards the body; the outer half is a soft, violet gray. The hindwing margin is slightly scalloped, and the species has no tail.

COULD BE CONFUSED WITH The Frosted and Henry's Elfins are similar, but both have a noticeable tail on the hindwing; the Hoary Elfin lacks a tail. The Frosted Elfin has a distinctive black spot above its small tail on the underside of its hindwing that the other two elfins lack. Henry's Elfin has a more defined pattern on the underside of its hindwing and is a woodland butterfly.

HABITAT/LIFE HISTORY In Illinois, the habitat of the Hoary Elfin is the Lake Michigan dunes, were bearberry, the caterpillar host, occurs. Each spring this butterfly nestles into bearberry bushes on the dunes, taking flight when disturbed. It flies low to the ground and settles down quickly. When not in flight, this diminutive creature resembles last year's bearberry leaves and is virtually invisible. It overwinters as a chrysalis. The adult can be found from April into May, but generally is only at peak numbers for a few days during that time span. The flight period varies each year, depending on the weather.

STATUS The Hoary Elfin's range is restricted to where bearberry grows, but it can be common to abundant at the right location. This species is at the extreme edge of its range in northeastern Illinois. With the exception of an old Cook County record from 1911, all records we are aware of are from Lake County. It continues to thrive in the dune areas of Lake County, and is reported in good numbers almost every year.

♂ T

♀ T

WINGSPAN
1.0 in

♂ U

♀ U

FROSTED ELFIN
Callophrys irus (Godart)

PREVALENCE
Rare

FLIGHT PERIOD

MAR	
APR	■
MAY	
JUN	
JUL	
AUG	
SEP	
OCT	
NOV	

FIELD NOTES

A. Small tail on hindwing

B. Black spot above tail (U)

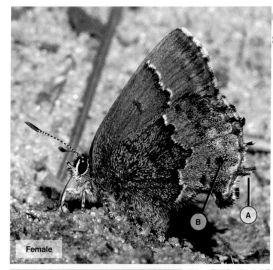

Female

Male

DESCRIPTION The Frosted Elfin has a wingspan of 1.0 inch. The sexes are similar, but the male has a stigma (sex patch) on his forewing. The upperside of both sexes is dark brown. The underside is dark brown towards the body; the outer half is lighter in color with a dusting of purplish-gray towards the outer margin of the hindwing. A small, but distinct tail occurs on the lower hindwing. The most diagnostic feature of this butterfly—not found on any of the other elfins—is a black spot just above the tail on the underside.

COULD BE CONFUSED WITH The Henry's Elfin and Hoary Elfin are similar to the Frosted Elfin. Henry's Elfin has a more defined pattern on the underside of its hindwing and a well-developed tail; also, it is a woodland butterfly. The Hoary Elfin has slightly scalloped hindwing margins with no tail, and stays close to its caterpillar host, bearberry. Unlike the Frosted Elfin, neither species has a black spot on its underside.

HABITAT/LIFE HISTORY The Frosted Elfin inhabits oak savannas and barrens that contain stands of lupine, its caterpillar host plant. Although there are reports of the caterpillar feeding on indigo, in Illinois it seems to be limited to lupine. The species is on the wing from April into May, and is gone before the trees have fully leafed out. It is easy to miss if a location is not checked regularly to catch its emergence. The Frosted Elfin overwinters as a chrysalis.

STATUS The Frosted Elfin has been found once in Illinois in 1922.[16] Illinois is at the extreme edge of its range (most records are from farther east). Due to the type of habitat it requires, the species is not very common in any part of its range.

♂ T

♀ T

WINGSPAN
1.0 in

♂ U

♀ U

HENRY'S ELFIN
Callophrys henrici (Grote & Robinson)

Male

PREVALENCE
Locally
encountered

FLIGHT PERIOD

MAR	
APR	███
MAY	
JUN	
JUL	
AUG	
SEP	
OCT	
NOV	

FIELD NOTES

A. Prominent, curved tail

B. Inner half of wings dark brown (U)

C. Middle line of hindwing ends in white (U)

Female

DESCRIPTION Henry's Elfin has a wingspan of 1.0 inch. The sexes are similar, but the female color is variable. The male upperside is brown with a slight orange tint and no forewing sex patch (stigma). The female can be slightly orange-brown, like the male, or a dull orange over brown. The underside of both sexes is dark brown on the inner half of the wings and a lighter, yellowish brown on the outer half. The line in the middle of the hindwing is white at each end, and protrudes outward in the center toward the wing margin. The hindwing has an outward-curving tail.

COULD BE CONFUSED WITH The Hoary and Frosted Elfins are both similar, but neither occur in the same habitat as Henry's Elfin; thus, location should help determine what species you have. The Hoary Elfin lacks a tail and the underside of its hindwing has a more uniform look. The Frosted Elfin has a distinctive, black spot on its underside above its tail.

HABITAT/LIFE HISTORY Henry's Elfin is a forest species, often seen taking moisture at damp spots along woodland trails or darting around the blooms of redbud, its caterpillar host. On occasion, it has been encountered on hill prairies, where it perches on red cedar, sometimes in the company of the Olive Hairstreak. The adult comes and goes with the blooming of redbud, and by the time the blossoms are gone, so is the butterfly. Depending on the year, it can be found from late March into May, but an individual adult flies for only about a week. Henry's Elfin has a single spring generation and overwinters as a chrysalis in the leaf litter.

STATUS Henry's Elfin is found in the southern two-thirds of the state—it has not been recorded north of I-80. It occurs commonly in the river valleys of west-central Illinois. Tap a few blooming redbuds with a stick and any perching Henry's Elfin will usually fly out. The species appears secure and can be locally common.

♂ T

♀ T

WINGSPAN
1.0 in

♂ U

♀ U

EASTERN PINE ELFIN
Callophrys niphon (Hübner)

Female

Female
(worn)

PREVALENCE
Locally
encountered

FLIGHT PERIOD

MAR	
APR	▓
MAY	▓
JUN	
JUL	
AUG	
SEP	
OCT	
NOV	

FIELD NOTES
A. Bold, dark-colored pattern (U)

DESCRIPTION The sexually dimorphic Eastern Pine Elfin has a wingspan of just over 1.0 inch—it is Illinois' largest elfin species. The male upperside is dark brown with a brown-and-white checkered fringe and a small sex patch (stigma). The female upperside is orange-brown with a checkered fringe (similar to the male's fringe pattern). The underside of both sexes is boldly patterned with offset black lines trimmed with white. The wings are edged with inwardly-facing black chevrons.

COULD BE CONFUSED WITH Although in flight the Eastern Pine Elfin superficially resembles the other elfins, once perched its unique underside pattern will separate it from all other elfin species. Habitat should also be noted; areas with stands of pine are the only places you are likely to see this elfin.

HABITAT/LIFE HISTORY Forested areas with either native or planted pine stands are the habitat of this elusive species. The Eastern Pine Elfin tends to stay high in the pines and seldom comes down. The best chance to see it is to travel a trail or back road through pines in Pope County, usually in late April on a sunny day, after a rain. Watch puddles, and if anything flies up, pinpoint where it lands and carefully approach. This method should provide an opportunity to see the species. As the common name implies, the caterpillar feeds on various species of pine. The Eastern Pine Elfin makes its once-a-year appearance from April into May and overwinters as a chrysalis.

STATUS While a few scattered records occur from throughout Illinois, the Eastern Pine Elfin is more commonly found in southern Illinois. The species is probably much more common than records indicate, but its habit of staying high in the tree canopy keeps its true distribution a secret. Based on the available data, we consider the species as local and uncommon. However, any pine woods in the state could potentially have Eastern Pine Elfins, as there is an old specimen labeled "Cicero, Ill."

♂ T

♀ T

WINGSPAN
>1.0 in

♂ U

♀ U

GRAY HAIRSTREAK
Strymon melinus Hübner

PREVALENCE
Widely
encountered

FLIGHT PERIOD

MAR	
APR	
MAY	
JUN	
JUL	
AUG	
SEP	
OCT	
NOV	

FIELD NOTES

A. Medium gray base color (T & U)

B. Orange-capped black spot on hindwing (T & U)

C. Broken, tri-colored line across hindwing, with inner orange line prominent (U)

Male

Male

DESCRIPTION The Gray Hairstreak has a wingspan of 1.25 inches. The sexes are similar, and the male has no stigma (sex patch) on his forewing. The upperside is a uniform grayish-brown, and the hindwing has two tails. The underside is pale gray with a tri-colored band—white, followed by black, and trimmed inwardly with a line of orange. An orange-capped, black spot—located between the tails—is present on both the upperside and underside.

COULD BE CONFUSED WITH The Northern Hairstreak is similar, but has more squared-off wings and is more brown than gray (see page 356). Further, the underside of the Northern Hairstreak is darker and has a two-colored band (it lacks the orange).

HABITAT/LIFE HISTORY The Gray Hairstreak is a habitat generalist, and can be found along weedy roadsides, pastures, cultivated areas, woodland margins, and in gardens. It is polyphagous. The caterpillar feeds on the flowers, seed pods, and fruits of hops, knotweeds, cultivated beans, and many other species. Ants often tend the caterpillar. Unlike most other hairstreaks, this species often perches with its wings open. Multiple generations occur each year, with records from April through October. The species overwinters as a chrysalis.

STATUS The Gray Hairstreak is by far our most common and widespread hairstreak, and likely occurs in every county. It is common to abundant in southern Illinois, becoming less common to rare farther north. This species is repeatedly listed as a pest of beans in regional publications, but it seems difficult to imagine the Gray Hairstreak could ever reach "pest" status in Illinois. Such epic numbers have certainly not been observed by the authors.

♂ T

♀ T

WINGSPAN
1.25 in

♂ U

♀ U

WHITE-M HAIRSTREAK
Parrhasius m-album (Boisduval & Le Conte)

Bill Bouton

Male

Female

PREVALENCE
Rare

FLIGHT PERIOD

MAR	
APR	
MAY	
JUN	
JUL	
AUG	
SEP	
OCT	
NOV	

FIELD NOTES

A. Metallic blue iridescence (T)

B. Bright orange spot (U)

C. Prominent "M" (U)

D. White mark on hindwing (U)

DESCRIPTION   The wingspan of the White-M Hairstreak is 1.5 inches. The sexes are slightly different. The male upperside is brilliant, iridescent blue with thin, black borders and a stigma (sex patch) on the forewing. The female upperside is basically the same, with thicker, black borders and no stigma. The underside of both sexes is grayish-brown with a prominent white "M" (or "W" depending on how you look at it), inwardly shadowed with dull brown. Note a single white mark towards the upper corner of the hindwing. Between the two tails and just off the outer margin is a conspicuous, reddish-orange spot.

COULD BE CONFUSED WITH   The Great Purple Hairstreak is also iridescent blue, but a darker shade. Further, the Great Purple Hairstreak is larger and its underside lacks the white "M". The only area in which the two species would ever occur together is the far southern tip of Illinois. The Red-banded Hairstreak is smaller, has less blue on its upperside, and has an orange-red band on its underside.

HABITAT/LIFE HISTORY   The White-M Hairstreak occurs along forest edges and in clearings, never far from oak woodlands. Search flowers and damp spots for this elusive butterfly. The caterpillar feeds on various species of oak. The adult's flight is fast and erratic; approach carefully, as once disturbed it is likely gone. The White-M Hairstreak has a long flight period with two, perhaps three generations spanning the summer. Most records are from June and September; however, it has been found every month from May into October. The species overwinters as a chrysalis in leaf litter.

STATUS   The White-M Hairstreak is a scarce, breeding resident. It is most often found singly, but occasionally appears in numbers. Specimens are known from more than a dozen counties across the state. Like other hairstreaks, the White-M Hairstreak stays high in the trees, keeping its presence a secret.

♂ T

♀ T

WINGSPAN
1.5 in

♂ U

♀ U

RED-BANDED HAIRSTREAK
Calycopis cecrops (Fabricius)

PREVALENCE
Locally
encountered

FLIGHT PERIOD

MAR	
APR	
MAY	
JUN	
JUL	
AUG	
SEP	
OCT	
NOV	

FIELD NOTES
A. Distinctive,
reddish-orange
band across both
wings (U)

Bill Bouton

Male

Female

DESCRIPTION The Red-banded Hairstreak has a wingspan of 1.0 inch. The sexes are similar, but the species is seasonally dimorphic. The upperside of spring individuals is black and usually has some iridescent, blue scaling (ranges from a little scaling to almost half the total wing area). In the summer generation, the blue scaling is reduced or absent. The underside of both generations is grayish-brown with a thick, red to reddish-orange band trimmed with black and white. A large, black spot is located along the outer margin between the two tails—it is sometimes capped with orange. A pale, blue-to-white spot occurs below the large black spot, at the outer angle of the hindwing.

COULD BE CONFUSED WITH The Red-banded Hairstreak should not be confused with anything else, as the reddish-orange band on its underside is distinctive.

HABITAT/LIFE HISTORY The Red-banded Hairstreak is equally at home in the open as it is in the deep forest. The species' strange life history has only recently been accepted. The caterpillar appears to feed on deteriorating leaf debris. Most field guides list oaks or sumacs as caterpillar hosts—it is the fallen leaves of these and other species that provide sustenance. When disturbed, the adult flies around briefly, but often settles back onto the perch it vacated. Multiple generations occur each season, with the adult on the wing from April through September. Most specimens we have seen are from late April. The species overwinters as an egg or a partially grown caterpillar.

STATUS The Red-banded Hairstreak is uncommon to locally common in southern Illinois, but becomes rare to absent north of St. Louis' latitude. That range line continues across the eastern U.S. to the Atlantic coast. At times, the Red-banded Hairstreak can be numerous in forest clearings and openings throughout the Shawnee National Forest region.

♂ T

♀ T

WINGSPAN
1.0 in

♂ U

♀ U

Summer Azure

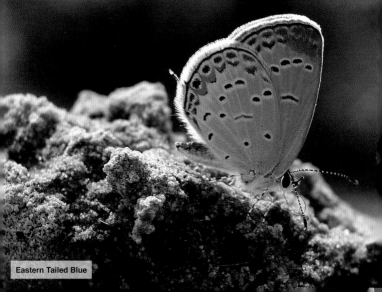

Eastern Tailed Blue

SUBFAMILY POLYOMMATINAE
Blues

The subfamily Polyommatinae is found throughout the world, with most species occurring in Eurasia. Over 30 species are found in North America, and of those, three regularly occur in Illinois—Eastern Tailed Blue, Spring Azure, and Summer Azure. The males are predominantly blue above, while the females are a duller color, usually brown. The blue on the males is a result of reflected light rather than pigmentation. The underside of both sexes is a light color, with a pattern of stripes and/or dots. Blues are avid flower visitors and puddlers. Due to their weak, fluttery flight they do not fly long distances and are usually found near their host plants. Many times they will rest with their wings partially open. Most overwinter as chrysalids.

SPECIES

- Marine Blue
- Eastern Tailed Blue
- Spring Azure
- Summer Azure
- Dusky Azure
- Silvery Blue
- Reakirt's Blue
- Karner Blue

MARINE BLUE
Leptotes marina (Reakirt)

PREVALENCE
Rare stray

FLIGHT PERIOD

MAR	
APR	
MAY	
JUN	
JUL	
AUG	
SEP	
OCT	
NOV	

FIELD NOTES

A. Purplish sheen (T)

B. Concentric bands of white and light brown (U)

C. Two dark spots on hindwing (U)

Bill Bouton

Female

Bill Bouton

Male

DESCRIPTION The sexually dimorphic Marine Blue has a wingspan of just under 1.0 inch. The male upperside is almost entirely blue, with a noticeable purplish cast. His wings are edged with a thin, brown border and white fringe. The male also has two small, dark spots on the bottom margin of his hindwing. The female upperside is mostly brown, with the blue scaling reduced to the wing areas near the body. Like the male, she also has the dark spots on her hindwing. The underside of both sexes has white and pale brown bands crossing the wings, with brown crescents bordering the wing edges. The two black spots at the end of the hindwing are encircled by a halo of iridescent, silvery blue.

COULD BE CONFUSED WITH A quick look at the underside of the Marine Blue reveals it to be different from any other Illinois blue. Even in flight this species has a purplish sheen that is lacking in the other species.

HABITAT/LIFE HISTORY The Marine Blue inhabits open fields, sand prairies, old railroad grades, and the margins of streams/rivers. This species occasionally wanders into Illinois. It may create a temporary breeding colony that produces a generation before winter; the colony may survive a year or two if the ensuing season is mild. The caterpillar hosts are the flowers of many different, abundant legumes. The adult has been found from July through September, with most records from August.

STATUS The Marine Blue is an inhabitant of the southwestern U.S and is a rare visitor to Illinois. It may turn up anywhere in the state, but encounters are rare.[17]

♂ T

♀ T

WINGSPAN
<1.0 in

♂ U

♀ U

EASTERN TAILED BLUE
Cupido comyntas (Godart)

PREVALENCE
Widely
encountered

FLIGHT PERIOD

MAR	
APR	
MAY	
JUN	
JUL	
AUG	
SEP	
OCT	
NOV	

FIELD NOTES

A. White-tipped tail

B. Two black spots topped with large orange crescents (U)

Male

Male

DESCRIPTION The wingspan of the Eastern Tailed Blue is less than 1.0 inch. The sexes are dimorphic and seasonally variable. As its name implies, each hindwing has a white-tipped tail. The male upperside is iridescent blue, with a narrow, black border and white fringe. The male has orange crescents just above his tail. The upperside of the spring generation female is dark brown with extensive blue scaling on the inner half of the wing; conversely, the upperside of the summer generation female is almost entirely dark brown. Like the male, the hindwing of both female forms has orange crescents just above the tail. The underside of both sexes is grayish-white with scattered black spots. Two black spots on the outer margin near the tail are capped with orange crescents.

COULD BE CONFUSED WITH The Eastern Tailed Blue is our only blue with tailed hindwings; however, seeing the tails is not easy. Its small size and low, bouncy flight are good clues to its identity.

HABITAT/LIFE HISTORY The Eastern Tailed Blue is a habitat generalist—open fields, urban yards, and pastures. It avoids deep, shaded forests, but may occur in forest openings. This species is often ignored because it is so common. The slow, bouncing flight of the Eastern Tailed Blue is low to the ground and seldom reaches over knee high. The caterpillar feeds on a wide variety of legumes. The adult is an avid "puddle club" attendee, and often gathers with dozens of others at a damp spot. At least three generations occur each year, as fresh adults fly in all months, from April through October. The species overwinters as a mature caterpillar.

STATUS The Eastern Tailed Blue is considered one of the most common Illinois species and appears secure. It no doubt occurs in every Illinois county.

♂ T

♀ T

WINGSPAN
<1.0 in

♂ U

♀ U

SPRING AZURE

Celastrina ladon (Cramer)

DESCRIPTION The sexually dimorphic Spring Azure has a wingspan of 1.0 inch. The male upperside is a uniform, iridescent violet-blue with a satin-like sheen. His outer

PREVALENCE
Widely
encountered

FLIGHT PERIOD

MAR	
APR	
MAY	
JUN	
JUL	
AUG	
SEP	
OCT	
NOV	

FIELD NOTES
A. Pale colored
with dark spots (U)

Male

Male

margin is black with a black fringe at the tip of the forewing that becomes checkered with white as it descends. The veins of his hindwing are bordered with black. The female upperside is the same iridescent violet-blue as the male upperside, but has a wide, black border on the outer wing margins and the leading edge of the forewing. A row of black spots runs down the outer margin of her hindwing. The female forewing has a central, dark spot near the leading edge. The underside of both sexes is light gray, though the hindwing can be either uniformly colored or contain blotchy, dark areas. A line of gray to black spots is located in from the wing margin, with other spots scattered about. The outer margin on both wings is lined with chevrons over dark spots.

♂ T

COULD BE CONFUSED WITH The Summer Azure and Dusky Azure female are similar. The Summer Azure is typically larger and lighter in color, but not always. The upperside of the Dusky Azure hindwing often has slight-to-extensive whitish scaling, which the Spring Azure lacks. The Dusky Azure female is darker in color; her wings are dark gray, not blue, near her body. Further, her upperside has a solid-looking hindwing border.

♀ T

WINGSPAN
1.0 in

HABITAT/LIFE HISTORY The Spring Azure is a woodland butterfly, and is best sought in river valleys near stands of dogwood. It has a rapid flight, not covering a great distance unless disturbed. In Illinois, the caterpillar likely uses dogwoods. The adult visits flowers and damp spots. This species is one of the earliest butterflies to emerge from its chrysalis. A single spring generation occurs from late March to mid-May, with individuals on the wing for about a week.

♂ U

STATUS A reevaluation of specimens in collections is needed to determine the true distribution and status of the Spring Azure. Our experience indicates that the species is a more localized, restricted, and uncommon than the Summer Azure. The Spring Azure is more common and widespread south of State Route 136—only a few records occur from the northern counties.

♀ U

SUMMER AZURE
Celastrina neglecta (W.H. Edwards)

DESCRIPTION The sexually dimorphic Summer Azure has a wingspan of 1.0–1.3 inches. The male upperside is an iridescent violet-blue, with the hindwing either completely uniform with the forewing, or a whitish-blue. The male

PREVALENCE
Widely
encountered

FLIGHT PERIOD

MAR	
APR	
MAY	
JUN	
JUL	
AUG	
SEP	
OCT	
NOV	

FIELD NOTES
A. Pale colored
with dark spots (U)

Bill Bouton

Male

Male

hindwing usually retains a blue band along the outer margin that is trimmed in black. The wing fringe on the male is black at the apex and along most of the forewing, turning pure white on the hindwing. The upperside of the female forewing is iridescent violet-blue and has a wider, dark margin that runs down the leading border of the wing to the body. A small, dark spot occurs near the leading edge of the female forewing. The female hindwing has a row of dark spots along its outer margin. The iridescent, violet-blue is replaced on the hindwings with variable amounts of white; the blue is limited to near the body. This white coloring is also evident on the upper forewing, though never as extensive as on the hindwing. A summer individual has more whitish coloring than the early spring generation. The underside of both sexes is a pale whitish-gray with a well-defined pattern of black spots. These spots form a band, located in from the wing margin; along the outer margin of the hindwing are diffuse, chevron-capped, dark spots.

COULD BE CONFUSED WITH The Spring Azure and Dusky Azure females can cause difficulty. The Spring Azure usually has a checkered fringe, a duller or softer-looking appearance, and no whitish scaling on its upperside. As its name suggests, the Spring Azure is strictly a spring butterfly, so anything after May is likely to be a Summer Azure.[18] The Dusky Azure female is darker in color; her wings are dark gray, not blue, near her body. Further, her upperside has a solid-looking hindwing border.

HABITAT/LIFE HISTORY The Summer Azure is at home in any habitat—natural and disturbed. Unlike the Spring Azure, it is not confined to woodlands. The caterpillar feeds on the buds and flowers of a variety of host plants. The adult is an avid flower visitor, and often congregates in puddle clubs. The Summer Azure has multiple generations from March to October, with late summer/fall individuals the largest and whitest. The species likely overwinters as a chrysalis.

STATUS The Summer Azure is common throughout the state, likely in every county.

♂ T

♀ T

WINGSPAN
1.0–1.3 in

♂ U

♀ U

DUSKY AZURE
Celastrina nigra (W. Forbes)

PREVALENCE
Rare

FLIGHT PERIOD

MAR	
APR	■
MAY	
JUN	
JUL	
AUG	
SEP	
OCT	
NOV	

FIELD NOTES
A. Row of dark spots along the hindwing margin (U)

Male

Male

DESCRIPTION The sexually dimorphic Dusky Azure has a wingspan of 1.0 inch. The male upperside is grayish-black, darkest in fresh individuals. His wings are edged with a fine, white fringe with faint black checkering. The female upperside has extensive dark gray scaling around all wing edges, more than any other azure female. The central area of her wings is a dirty, blue-white color, giving her a dull appearance, and her wing veins are outlined in gray. The underside of both sexes has the typical azure pattern of grayish-white with a scattering of black spots. Even in the freshest specimen, the wings always look faded or pale, never crisp and defined as in the other azures.

COULD BE CONFUSED WITH From the underside, the Dusky Azure could be mistaken for any of the other azures. However, the male upperside is entirely grayish-black and the female upperside has exaggerated dark borders. Both sexes have an overall dull look. These features are discernible even in flight.

HABITAT/LIFE HISTORY The Dusky Azure is a forest butterfly, prevalent before the trees leaf out in spring. Look for it in deep, wooded, east-west running ravines, and on north-facing slopes, always near its caterpillar host, goat's beard (*Aruncus dioicus*). The species overwinters as a chrysalis. Flight times vary and can be from late March until mid-May. The butterfly is on the wing only about a week during that time period. Be persistent and check goat's beard blooms for the caterpillar—it is sometimes easier to locate than the adult.

STATUS The Dusky Azure is scattered and very localized across the state. While probably more widespread than records indicate, it will always be limited in numbers, uncommon, and difficult to locate due to its specific habitat requirements and short, early flight season.[19]

♂ T

♀ T

WINGSPAN
1.0 in

♂ U

♀ U

SILVERY BLUE
Glaucopsyche lygdamus (E. Doubleday)

Male

Female

Male

PREVALENCE
Rare

FLIGHT PERIOD

MAR	
APR	■
MAY	
JUN	
JUL	
AUG	
SEP	
OCT	
NOV	

FIELD NOTES

A. Silvery sheen (T)

B. Row of white-ringed, black spots on wings (U)

DESCRIPTION The sexually dimorphic Silvery Blue has a wingspan of 1.0 inch. The male upperside is a uniform, iridescent, silvery-blue color (quite flashy) with thin, black wing borders. The female upperside is duller and the black wing borders are wider. The underside of both sexes is steel gray, with a row of prominent, white-ringed black spots.

♂ T

COULD BE CONFUSED WITH[20] In flight, the Silvery Blue superficially resembles the other blues, especially Reakirt's Blue. However, Reakirt's Blue is smaller and has an underside pattern of spots, marks, and crescents.

♀ T

HABITAT/LIFE HISTORY The seldom encountered Silvery Blue occurs in dry, open areas; oak savannas; and old railroad grades where the caterpillar host plant occurs. In Illinois, the caterpillar feeds on the flowers of veiny pea during May. Pupation occurs at the base of the plant, making it fire sensitive. Any fire management where this species occurs should be carefully evaluated. A single generation occurs each spring. The adult flies from April into mid-May, and is gone by the time most trees and shrubs leaf out. The species overwinters as a chrysalis.

WINGSPAN
1.0 in

STATUS The Silvery Blue is a rare species in Illinois—it occurs in localized colonies and is never widespread. With one exception, the species has only been found in the northeast corner of the state.[21] The Chicago area has had known populations for over a century; the best of these occurs in the Palos Park area. A few additional viable populations are known in the northern tier of Illinois counties, from Winnebago to the east. Additional unknown Silvery Blue colonies may exist in that region, but the species' appearance in spring is so brief that it is easily missed.

♂ U

♀ U

REAKIRT'S BLUE
Echinargus isola (Reakirt)

Male

A

FLIGHT PERIOD

MAR	
APR	
MAY	
JUN	■
JUL	■
AUG	■
SEP	
OCT	
NOV	

FIELD NOTES

A. Two small, black spots on hindwing (T)

B. Row of dark, round spots on forewing (U)

A

Female

A

B

Female

DESCRIPTION   The sexually dimorphic Reakirt's Blue has a wingspan of about 1.0 inch. The male upperside is violet-blue with a dark border, edged with an off-white fringe. Two small, black spots occur at the outer angle of the male hindwing. The female upperside has a dark border extending at least halfway into the wings, confining the blue areas to near the body. The female also has two black spots at the outer angle of the hindwing. The underside of both sexes has a ground color of light, grayish brown. The underside of the forewing has a middle row of white-ringed, black spots with crescents along the outer edge. The underside of the hindwing has a few, scattered, dark markings with prominent crescents along the outer margin, as well as two or three black spots ringed with iridescent white and orange.

♂ T

♀ T

COULD BE CONFUSED WITH   The Silvery Blue is larger than Reakirt's Blue and flies in early spring. In flight, the Eastern Tailed Blue and Reakirt's Blue are difficult to tell apart; however, when perched the tail on the Eastern Tailed Blue will separate them. This species may be overlooked, so always take a second glance at all small, blue butterflies.

WINGSPAN
~1.0 in

HABITAT/LIFE HISTORY   Reakirt's Blue inhabits prairie remnants, open fields, railroad grades, and sandy areas. The caterpillar hosts are the buds and flowers of various legumes. The adult is an avid flower visitor and will spend a long time probing a flower for nectar. The adult has been found in June, July, and August.

♂ U

STATUS   The Reakirt's Blue normally resides far to the south and west of Illinois (Texas to southern California). It is an irregular, but consistent stray, able to establish temporary colonies that have the potential to last for several years before disappearing. The species can show up anywhere in Illinois—scattered records occur from all over the state.[22]

♀ U

KARNER BLUE
Plebejus samuelis (Nabokov)

PREVALENCE
Rare

FLIGHT PERIOD

MAR	
APR	
MAY	
JUN	
JUL	
AUG	
SEP	
OCT	
NOV	

FIELD NOTES
A. Row of orange-capped spots (U)

Male

Female

Male

A

DESCRIPTION The sexually dimorphic Karner Blue has a wingspan of 1.25 inches. The male upperside is a darker blue than other species in this subfamily; it is slightly iridescent, has a thin, black border around all wings, and is outlined by fine, white fringe. The upperside of the female forewings is dark, with some blue scaling on the inner half of the wings, and a black spot near the center of the forewing. The upperside of the female hindwing is usually half dark and half blue (the inner half). The outer margin of the female hindwing has a row of orange-capped black spots. All female wings have a fine, white fringe. The underside of both sexes is pale gray with many black spots ringed in white; the outer margin of the hindwing has several silver spots capped with deep orange crescents.

COULD BE CONFUSED WITH In flight, the Karner Blue is similar to all other blues. However, the row of orange-capped spots on its underside distinguishes it from other Illinois species.

HABITAT/LIFE HISTORY The Karner Blue is found in open, oak savannas and sandy barrens with lush stands of lupine, the caterpillar host plant. The adult is low-flying and stays close to vegetation, often sitting in plain view with its wings open. Research suggests that an individual never strays farther than a few hundred feet from where it emerges. The caterpillar is often tended and protected by ants for the "honeydew" it produces. The limited records of the Karner Blue suggest that it has two generations in Illinois, one from late May into June and another from July into August. The species overwinters in the egg stage.

STATUS The Karner Blue is a very rare, sporadic species that is at the extreme edge of its range in Illinois. All blue butterflies found in the vicinity of lupine should be carefully observed as a potential Karner Blue.[23]

♂ T

♀ T

WINGSPAN
~1.25 in

♂ U

♀ U

A tropical Riodinidae species, the
Northern Clearmark (*Chorinea bogota*)

A tropical Riodinidae species, the
Neglected Jewelmark (*Sarota neglecta*)

FAMILY RIODINIDAE
Metalmarks

Only one member of this family has been collected in Illinois—the Swamp Metalmark. Worldwide, this family has over 1,000 species, with most of them found in the American tropics. The common name of *metalmark* refers to the small, metallic spots often found on their wings. The females have three pairs of walking legs, while the males have two pairs—their front pair of legs is reduced and not used for walking. Although closely related to the hairstreaks (Lycaenidae), metalmarks have longer antennae and distinctive, upperside wing patterns.

Metalmarks are rather localized, seldom flying far—their flight is weak and somewhat erratic. The adults perch with their wings open to rest, nectar, and bask. They will often land on a leaf and crawl underneath it, much the way many moths do, to avoid detection—this may lead to the species being overlooked. Metalmarks overwinter as caterpillars.

SPECIES
- Swamp Metalmark

SWAMP METALMARK
Calephelis muticum McAlpine

Female

Female

A

Male

PREVALENCE
Rare

FLIGHT PERIOD

MAR	
APR	
MAY	
JUN	
JUL	
AUG	
SEP	
OCT	
NOV	

FIELD NOTES
A. Square-shaped metallic markings (U)

DESCRIPTION The Swamp Metalmark has a wing-span of about 1.0 inch and similar sexes. The upperside is reddish-brown with scattered black marks distributed uniformly across all wings. Two silvery-blue, metallic bands run the length of the wings—one interior to the wing edge, and one on the outer margin. A row of black dots is located between the bands. The underside is orange with markings similar to the upperside. The outer, silvery band is continuous, while the inner, silvery markings are broken and square-shaped.

COULD BE CONFUSED WITH The Northern Metalmark[24] is similar, only with more rounded forewings and a noticeable dark band on its upperside. On the underside, the innermost silvery marks are crescent-shaped (Northern) instead of square-shaped (Swamp).

HABITAT/LIFE HISTORY The Swamp Metalmark is secretive and behaves much more like a geometrid moth than a butterfly, with its erratic flight and habit of landing and crawling to the underside of a leaf. As the name implies, the Swamp Metalmark favors wet areas (generally seeps in open woodlands), but can also be found in larger, marshy thickets—it seems to prefer some shade. In Illinois, the caterpillar is known to feed on both swamp and tall thistle; it has nine instars and overwinters in the fourth. Two generations occur in central Illinois; the first one emerges in June and another in late August into September. In northern Illinois, only one generation occurs, and it flies mainly in July.

STATUS This species is uncommon to rare and intensely local.[25] A colony often stays within a few-hundred-square-foot area and the adult seldom ventures out.

♂ T

♀ T

WINGSPAN
~1.0 in

♂ U

♀ U

Great Spangled Fritillaries and an Ozark Checkerspot

FAMILY NYMPHALIDAE
Brush-footed Butterflies

The Nymphalidae, the brush-footed butterflies, are named for their small, furry forelegs. They have three pairs of legs; however, the front pair is atrophied and is sensory in function. Only the middle and hind legs are used in walking; so, in effect, these butterflies are quadrupeds (appear to have only four functioning legs). The female American Snout is the sole exception. Nymphalids are highly variable and found worldwide. Cech and Tudor (2005) write in *Butterflies of the East Coast*, "The nymphalids are an unlikely assemblage of butterflies. They encompass, in one family, much of the biological diversity of all the other five families combined—in shape, appearance, ecological life-style, early stages, host plant use, and seasonal movements."

Within this diverse family are the longest-lived butterflies (those that emerge during the summer and overwinter in a state of diapause until spring—Mourning Cloak, Comma, and Question Mark) and the furthest travelers (Monarch and Painted Lady). The shades of Autumn—brown, orange, black, and yellow—are recurring colors of the Illinois species.

At one time, many of the Nymphalidae subfamilies were classified as separate families.

SUBFAMILIES
- Libytheinae (Snout)
- Danainae (Monarchs)
- Heliconiinae (Longwings & Fritillaries)
- Limenitidinae (Admirals)
- Apaturinae (Emperors)
- Nymphalinae (True Brush-foots)
- Charaxinae (Leafwings)
- Satyrinae (Satyrs)

American Snout

SUBFAMILY LIBYTHEINAE
Snouts

Fewer than a dozen members of the subfamily Libytheinae, the snouts, occur worldwide. All those with known life histories feed on hackberry. They are an ancient group, as snouts have been found in 35 million-year-old fossil shales. Preserved hackberry leaves and flowers have also been found in the same shales, leading Samuel Scudder, the first North American paleoentomologist, to note that it is highly probable that snouts fed on hackberry even then (Emmel, T.C. et. al., 1992). We have only one species in North America.

Snouts have thickened mouthparts (palps) that look like a beak or a snout. The adults often perch with their heads down on twigs or small branches, where they mimic dead leaves. They are orange and brown with square forewing tips, and are strong fliers. Snouts puddle and nectar, but are easily disturbed. They overwinter as adults, and they migrate like some members of the Nymphalid family.

SPECIES
• American Snout

AMERICAN SNOUT
Libytheana carinenta bachmanii (Cramer)

PREVALENCE
Widely
encountered
migrant

FLIGHT PERIOD

MAR	
APR	
MAY	
JUN	
JUL	
AUG	
SEP	
OCT	
NOV	

FIELD NOTES

A. Distinctive
mouth parts (i.e.,
snout)

B. Squared-off
forewings

DESCRIPTION The American Snout has a wingspan of 1.5–2.0 inches and similar sexes. A prominent "snout" distinguishes this species from all other North American butterfly species. The snout is formed by elongated mouthparts. The upperside of the American Snout is drab brown with white markings on the forewing and orange areas on both wings. The forewing tip is squared off. The underside of the hindwing is cryptically colored—at rest, with its wings closed, the American Snout resembles a dead leaf. The "snout" gives the illusion of a leaf petiole.

♂ T

COULD BE CONFUSED WITH No other butterfly has a snout.

HABITAT/LIFE HISTORY Look for the American Snout along roadsides, rivers, and streams as well as in woods, fields, and open country—anywhere its caterpillar host plant, hackberry, is found. While the adult nectars at flowers, it also actively seeks salts and minerals by puddling, perching on the sweaty arm of a butterfly observer, or sitting on the ground. The adult is on the wing from late April through September. Unfortunately, Illinois does not have the huge mass migrations in late summer through early fall that occur in the southwestern United States, during which the American Snout can darken the sky (Cech and Tudor, 2005).

WINGSPAN
1.5–2.0 in

STATUS The American Snout is a widely encountered migrant that colonizes the state each year. It cannot survive an Illinois winter; all stages of its life cycle are cold intolerant. It may be found throughout Illinois, with greater numbers and sightings in the southern two-thirds of the state.

♂ U

Monarch

Queen

SUBFAMILY DANAINAE
Milkweed Butterflies

The members of the subfamily Danainae are mostly tropical, but Illinois does have two representatives—our familiar state insect, the Monarch, and a rare stray, the Queen. The North American Danaids are referred to as milkweed butterflies, because their caterpillars eat only milkweed. Milkweed plants contain heart poisons (cardiac glycosides) that are toxic to most insects, yet the Danaids seem immune to their effects. These chemicals not only protect Danaid caterpillars, but also the adults as they retain the stored toxins. If a predator should happen to eat a Danaid, it would literally "throw up."

Danaid caterpillars, which lack any hairs or spines, are boldly marked in black and yellow, while the adults are orange with black and white markings, coloration that advertises, "Leave me alone." Their chrysalids resemble jewels—green, with gold and black markings.

Adult Danaids have tough, flexible bodies that help them survive attacks by predators. They also have an elegant, gliding flight and are avid nectar feeders. Males have abdominal hair pencils and hindwing scent patches that are used in courtship. No frost tolerance is present in any life stage, so members of this family take part in seasonal movements or migrations; these can be short range, or in the case of the Monarch, quite lengthy.

SPECIES

· Monarch
· Queen

MONARCH
Danaus plexippus (Linnaeus)

Male

Female

Male

PREVALENCE
Widely
encountered

FLIGHT PERIOD

MAR	
APR	
MAY	
JUN	
JUL	
AUG	
SEP	
OCT	
NOV	

FIELD NOTES

A. Bright orange
base color (♂ T)

B. Duller orange
base color (♀ T)

C. All wing veins
outlined in black
(T & U)

D. Black borders
with white spots
(T & U)

E. Androconium
(♂ T & U)

DESCRIPTION   Perhaps no butterfly is more familiar than the highly visible Monarch. It has a wingspan 3.5–4.5 inches. The sexes are similar, but the male has a sex patch (androconium) on his hindwing. The upper- and underside of both sexes is orange; however, the male is bright orange while the female is duller orange. All wings have black borders containing two rows of white spots; these spots are more prominent on the underside. A few scattered white and orange spots occur in the outer half of the upper- and underside of the forewing. All wing veins are lined in black.

COULD BE CONFUSED WITH   The Monarch and Viceroy form a mimicry complex, and are quite similar (see page 358); however, the Viceroy is smaller and has a black band that traverses its hindwing. The Queen, a rare stray in Illinois, could be confused with the Monarch, but it is orange-brown and only has the hindwing veins on its underside traced in black—all of the Monarch's wing veins are boldly outlined in black.

HABITAT/LIFE HISTORY   The Monarch prefers open areas, and is equally at home in city flower gardens or country pastures and roadsides. The caterpillar—almost as recognizable as the adult with its bold black, white, and yellow stripes—sits in plain view on the leaves of various milkweed species. The adult arrives in Illinois as early as late March, but it is usually not seen regularly before May. The Monarch will have two, sometimes three nonmigratory generations before the September generation congregates and starts its journey to the mountains of Mexico. In North America, the annual migratory flight of the Monarch is legendary (see *Models, Migration, and Mimicry*, page 63).

STATUS   In 1975, schoolchildren voted the Monarch as the official state insect of Illinois. The species undoubtedly occurs in every county in Illinois.

♂ T

WINGSPAN
3.5–4.5 in

♂ U

QUEEN
Danaus gilippus (Cramer)

Male

Female

Female

PREVALENCE
Rare stray

FLIGHT PERIOD

MAR
APR
MAY
JUN
JUL
AUG
SEP
OCT
NOV

FIELD NOTES

A. Orange abdomen top

B. Scattered white spots (T)

C. Orange-brown base color (T & U)

D. Androconium (♂ T & U)

E. Black-lined veins only on hindwing (U)

DESCRIPTION The wingspan of the Queen is about 3.0 inches. The sexes are similar, but the male has a dark sex patch (androconium) on his hindwing. The upper- and underside of both sexes is rich, orange-brown with black wing borders containing white spots. A few scattered, white spots also occur on the outer half of the forewing. The veins on the underside of the hindwing are outlined boldly in black and edged with white. The top of the abdomen is orange.

COULD BE CONFUSED WITH The Queen's pattern is much like the Monarch's; however, the Queen's rich, orange-brown color is unmistakable. Further, only the veins on the underside of the hindwing are traced in black on the Queen, whereas all of the Monarch's wing veins are outlined in black.

HABITAT/LIFE HISTORY The Queen is an open-land butterfly that occurs in fields, pastures, roadsides, and city gardens. The caterpillar feeds on milkweeds, and could perhaps complete a generation in Illinois, but certainly could not survive an Illinois winter. The adult would most likely be encountered anytime from May to September.

STATUS The Queen can only be considered a rare stray from the south that occasionally finds its way to Illinois. About a half dozen records are known from the state, north of St. Louis; no records occur from the southern part of Illinois, where you would expect to find it. The Queen probably passes through Illinois more often than records indicate, and could be found anytime, anywhere.

♂ T

WINGSPAN
~3.0 in

♂ U

Regal Fritillary

SUBFAMILY HELICONIINAE
Longwings and Fritillaries

The subfamily Heliconiinae is most abundant in the tropics, but Illinois does have several representatives. The species in this group have slender bodies, large eyes, and long antennae, and most have some orange coloration. The males search for recently emerged females or chrysalids that are about to produce an adult.

In Illinois, the longwings include the Zebra (collected once in Illinois), Gulf Fritillary (a rare stray), and Variegated Fritillary (a yearly migrant into the state). Like the common name suggests, the longwings have elongated forewings; the Variegated Fritillary's forewings, while not as long as its tropical cousins, are elongated as well. This group's caterpillars feed on several hosts, including passionflower. The adults can be migratory, and the group has more than one generation per year. Note: both the Gulf Fritillary and Variegated Fritillary are not "true" fritillaries, and thus are not closely related to those listed below.

The Fritillaries are divided into two subgroups—the greater (genus *Speyeria*) and lesser (genus *Boloria*). The greater fritillaries include Diana, Regal, Great Spangled, Aphrodite, and Atlantis. Males emerge first and begin to patrol for females—they use not only visual cues, but also scent cues to recognize a female. This subgroup has only one generation per year. The females lay their eggs on or near violets, even though the plant may have senesced and not be visible to us. Violets are their only hosts. As is typical for the group, when the caterpillars hatch they eat their eggshell, crawl to a protected site in the leaf litter, and enter diapause until spring. The lesser fritillaries—Silver-bordered and Meadow—resemble miniature *Speyeria* fritillaries and also use violets for their life cycle. They have multiple generations per year.

SPECIES
- Gulf Fritillary
- Zebra
- Variegated Fritillary
- Silver-bordered Fritillary
- Meadow Fritillary
- Diana
- Great Spangled Fritillary
- Aphrodite Fritillary
- Regal Fritillary
- Atlantis Fritillary

GULF FRITILLARY
Agraulis vanillae (Linnaeus)

Male

Nectaring Activity

PREVALENCE
Rare

FLIGHT PERIOD

MAR	
APR	
MAY	
JUN	
JUL	
AUG	
SEP	
OCT	
NOV	

FIELD NOTES

A. Black-ringed, white spots (T & U)

B. Oval-shaped, silver spots (U)

DESCRIPTION The Gulf Fritillary has a wingspan of 2.5–3.75 inches. The sexes are similar in pattern; however, the male is brighter orange and the female has darker markings. The upperside of both sexes is orange with black marks, especially along the outer margin of the hindwing. A few (usually three) black-ringed, white spots occur near the leading edge of the forewing. The upperside of the forewing also has several scattered black spots. The underside is orange-brown with many, mostly oval-shaped, silver spots. The centers of the black spots on the underside of the forewing are silver.

COULD BE CONFUSED WITH At first glance the Gulf Fritillary could be mistaken for one of our *Speyeria* fritillaries, but the shape of its wings and its overall pattern should separate it.

HABITAT/LIFE HISTORY This butterfly occurs near the edge of woods, searching for its caterpillar host, passion-flower.[26] It may frequent open fields with flowers and perhaps wander into flower gardens.

STATUS This species is a rare stray to Illinois. It can occasionally breed here and form temporary colonies in areas where its caterpillar host is found. Records are scattered across Illinois. In recent years at least one individual has been recorded annually from somewhere in the state.

♂ T

♀ T

WINGSPAN
2.5–3.75 in

♂ U

ZEBRA
Heliconius charithonia (Linnaeus)

PREVALENCE
Rare stray

FLIGHT PERIOD

MAR	
APR	
MAY	
JUN	
JUL	
AUG	
SEP	
OCT	
NOV	

FIELD NOTES

A. Elongated wings

B. Distinctive black-and-yellow striping pattern (T & U)

Female

Male

DESCRIPTION The Zebra, a tropical longwing butterfly, has a wingspan of 3.0 inches and similar sexes. Its upperside is black with three yellow stripes across the forewing. A single stripe and a row of yellow spots cross the underside of the hindwing. The upperside pattern is repeated on the underside, except the yellow coloring is paler and a reddish spot occurs on the inner wing margin.

COULD BE CONFUSED WITH The Zebra is unmistakable; nothing like it occurs in Illinois.

HABITAT/LIFE HISTORY The Zebra is a butterfly of the deep south, mainly Florida, southern Texas, and the American tropics. It occurs in open woodlands and the borders of hammocks, where its caterpillar feeds on passion-flower. The Zebra could be found in late summer.

STATUS The Zebra is a rare stray in Illinois.[27] Even though it flies with shallow, fluttery wing beats and is slow moving, the Zebra seems to occasionally accomplish this northward pilgrimage.

♂ T

WINGSPAN
~3.0 in

♂ U

VARIEGATED FRITILLARY
Euptoieta claudia (Cramer)

PREVALENCE
Locally
encountered
migrant

FLIGHT PERIOD

MAR	
APR	
MAY	
JUN	
JUL	
AUG	
SEP	
OCT	
NOV	

FIELD NOTES

A. Tawny, yellow-orange base color (T)

B. Dark spots near wing margins (T)

C. Light band across center of hindwing (U)

Female

Male

DESCRIPTION The Variegated Fritillary has a wing-span of 1.75–3.0 inches and similar sexes. The upperside is tawny, yellow-orange, with dark veins and markings, black spots near the wing margins, and a light-colored band that runs through the middle of both wings. The underside of the hindwing is mottled with orange, brown, and gray; it resembles a dead leaf. A lighter band passes through the middle of the hindwing. There are no bold, silver spots on the underside of the wings.

COULD BE CONFUSED WITH The *Speyeria* fritillaries have silver spots on the underside of their wings, and a red-orange instead of a yellow-orange upperside. The Tawny Emperor does not have a row of black spots near its upperside wing margins, nor a light colored band on the underside of its hindwing; further, it is not normally found in the same habitat as the Variegated Fritillary. From a distance, the Variegated's wing shape may suggest a Painted Lady, but the Painted Lady has distinctive, white spots on the upperside of the forewing tip.

HABITAT/LIFE HISTORY The Variegated Fritillary prefers open, sunny areas including prairies, old fields, road edges, and disturbed habitats. Unlike the *Speyeria* fritillaries, the Variegated Fritillary caterpillar is a generalist. It feeds on a wide range of hosts, including passion-flower. It overwinters in frost-free areas of the southern United States and flies north each spring and summer. The adult flies from late April through November, but is most often encountered in late summer or fall. There are two to three generations per year in Illinois.

STATUS While Illinois is repopulated each year with the Variegated Fritillary, finding it may be problematic. It occurs throughout the state, but is usually never very common.

REMARK With its low, swift flight, the Varigated Fritillary is difficult to approach; the genus name is from the Greek *euptoietos*, which means "easily scared."

♂ T

WINGSPAN
1.75–3.0 in

♂ U

SILVER-BORDERED FRITILLARY
Boloria selene (Denis & Schiffermüller)

PREVALENCE
Locally
encountered

FLIGHT PERIOD

MAR	
APR	
MAY	
JUN	
JUL	
AUG	
SEP	
OCT	
NOV	

FIELD NOTES

A. Narrow, black
wing margins with
cream spots along
the edge (T)

B. Silver border of
spots along outer
wing margins (U)

C. Scattered
silver spots (U)

Female

Female

DESCRIPTION The Silver-bordered Fritillary has a wingspan of 1.5–2.25 inches. The sexes are similar, but the female has a slightly more rounded wing shape. The upperside of both sexes is tawny to red-orange with black spots and dashes. The upperside wing margins have a narrow, dark border with cream spots along the edge. The underside is various shades of orange, with a silver border along both outer wing margins. The underside of the hindwing has additional scattered, silver spots.

COULD BE CONFUSED WITH The Meadow Fritillary is about the same size and found in the same habitat as the Silver-bordered Fritillary; however, it lacks a dark border on the upperside of its wings, as well as a silver border and silver spots on its underside (see page 360).

HABITAT/LIFE HISTORY The fast-flying Silver-bordered Fritillary is found in wet prairies, marshes, and sedge meadows. It seems to prefer some structure to its habitat, with willows, alder, or other shrubs present. The species overwinters as a caterpillar, and like the *Speyeria* fritillaries, is in close association with the caterpillar food plant, various species of violets. Unlike the *Speyeria* fritillaries which have a single generation per year, the Silver-bordered Fritillary has two to three generations. It has been recorded flying from mid-May to the end of September.

STATUS The Silver-bordered Fritillary is found in the northern half of Illinois and is never very abundant. An observer may see only one or two individuals at a site.

♂ T

♀ T

WINGSPAN
1.5–2.25 in

♂ U

♀ U

MEADOW FRITILLARY
Boloria bellona (Fabricius)

FLIGHT PERIOD

MAR
APR
MAY
JUN
JUL
AUG
SEP
OCT
NOV

FIELD NOTES

A. Squared-off
forewing tip

B. Hindwing has
a purple cast,
giving it a dull
appearance (U)

Male

Male

DESCRIPTION The Meadow Fritillary has a wingspan of 1.25–2.0 inches. The sexes are similar, but the female has rounder wings. The upperside is red-orange with black zigzags, dots, and crescents on the interior of the wings, and two rows of dark spots on the outer wing edges. The forewing is squared off below the tip, giving the wing a clipped appearance. The underside of the hindwing is various shades of orange, with a purple sheen (a hoariness) over the outer half of the wing.

COULD BE CONFUSED WITH The Silver-bordered Fritillary is about the same size and found in the same habitat; however, it has a dark border on the upperside of both its wings. Additionally, the underside of the Silver-bordered Fritillary has many silver spots (see page 360).

HABITAT/LIFE HISTORY The Meadow Fritillary is found in wet to dry meadows, prairies, and marshes, but can also stray into roadsides, pastures, and gardens. The adult pauses frequently to nectar on a variety of flowers, while the caterpillar will eat only various species of violets. The species overwinters as a partially developed caterpillar, usually at the base of the food plant. Unlike the larger fritillaries (*Speyeria*), the Meadow Fritillary has more than one generation per year in Illinois. It has been recorded flying from May to mid-September.

STATUS The Meadow Fritillary primarily occurs in the northern half of Illinois, where it may be locally common; however, scattered records exist for the Meadow Fritillary throughout Illinois.

♂ T

♀ T

WINGSPAN
1.25–2.0 in

♂ U

♀ U

DIANA
Speyeria diana (Cramer)

Male

Female

Male

PREVALENCE
Extirpated

FLIGHT PERIOD

MAR	
APR	
MAY	
JUN	
JUL	
AUG	
SEP	
OCT	
NOV	

FIELD NOTES

A. Large, orange border on both wings (♂ **T**)

B. Large, blue band on hindwing (♀ **T**)

DESCRIPTION The sexually dimorphic Diana—named to honor the Roman goddess Diana—has a wingspan of 3.0–4.5 inches. The male upperside is dark brown with a large orange border—he is the "typical" orange and brown, like other *Speyeria*. The underside of the male hindwing is burnt orange, with a lighter orange band containing a thin line of silver dashes near the margin. The female upperside is blue and black with white patches and spots on the forewing and large, faded-denim-colored patches near the hindwing edge. The underside of the female forewing is mottled blue and off-white, while the female hindwing is blue-brown, with two thin, ivory lines.

COULD BE CONFUSED WITH The Diana male may be confused with the Monarch, Great Spangled Fritillary, and Regal Fritillary. The Monarch is orange with black veins, and both the Great Spangled and Regal have silver spots on the underside; the male Diana has a faint line of silver, and no large spots. The Diana female may be confused with the Red-spotted Purple and Pipevine Swallowtail, but lacks tails and a row of orange spots on the underside of her hindwing. The Diana female is thought to be a Batesian mimic of the Pipevine Swallowtail.

HABITAT/LIFE HISTORY The Diana prefers moist, mature, forested areas where it nectars on flowers in openings and along roadsides. The caterpillar feeds only on violets. The female lays her eggs in the vicinity of violets in late summer, and when the caterpillar hatches it goes into diapause, emerging in spring with a voracious appetite for violets. The adult flies from late May through early fall.

STATUS The Diana is a resident of the southern Appalachians and the Ozark Mountains of Missouri, Arkansas, and eastern Oklahoma.[28] It has been extirpated from Illinois.

WINGSPAN
3.0–4.5 in

GREAT SPANGLED FRITILLARY
Speyeria cybele (Fabricius)

PREVALENCE
Widely
encountered

FLIGHT PERIOD

MAR	
APR	
MAY	
JUN	
JUL	
AUG	
SEP	
OCT	
NOV	

FIELD NOTES
A. Wings darker
near body (T)

B. Hindwing with
wide, buff-colored
band (U)

Male

Male

DESCRIPTION The Great Spangled Fritillary has a wingspan of 3.0–4.0 inches, and similar sexes. The upperside has a variety of markings—bars, crescents, and black spots—and is darker nearer the body. The underside of the hindwing has a wide, buff-colored band between two rows of silver spots along the wing margin. The common name is derived from these spots—the "spangles."

COULD BE CONFUSED WITH In flight, the Diana male is similar, but the underside of his hindwing is orange and has no silver spots. The Aphrodite is smaller and lighter in color than the Great Spangled; further, the underside of its hindwing is reddish-brown, with a narrow, buff-colored band (see page 362). The Regal Fritillary's hindwing is dark, and its underside is a jumble of silver-white marks.

HABITAT/LIFE HISTORY The Great Spangled Fritillary is found in open, sunny habitats—fields, roadsides, wet meadows, woodland edges, and gardens. The adult nectars at a variety of plants, while the caterpillar only eats violets. The female deposits a single egg on or near violet plants in late summer (Note: any evidence of violets is usually gone by this point). Once the caterpillar hatches it crawls to a protected site in the leaf litter where it enters diapause until spring. It then finds violet leaves and begins to feed. The adult may be found from mid-April through early October. Illinois has one generation per year, with the male emerging two to three weeks before the female.

STATUS The Great Spangled Fritillary occurs throughout Illinois, where it can be quite common. It has a single, extended generation with continual emergence of adults throughout the season.

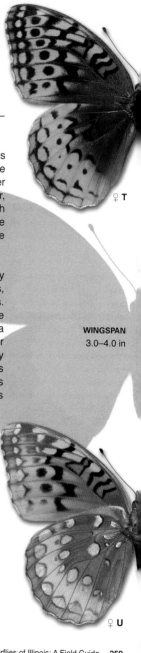

♀ T

WINGSPAN
3.0–4.0 in

♀ U

APHRODITE FRITILLARY
Speyeria aphrodite alcestis (W.H. Edwards)

PREVALENCE
Locally
encountered

FLIGHT PERIOD

MAR	
APR	
MAY	
JUN	■
JUL	■
AUG	
SEP	
OCT	
NOV	

FIELD NOTES

A. Small,
distinctive, black
mark (T)

B. Very narrow,
buff-colored
hindwing band (U)

Male

Female

DESCRIPTION The Aphrodite Fritillary—named for the ancient Greek goddess of beauty—has a wingspan of 2.5–3.5 inches, with the female larger than the male. The upperside is orange, with a variety of black markings. Also, at least in most individuals, note a single black mark in the diffuse, brown area near the forewing base. The underside of the hindwing is reddish-brown and can have a faint, narrow, buff-colored band between two parallel rows of silver spots.

COULD BE CONFUSED WITH The Aphrodite Fritillary appears to be the intermediate between the Great Spangled and Atlantis Fritillaries, sharing characteristics of both species. The Great Spangled has a wider, buff-colored band on the underside of its hindwing, while Aphrodite's band is narrower. Aphrodite's orange wing color is noticeably more vibrant and brighter. The Atlantis is smaller, and has only been documented once in Illinois.

HABITAT/LIFE HISTORY The Aphrodite Fritillary occurs in open fields and woodland edges. It does not seem to matter whether the habitat is wet or dry, as the authors have watched the species nectar in both moist prairies and dry savannas. The adult is a strong flier and nectars at a variety of plants, while the caterpillar only eats violets. The female deposits a single egg on or near violet plants in late summer. (Note: any perceivable evidence of violets is usually gone.) When the caterpillar hatches, it crawls to a protected site in the leaf litter, and enters diapause until spring. It then finds violet leaves and begins to feed. The Aphrodite Fritillary is on the wing from mid-June to early September, and has one generation per year in Illinois.

STATUS The Aphrodite Fritillary is found in the northern third of Illinois. It is not as common as the Great Spangled Fritillary, and for every dozen individuals of the Great Spangled, one might see a single Aphrodite.

♂ T

WINGSPAN
2.5–3.5 in

♂ U

REGAL FRITILLARY
Speyeria idalia occidentalis B. Williams

DESCRIPTION The sexually dimorphic Regal Fritillary has a wingspan of 2.75–4.25 inches. The upperside of the forewing is red-orange with black markings; the female

PREVALENCE
Locally
encountered

FLIGHT PERIOD

MAR	
APR	
MAY	
JUN	
JUL	
AUG	
SEP	
OCT	
NOV	

FIELD NOTES

A. Two rows
of spots on
hindwings: ivory-
colored in female,
one row ivory and
one row orange in
male (T)

B. Numerous,
large, silvery-white
spots on hindwing
(U)

Male

Female

forewing also has white spots in the black wing margin. The upperside of the hindwing is dark with spots in two curved rows—on the male, the inner row of spots is ivory and the outer row is pale orange, whereas on the female both rows of spots are ivory. The underside is similar. The forewing is orange with black markings and white spots in the dark margins. The hindwing is dark brown, with silvery-white spots and bars—more than half the wing is actually white.

COULD BE CONFUSED WITH The Regal Fritillary is sometimes confused with the Monarch because they are the same size.[29] The Great Spangled Fritillary is similar, but the upperside of its hind-wing is orange and the underside of its hindwing has a buff-colored band between two rows of silvery-white spots. The Aphrodite Fritillary is smaller, and the markings on the underside of its orange hindwing are not as bold as the Regal's.

HABITAT/LIFE HISTORY The Regal Fritillary occurs in sand prairies, dunes, and wet areas in sandy regions, as well as tallgrass prairies and savan-nas. In Illinois, the caterpillar feeds primarily on Johnny-jump-up. The adult nectars on a variety of plants, with thistles and milkweeds preferred. The Regal Fritillary's flight is swift, often coasting close to the ground. It quickly drops into the vegetation and emerges when an observer approaches. After mating, the female will not lay her eggs for at least six to eight weeks. The egg hatches in early fall, whereupon the caterpillar seeks cover in the leaf litter and overwinters. In the spring, the caterpillar emerges and begins to feed. In Illinois, the flight period is from mid-May through September, with the male appearing and disappearing earlier than the female. There is only one generation per year.

STATUS The Regal Fritillary is a threatened spe-cies in Illinois. In the past it probably occurred throughout the Grand Prairie region of the state. At present, it is known from a dozen counties where the populations may be common to scarce during any given year.

♂ T

♀ T

WINGSPAN
2.75–4.25 in

♀ U

ATLANTIS FRITILLARY
Speyeria atlantis (W.H. Edwards)

PREVALENCE
Rare stray

FLIGHT PERIOD

MAR
APR
MAY
JUN
JUL
AUG
SEP
OCT
NOV

FIELD NOTES

A. Dark wing margins (no orange) (T)

B. Medium-width, buff-colored band on hindwing (U)

Female

Female

DESCRIPTION The Atlantis Fritillary has a wingspan of 2.0–2.75 inches, and similar sexes. It has been described as "trim and crisply marked." The upperside is orange (various shades) with dark markings. The wing margins are dark and contain little or no orange. The underside of the hindwing has a narrow, buff-colored band separating two rows of silver spots; other silver spots are scattered near the base of the hindwing.

♂ T

♀ T

WINGSPAN
2.0–2.75 in

♂ U

COULD BE CONFUSED WITH The Great Spangled and Aphrodite are the "common" fritillaries to look for in Illinois—the Atlantis Fritillary is a rare stray from the north. The Atlantis is smaller and has a darker upperside than the other species; it also has prominent, dark wing margins.

HABITAT/LIFE HISTORY The Atlantis Fritillary is a northern (boreal) species, and there it prefers meadows and forest openings. The adult nectars at a variety of plants, while the caterpillar eats only violets. The female deposits a single egg on or near violet plants in late summer (Note: any evidence of violets is usually gone by this time). Once the caterpillar hatches, it crawls to a protected site in the leaf litter where it enters diapause until spring. It then finds violet leaves and begins to feed. The Atlantis Fritillary is on the wing from early June through very early August, and has one generation per year.

STATUS Illinois has a single record of the Atlantis Fritillary, from Cook County in 1930. Irwin and Downey (1973) report that the specimen from Illinois was probably casual and "the species does not normally range as far south as Illinois." It is not likely that the species will soon become a "resident." Cech and Tudor (2005) surmise this about the Atlantis Fritillary: "…common northward, it is a boreal specialist that cannot easily adapt to modern land use patterns and warming climate conditions."

Red-spotted Purple

Viceroy

SUBFAMILY LIMENITIDINAE

Sisters and Admirals

In Illinois, the subfamily Limenitidinae includes the Red-spotted Purple/White Admiral and Viceroy; it does not include the Red Admiral. Many members of this subfamily have names associated with military ranks or titles of nobility. One reason could be that many of the species have a stripe running lengthwise across the wings, reminding earlier authors of an officer's stripes.

Limenitidines have a characteristic flap and glide flight, where several wingbeats are followed with short, open-winged glides. This gives a butterfly observer a look at their bright upperside and a view of their more cryptically colored underside. All Illinois members of this subfamily are mimics.

Adult Limenitidines not only feed on flower nectar, but also use nonfloral moisture sources (dung, sap, rotting fruit). Illinois members overwinter as partially grown caterpillars.

SPECIES
- White Admiral
- Red-spotted Purple
- Viceroy

WHITE ADMIRAL
Limenitis arthemis arthemis (Drury)

PREVALENCE
Rare

FLIGHT PERIOD

MAR
APR
MAY
JUN
JUL
AUG
SEP
OCT
NOV

FIELD NOTES
A. Wide, white band across both wings (T & U)

Female

Male

DESCRIPTION Note: the White Admiral and the Red-spotted Purple are the same species, but are polytypic (have two subspecies and many hybrids or intergrades where their ranges overlap). The "classic" White Admiral has a wingspan of 3.0–4.0 inches and similar sexes. The upperside is a deep, blackish-blue, with a wide, white band that traverses both wings. The underside also has a wide, white band and a cluster of red-orange spots at the base of the wings. The intergrades (offspring between two different subspecies) are extremely variable on the upper- and underside; for example, the white band may be mostly white or only show up as a lighter region.

COULD BE CONFUSED WITH The White Admiral is distinctive, and should not be confused with any other species. However, intergrades are quite variable, and observers should be aware that these occasionally occur in the northern third of Illinois.

HABITAT/LIFE HISTORY The habitat and life history of the White Admiral are nearly identical to those of the Red-spotted Purple. What makes these two subspecies interesting is that the White Admiral has the ancestral color pattern, while the Red-spotted Purple is actually a Batesian mimic of the toxic Pipevine Swallowtail. Thus, where the range of the Red-spotted Purple overlaps with the Pipevine Swallowtail, the Red-spotted Purple subspecies occurs. North of the Pipevine Swallowtail's range, the White Admiral is the common subspecies. Integrades occur where the two forms overlap—in southern Wisconsin and occasionally in northern Illinois.

STATUS The White Admiral is a northern butterfly, found across Michigan, Wisconsin, and Minnesota. While it may stray into northern Illinois, the intergrades between it and the Red-spotted Purple are likely more common, and have been found as far south as Urbana, IL.

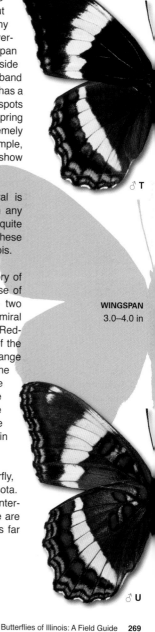

♂ T

WINGSPAN
3.0–4.0 in

♂ U

RED-SPOTTED PURPLE
Limenitis arthemis astyanax (Fabricius)

Female

PREVALENCE
Widely
encountered

FLIGHT PERIOD

MAR	
APR	
MAY	
JUN	
JUL	
AUG	
SEP	
OCT	
NOV	

FIELD NOTES
A. Iridescent blue
sheen on both
wings (T)

B. Red-orange
spots located at
both the wings'
margins and at
their bases (U)

Female

Male

DESCRIPTION Note: the White Admiral and the Red-spotted Purple are the same species, but are polytypic (have two subspecies and many hybrids or intergrades where their ranges overlap). The Red-spotted Purple has a wingspan of 2.5–4.0 inches, and similar sexes. The upperside is black, with iridescent blue on both wings. The underside of the hindwing has a row of red-orange spots near the wing edge as well as a scattering of red-orange spots near the body.

♂ T

COULD BE CONFUSED WITH A quick glance at a Red-spotted Purple brings to mind a small swallowtail, but closer inspection reveals no hindwing tails (see page 352). The Pipevine Swallowtail also has a row of red-orange spots near the wing edge, but it has no red-orange spots near the wing base.

HABITAT/LIFE HISTORY The Red-spotted Purple can be found at forest edge openings, roadsides, and along trails through wooded areas. The adult feeds on sap flows, rotting fruit, carrion, and dung. It also takes nutrients from moist, gravel patches. The male is fond of perching on gravel or dirt roads. The eggs are laid singly on the host plants, which include a wide range of plant families; black cherry seems to be a favorite. The species overwinters as a caterpillar attached to vegetation in a hibernaculum (a rolled up dead leaf). In Illinois, there are two generations and the adult flies from late April through September.

WINGSPAN
2.5–4.0 in

STATUS The Red-spotted Purple is found throughout Illinois, and mimics the toxic Pipevine Swallowtail where their ranges overlap. For further information see White Admiral (page 268) and *Models, Migration, and Mimicry* (page 63).

REMARK The Red-spotted Purple's wings are the same shape as the Viceroy's, just a different color; the two species sometimes interbreed. The authors have observed and photographed a Viceroy courting a Red-spotted Purple (see *Models, Migration, and Mimicry*, page 74).

♂ U

VICEROY
Limenitis archippus (Cramer)

Female

PREVALENCE
Widely
encountered

FLIGHT PERIOD

MAR
APR
MAY
JUN
JUL
AUG
SEP
OCT
NOV

FIELD NOTES

A. Bright orange
base color (T)

B. All wing veins
outlined in black
(T & U)

C. Black band
traverses the
hindwing (T & U)

Male

DESCRIPTION The Viceroy has a wingspan of 2.5–3.0 inches and similar sexes. The upperside is orange with black veins and has a row of white spots along the wing margins. The upperside of the hindwing has a black band that runs across the veins. The underside is a paler orange, with pronounced, black veins and a black line extending across the hindwing.

♂ T

COULD BE CONFUSED WITH The Viceroy resembles the Monarch and the two species are often confused in various venues; however, the Monarch is larger and does not have a black band traversing its hindwing (see page 358).

HABITAT/LIFE HISTORY The Viceroy occurs along roadsides and in meadows, marshes, and river-beds—any wet area where willow species, the caterpillar host plants, grow. These plants contain salicylic acid, which the caterpillar sequesters in its body. As a result, both caterpillar and adult taste bitter. The Viceroy overwinters as a partially grown caterpillar, attached to its food plant in a rolled up leaf (hibernaculum). The adult prefers to fly from late morning to early afternoon, and while it seeks nutrients from dung, sap flows, carrion, fruit, and moist areas, it also nectars at flowers. In Illinois, multiple generations occur per year. The adult is on the wing from late April through October, with the greatest numbers in July and August.

WINGSPAN
2.5–3.0 in

STATUS The Viceroy is found throughout Illinois.

REMARK As children, we learned the simple fact that the good-tasting Viceroy looks like the nasty tasting Monarch so birds will not eat it. If only it were that simple. Both Viceroy and Monarch caterpillars consume food plants that result in both species tasting bitter. So, does the Viceroy really mimic the Monarch or does the Monarch mimic the Viceroy? The answer is that they form a Müllerian mimicry complex; the story is detailed in *Models, Migration, and Mimicry* (see page 63).

♂ U

Puddle club of Hackberry Butterflies

SUBFAMILY APATURINAE
Emperors

The Apaturinae is a small subfamily, with about 50 species worldwide; Illinois has two members—Hackberry Butterfly and Tawny Emperor. Adults rarely nectar; instead, they imbibe nutrient-rich liquids at sap flows, rotting fruit, carrion, and moist roadsides. Often, a perspiring observer is also a moisture source. Adults are stout-bodied, and have triangular-shaped forewings. Males aggressively defend their territories, dashing out to challenge intruders, all the while on the lookout for a mate. Many times emperors will perch very high in the branches of a host tree. Only hackberry species (*Celtis*) serve as caterpillar hosts. The caterpillars feed communally and overwinter in small groups, clustered inside dead leaves.

SPECIES
- Hackberry Butterfly
- Tawny Emperor

HACKBERRY BUTTERFLY
Asterocampa celtis (Boisduval & Le Conte)

Male

Male

Puddle Club

PREVALENCE
Widely encountered

FLIGHT PERIOD

MAR	
APR	
MAY	
JUN	
JUL	
AUG	
SEP	
OCT	
NOV	

FIELD NOTES

A. Yellowish-brown base color (T)

B. Two rows of distinctive white markings (T)

C. Forewing eyespot encircled in yellow (T)

D. Row of eyespots (U)

DESCRIPTION The Hackberry Butterfly has a wing-span of 1.75–2.5 inches. The sexes are similar, but the female is larger, paler, and her wings are more rounded. The upperside is yellow-brown, with a forewing eyespot and a smattering of white spots near the forewing tip. The upperside of the hind-wing has a band of dark spots, and two lines that follow the wing margin. The underside is tan with a series of chevrons, eyespots, and wavy lines.

COULD BE CONFUSED WITH The Tawny Emperor is rusty-brown and does not have an eyespot or white markings on its forewing.

HABITAT/LIFE HISTORY The Hackberry Butterfly is found wherever its caterpillar food plant, hackberry, grows. The adult rarely visits flowers, preferring sap, rotting fruit, carrion, dung, or wet spots along streams or roads. Its flight is fast and erratic. While the Hackberry Butterfly frequently rests high in trees, it is also salt-loving, allowing a close look when it lands on the arm or clothes of a sweaty observer. The adult male can be quite pugnacious in defending his territory, returning again and again to the same perch. The female lays her eggs, either singly or in small clusters, on young hackberry foliage throughout the tree. The Hackberry Butterfly overwinters as a partially grown caterpillar in rolled leaves. In spring, the caterpillar disperses and feeds. Look for the Hackberry Butterfly from late April through September. It has two generations in Illinois.

STATUS The Hackberry Butterfly is found throughout Illinois. While several sources say the species is most plentiful in the state during August, the authors would have to disagree. During many field seasons, we have observed thousands of Hackberry Butter-flies during early June as they puddle on sap, dung, or the bodies of their smashed brethren. So many butterflies are present that you can hear their wings (a crinkly paper sound) as they take off.

♂ T

♀ T

WINGSPAN
1.75–2.5 in

♂ U

♀ U

TAWNY EMPEROR
Asterocampa clyton (Boisduval & Le Conte)

PREVALENCE
Locally
encountered

FLIGHT PERIOD

MAR	
APR	
MAY	
JUN	
JUL	
AUG	
SEP	
OCT	
NOV	

FIELD NOTES

A. Rusty-brown
base color (T)

B. Two rows of
cream-colored
markings on
forewing (T)

C. Violet spots on
hindwing (U)

Male

Male

DESCRIPTION The Tawny Emperor has a wingspan of 1.75–2.5 inches. The sexes are similar, but the female is larger, lighter in color, and has more rounded wings. The upperside of both sexes is rusty-brown; the forewing has dark lines and two rows of cream-colored spots, while the hindwing has a row of dark spots. The underside of the forewing has cream spots, while the hindwing has violet spots. A less common color form (morph) has the upperside of the hindwing almost completely dark.

COULD BE CONFUSED WITH The Hackberry Butterfly is grayer and has an eyespot on its forewing.

HABITAT/LIFE HISTORY The Tawny Emperor occurs wherever its caterpillar food plant, hackberry, is found—usually along shaded, woodland paths and trails. The adult rarely visits flowers, preferring instead sap, rotting fruit, carrion, dung, or wet spots along streams and roads. The female lays her eggs in large clusters (up to 500 eggs) on hackberry foliage. Despite the large quantity of eggs that are produced, few caterpillars seem to survive to adulthood. It is thought that once a predator finds a cluster of eggs or young caterpillars, all are consumed. The caterpillars stay together (gregarious), overwintering in small groups as partially grown caterpillars in rolled leaves. In the spring, each caterpillar disperses and feeds singly. Illinois has one generation per year. The adult is on the wing from June through August.

STATUS The Tawny Emperor is found throughout Illinois, and usually occurs in association with the Hackberry Butterfly. For every 100 Hackberry Butterflies encountered, one will be a Tawny Emperor.

♂ T

♀ T

WINGSPAN
1.75–2.5 in

♂ U

♀ U

Ozark Checkerspot

Silvery Checkerspots

SUBFAMILY NYMPHALINAE
True Brush-foots

The members of the subfamily Nymphalinae are some of the state's more familiar butterflies—the punctuation butterflies (i.e., commas and the Question Mark), crescents, ladies, Buckeye, Mourning Cloak, and checkerspots. It is a diverse group. Adults are orange, black, or brown, and their wing shape is variable. Males patrol, perch, or both, with some species being quite territorial. This group includes our longest-lived butterflies—the Mourning Cloak and the punctuation butterflies, which overwinter as adults. Some members are also migrants—the punctuation butterflies, ladies, and tortoiseshells.

SPECIES[30]

- American Painted Lady
- Painted Lady
- Red Admiral
- Milbert's Tortoiseshell
- Compton Tortoiseshell
- California Tortoiseshell
- Mourning Cloak
- Question Mark
- Comma
- Gray Comma
- Green Comma
- Buckeye
- Baltimore
- Ozark Checkerspot
- Silvery Checkerspot
- Gorgone Checkerspot
- Harris' Checkerspot
- Pearl Crescent
- Tawny Crescent

AMERICAN PAINTED LADY
Vanessa virginiensis (Drury)

PREVALENCE
Widely
encountered

FLIGHT PERIOD

MAR
APR
MAY
JUN
JUL
AUG
SEP
OCT
NOV

FIELD NOTES

A. Tiny, white spot in orange forewing cell (T & U)

B. Two large eyespots on hindwing (U)

C. White, spider web pattern on hindwing (U)

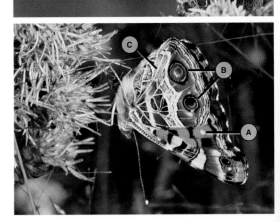

DESCRIPTION The American Painted Lady has a wingspan of 1.75–2.5 inches and similar sexes. The upperside of the forewing is shades of orange, with dots and splashes of black. The upperside of the forewing tip is dark with white spots. Note a white spot in one of the orange forewing cells that can also be seen from the underside. The upperside of the hindwing is shades of orange, with a row of dark spots (some with blue centers) near the wing margin. The underside of the hindwing is mottled gray and tan, with a white "spider web pattern" and two large eyespots.

♂ **T**

COULD BE CONFUSED WITH The Painted Lady is similar in color and pattern; however, the underside of its hindwing has four equally-sized, yellow-ringed eyespots, instead of two large eyespots.

HABITAT/LIFE HISTORY The American Painted Lady favors open places with low vegetation and flowers—yards, meadows, parks, and forest edges. The female flies low to the ground, searching for hosts for her eggs; she prefers everlastings and pussy toes, but will use many members of the daisy family. The adult nectars at flowers, and is on the wing from April through October. The American Painted Lady has multiple generations per year, with the last generation either hibernating as adults or overwintering as chrysalids. The species tolerates colder temperatures better than its cousin, the Painted Lady. Migrants from the south also repopulate the state each year.

WINGSPAN
1.75–2.5 in

STATUS The American Painted Lady is found throughout Illinois, and can become quite common later in the season. Irwin and Downey (1973) state, "Like *V. atalanta*, *V. virginiensis* is characteristic of spring when overwintered individuals appear, but it flies throughout the season until autumn."

♂ **U**

PAINTED LADY
Vanessa cardui (Linnaeus)

PREVALENCE
Widely
encountered

FLIGHT PERIOD

MAR	
APR	
MAY	
JUN	
JUL	
AUG	
SEP	
OCT	
NOV	

FIELD NOTES
A. Four equally-sized, yellow-ringed eyespots on hindwing (U)

DESCRIPTION The Painted Lady has a wingspan of 2.0–2.5 inches and similar sexes. The upperside of the forewing is orange with dots and splashes of black. The black forewing tip contains white spots. The underside of the hindwing is mottled with gray, tan, and white, and has four equally-sized, yellow-ringed eyespots.

♂ T

COULD BE CONFUSED WITH The American Painted Lady is similar in color and pattern; however, the underside of its hindwing has two large eyespots instead of four.

HABITAT/LIFE HISTORY The Painted Lady occurs in open areas—gardens, roadsides, pastures, and old fields—any sunny place that provides nectar for the adult and host plants for the caterpillar. The caterpillar host plants include several plant families, yet thistles are a favorite for nectaring and egg-laying. The adult is a rapid flier, and when disturbed, it may fly a considerable distance before resettling. While it occasionally visits rotting fruit and wet areas, the adult is an avid flower visitor. The adult is on the wing from April through October, with peak populations in August and September. Illinois is usually recolonized each year by individuals from the south (Mexico), with several generations produced. On April 9, 2011, the authors noted a glint of orange in a local woods and immediately thought—an early spring Question Mark or comma. A closer look, though, revealed that the ragged, faded butterfly flitting about and nectaring on a spring beauty was actually a Painted Lady. One did survive an Illinois winter!

WINGSPAN
2.0–2.5 in

STATUS The Painted Lady is found throughout Illinois. Populations fluctuate such that an observer may see many individuals one year and only one or two the next. In some years, Painted Ladies congregate in the fall and move *en masse* for unknown reasons.

♂ U

RED ADMIRAL
Vanessa atalanta (Linnaeus)

PREVALENCE
Widely
encountered

FLIGHT PERIOD

MAR	
APR	
MAY	
JUN	
JUL	
AUG	
SEP	
OCT	
NOV	

FIELD NOTES

A. Red-orange
bands on wings
(T)

B. Bluish area
and red bar across
forewing (U)

DESCRIPTION The Red Admiral has a wingspan of 1.75–3.0 inches and similar sexes. The upperside of the forewing is brownish-black with white spots near the wing tip. Also, a red-orange band crosses the forewing. The upperside of the hindwing has an orange band near the wing margin. The underside of the forewing has splashes of blue and white as well as a pinkish-red bar. The underside of the hindwing is mottled with gray and brown and contains faint spots.

COULD BE CONFUSED WITH If seen resting with its wings closed, the Red Admiral might be mistaken for the Painted Lady or American Painted Lady, but once its wings open, there is no doubt as to its identity.

HABITAT/LIFE HISTORY The Red Admiral prefers woodland and clearing edges, bottomland forests, stream banks, and roadsides; however, it can also be found in fields, yards, parks, and gardens. The caterpillar host plants are nettles—finally, a reason for us to appreciate stinging nettle! While the adult will nectar at flowers, it prefers sap flows and rotting fruit. The male stays active at dusk (crepuscular)—resting on buildings or chasing other males to defend his territory—and is often seen after other butterflies have gone to roost for the evening. In Illinois, the Red Admiral overwinters as an adult or a chrysalis, but also colonizes the state as a spring migrant from the South. The species cannot tolerate severe winter temperatures, so if the winter is mild the adult and chrysalis will survive. Early April, 2012, was an example as Red Admirals were so abundant that even nonbutterfly observers were noticing them. The Red Admiral, with its rapid and erratic flight, is one of the earliest Nymphalids to appear each spring. It is on the wing from late March until early November. There are multiple generations per year.

STATUS The Red Admiral is found throughout Illinois and can be quite common.

♂ T

WINGSPAN
1.75–3.0 in

♂ U

MILBERT'S TORTOISESHELL
Aglais milberti (Godart)

Mike Reese

Courting pair

Male

PREVALENCE
Rare

FLIGHT PERIOD

MAR	
APR	
MAY	
JUN	
JUL	
AUG	
SEP	
OCT	
NOV	

FIELD NOTES
A. "Flamelike" orange bands (T)

DESCRIPTION Milbert's Tortoiseshell has a wingspan of 1.75–2.5 inches and similar sexes. The tip of the forewing is squared off. The upperside is brownish-black, with dark brown wing margins and a wide, carrot-orange band that grades to yellow at its inner edge. This band has been described as "flamelike." The upperside of the hindwing has blue spots in the dark border. The underside is shades of dead-leaf gray and brown, with a lighter tan band toward the outer edges.

♀ T

COULD BE CONFUSED WITH A quick glimpse might elicit "Red Admiral;" however, the Milbert's Tortoiseshell's wing bands are carrot-orange and found along both wing edges, whereas the Red Admiral's forewing band is red-orange and located in the middle of the wing.

HABITAT/LIFE HISTORY The swift-flying Milbert's Tortoiseshell is found in woodland edges and along streams where the caterpillar food plant, nettle, grows. The female lays eggs in clusters on the underside of nettle leaves. The young caterpillar will feed with other young caterpillars in a web, whereas the older caterpillar feeds singly. While Milbert's Tortoiseshell has been known to overwinter as an adult and breed in Illinois, most records are from August to late October, when the population builds in Wisconsin or Michigan and migrates south. There are two generations per year with the adult on the wing anytime between mid-June and October.

WINGSPAN
1.75–2.5 in

STATUS The Milbert's Tortoiseshell is a butterfly of boreal North America. While common in Canada, even observers in Wisconsin may not see one every year. The species varies in abundance, having periodic outbreaks followed by long absences. The species is not common in Illinois and the majority of Illinois' records are from the northern half of the state. During an outbreak in 1997, Jeffords and Post noted one nectaring in their Champaign County front yard during Labor Day weekend.

♀ U

COMPTON TORTOISESHELL
Nymphalis l-album j-album (Boisduval & Le Conte)

PREVALENCE
Rare stray

FLIGHT PERIOD

MAR	
APR	
MAY	
JUN	
JUL	
AUG	
SEP	
OCT	
NOV	

FIELD NOTES

A. Small tail on hindwing

B. White spot on leading edge of both wings (T)

C. Silvery-white dash on hindwing (U)

DESCRIPTION The Compton Tortoiseshell has a wingspan of 2.5–3.0 inches and similar sexes. Its forewing is angular and it has a small tail on its hindwing. The upperside is orange-brown with darker wing bases, spots, and a single, white spot on the leading edge of both wings. The underside is a mottled gray and brown with a small, silvery-white dash in the middle of the hindwing.

♂ T

COULD BE CONFUSED WITH The underside of Milbert's Tortoiseshell is similarly colored but lacks the silver dash; it is also smaller than the Compton Tortoiseshell. The undersides of the Comma and Gray Comma are also similar, but these two species are smaller and their wings are more "cut out" or ragged on the edges. Once the Compton Tortoiseshell reveals its upperside, the single, white spot on the leading edge of both wings will alleviate confusion.

HABITAT/LIFE HISTORY The Compton Tortoiseshell prefers deciduous woods (especially along trails), woodland edges, and forest openings. The adult feeds on tree sap and rotting fruit, or on the ground where it takes minerals. While this species is usually hard to approach, it will often land on a perspiring observer! The overwintered adult emerges and mates in the spring, with the female laying clusters of eggs on aspen, birch, cottonwood, or willow. The adult emerges during the summer, flies from July through November, and then overwinters.

WINGSPAN
2.5–3.0 in

STATUS In North America, the Compton Tortoiseshell is found from the northern United States and across Canada, south of the tundra. Populations occur in both Wisconsin and Michigan. However, the Compton Tortoiseshell is known for its wandering, and there are several records from Carroll, Cook, Kane, and Lake counties in Illinois. For Illinois, Irwin and Downey (1973) report, "The species is notably periodic, and it is probable that these seasons of comparative numbers coincide with its years of abundance farther north in the main portion of its range. It probably does not breed in our area."

♂ U

CALIFORNIA TORTOISESHELL

Nymphalis californica (Boisduval)

Male

PREVALENCE
Accidental
occurrence

FLIGHT PERIOD

MAR	
APR	
MAY	
JUN	
JUL	
AUG	▉
SEP	
OCT	
NOV	

FIELD NOTES

A. Bright orange
base color (T)

B. Irregular, blue-
green line across
both wings (U)

Male

Male

DESCRIPTION The California Tortoiseshell has a wingspan of 2.5 inches and similar sexes. The upperside is orange with black spots on the inner half of the forewing. A black outer margin on the upperside of both wings widens at the forewing tip. The underside is mottled gray-brown with the outer half of the wing lighter than the inner half. An irregular, blue-green line follows the wing margins. No silver markings are present on the underside.

COULD BE CONFUSED WITH The only butterfly that might be mistaken for the California Tortoiseshell is the Compton Tortoiseshell; however, the Compton Tortoiseshell is larger, more heavily marked, and has a distinctive, silver dash on the underside of its hindwing. Further, the California Tortoiseshell has extensive, bright orange color on its upperside which the Compton lacks.

HABITAT/LIFE HISTORY The California Tortoiseshell is generally a woodland butterfly. The caterpillar hosts are several species of buckthorn. The adult could be found in late summer.

STATUS The California Tortoiseshell is found mainly west of the Rocky Mountains, but in years of large population outbreaks, it is known to travel great distances. Individuals have been found as far east as Pennsylvania. Outbreak years are often followed by years of scarcity in its home range.

The California Tortoiseshell is an extremely rare stray to Illinois, and was found once at a light inside a building on the Illinois Institute of Technology Campus, Chicago, August 20, 1952, by L.S. Phillips. This specimen was probably brought in as a chrysalis on packaging material and emerged inside the building. A few scattered records from neighboring states indicate that, at least on rare occasions, it finds its way to the Midwest.

♂ T

WINGSPAN
2.5 in

♂ U

MOURNING CLOAK
Nymphalis antiopa (Linnaeus)

PREVALENCE
Locally
encountered

FLIGHT PERIOD

MAR	
APR	
MAY	
JUN	
JUL	
AUG	
SEP	
OCT	
NOV	

FIELD NOTES

A. Burgundy-brown base color (T)

B. Yellow border (T)

C. Row of blue spots (T)

D. Resembles bark with buff-colored border (U)

DESCRIPTION The Mourning Cloak is named for the velvety, crepe-like appearance of its dark, jagged wings. It has a wingspan of 2.5–3.75 inches and similar sexes. The upperside is burgundy-brown and has yellow wing margins that fade to nearly white as the individual ages. A row of blue spots is adjacent to the yellow border on the upperside of both wings. The underside is brownish-gray and striated with dark lines to resemble bark.

COULD BE CONFUSED WITH This butterfly is very distinctive and should be easy to identify.

HABITAT/LIFE HISTORY The Mourning Cloak is characteristic of hardwood forests, but can be found in any habitat—forest edges, open woodlands, backyards, and parks. The female lays her eggs in clusters on willow, elm, hackberry, cottonwood, and poplar. Once the eggs hatch, the caterpillars stay together and will line up—heads aligned along the edge of the leaf—and eat communally. When disturbed, the whole aggregation rears up and shakes menacingly. The adult emerges in June and July and flies until cold, fall weather. It nectars at flowers, but prefers to feed on overripe fruit, sap flows, and carrion. The Mourning Cloak hibernates as an adult in hollow logs and tree holes, temporarily becoming active on warm winter days, and returning to winter quarters when the temperature drops. Its dark wing color and basking behavior help raise its body temperature above that of the ambient air. In flight, the species is powerful, wary, and not easily approached, unless distracted by feeding. The Mourning Cloak has one of the longest seasons of any Illinois butterfly—it flies during every month of the year.

STATUS The Mourning Cloak occurs statewide.

REMARK In Great Britain, this species is known as the Camberwell Beauty or the Grand Surprise. In recent years, the Mourning Cloak is not as common as it once was. This species is not very "viewer friendly," and often provides just a glimpse. For most, it is a "grand surprise" when the species sits and basks for that rare photo opportunity.

♂ T

WINGSPAN
2.5–3.75 in

♂ U

QUESTION MARK
Polygonia interrogationis (Fabricius)

PREVALENCE
Widely
encountered

FLIGHT PERIOD

MAR	
APR	
MAY	
JUN	
JUL	
AUG	
SEP	
OCT	
NOV	

FIELD NOTES
A. Horizontal
dash on forewing
(T)

B. Silvery dot
and crescent on
hindwing (U)

Summer
Form

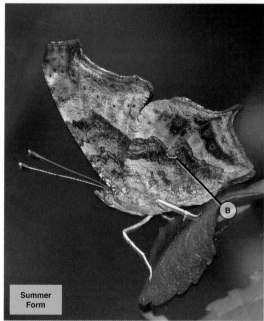

Summer
Form

DESCRIPTION The Question Mark is the largest of the "punctuation" butterflies, with a wingspan of 2.25–3.0 inches. The species has similar sexes and a squared off forewing. The upperside is orange to red-orange, with dark spots. Look for a horizontal dash at the end of a row of dots on the forewing. Two forms of this butterfly occur: a summer form in which the hindwing is two/thirds dark, has a shorter tail, and the violet edging reduced to a thin line; and a fall form in which the hindwing is almost completely orange, with a longer tail, and in "fresh" individuals, the violet edging is quite vivid. The underside is shades of dead-leaf brown and gray, with a silver crescent and dot on the hindwing that together resemble a question mark.

COULD BE CONFUSED WITH Commas do not have the horizontal dash at the end of the dot row on the upperside of the forewing, nor do they have the crescent and silver dot combination on the underside of the hindwing.

HABITAT/LIFE HISTORY The Question Mark is a butterfly of open, deciduous woodlands. It prefers trails, streamsides, and forest edges, but can often be found in a home garden. The adult prefers to feed on rotting fruit, dung, tree sap, or carrion; however, if none of these are available, it will nectar at flowers. Both sexes bask in a sunny spot during the morning, and by afternoon the male is defending his territory, before returning to his preferred perch. The female lays eggs on several different hosts, including elm, nettle, hops, and hackberry. There are two generations in Illinois, with the adult (fall form) overwintering. The species flies from mid-March through early November, with the early spring population (which consists of the fall form) laying eggs. These eggs hatch and produce summer form adults.

STATUS The Question Mark occurs statewide, and while common, only one or two will usually be seen at a site.

♀ **T**
summer
form

♂ **T**
fall form

WINGSPAN
2.25–3.0 in

♀ **U**
summer
form

♂ **U**
fall form

COMMA
Polygonia comma (T. Harris)

FLIGHT PERIOD

MAR	
APR	
MAY	
JUN	
JUL	
AUG	
SEP	
OCT	
NOV	

FIELD NOTES
A. C-shaped
hook with open
end pointing away
from the body on
hindwing (U)

Fall Form

Fall Form

DESCRIPTION The Comma has a wingspan of 1.75–2.5 inches and similar sexes. Its wing margins are irregular, and it has a short tail on its hindwing. The upperside of the forewing is orange with dark brown to black spots; note a row of three black dots mid-forewing. Two forms exist—a summer form and a fall form—that vary in the color of their hindwing upperside. In the summer form, the upperside of the hindwing is mostly dark, while in the fall form the hindwing is orange with black spots. Both forms have a dark border with pale spots, though the spots are more apparent in the fall form. The underside of both forms is shades of dried-leaf brown, with the hindwing having a central silver or white comma—a C-shaped hook with the open end pointing away from the body.

COULD BE CONFUSED WITH Many times you will see the Comma and Question Mark together; however, the Question Mark is larger and has a longer hindwing tail and a crescent with a dot on the underside of its hindwing. The underside of the Gray Comma forewing has a grayish patch, and the comma on the hindwing comes to a point in the middle.

HABITAT/LIFE HISTORY The Comma is a woodland species, most often seen along sunny, woodland edges and trails.[31] The caterpillar is solitary and feeds on elm, nettle, or hops. The adult feeds at rotting fruit, tree sap flows, and dung, and is wary, quick, and agile in flight. The male defends his territory with "attacks" on anything that passes, and afterward will quickly return to the same flight perch. The female lays her eggs singly, or in stacks under caterpillar host plant leaves or stems. The caterpillars are solitary. The Comma is on the wing from March to November. Illinois has multiple generations, with the adult overwintering.

STATUS The Comma is found throughout Illinois, and while common, an observer will usually only see one or two at a location.

♀ T
summer
form

♂ T
fall form

WINGSPAN
1.75–2.5 in

♀ U
summer
form

♂ U
fall form

GRAY COMMA
Polygonia progne (Cramer)

PREVALENCE
Locally
encountered

FLIGHT PERIOD

MAR
APR
MAY
JUN
JUL
AUG
SEP
OCT
NOV

FIELD NOTES

A. Very jagged
wing margins

B. Light gray
forewing tip (U)

C. L-shaped silver
mark on hindwing
(U)

Summer
Form

Fall
Form

DESCRIPTION The Gray Comma has a wingspan of 1.6–2.5 inches and similar sexes. Its wing margins are irregular, and its hindwing has a short, broad tail. The upperside of the forewing is orange, with dark brown to black spots. A row of three black dots occurs mid-forewing, with the outer dot small or sometimes absent. Two forms exist—a summer form and a fall form—that vary in the upperside of their hindwing. In the summer form, the hindwing has a wide, dark border, whereas the fall form hindwing has a narrow border. In both forms the border has small yellow dots. The underside is charcoal gray, with the outer half of the forewing a lighter gray. The underside of the hindwing has a central, silver, L-shaped mark.

COULD BE CONFUSED WITH The underside of the Comma does not have a light gray, frosted forewing tip, and the silver mark on the hindwing is arched instead of pointed. The Question Mark is larger, and the silver mark on the underside of its hindwing is accented with a dot. The Green Comma has an irregular, greenish band on its underside.

HABITAT/LIFE HISTORY The Gray Comma is most likely to be seen at dung, tree sap, and rotting fruit in high-quality woods, or at moist spots along dirt or gravel roads. Caterpillar food plants include gooseberry, currant, and elm.[32] The adult is swift in flight and wary, and, like the Comma, will return to a spot if disturbed. Illinois has multiple generations. The overwintered adult (fall form) breeds in spring, with the first generation (summer form) appearing in June and July. The final, overwintering generation appears in fall (fall form). The Gray Comma can be found from April through October.

STATUS The Gray Comma is not common in Illinois. Most sightings occur in central Illinois; northern sightings are uncommon, and the species is nearly absent from the southern third of the state.

♂ T
summer
form

♂ T
fall form

WINGSPAN
1.6–2.5 in

♂ U
summer
form

♂ U
fall form

GREEN COMMA
Polygonia faunus (W. H. Edwards)

Mike Reese

Mike Reese

PREVALENCE
Rare

FLIGHT PERIOD

MAR	
APR	
MAY	
JUN	
JUL	
AUG	
SEP	
OCT	
NOV	

FIELD NOTES

A. Irregular, jagged wing margins

B. Double forewing dot across vein (T)

C. Silver boomerang-shaped mark (U)

D. Irregular greenish bands (U)

DESCRIPTION The Green Comma has a wingspan of 1.75–2.5 inches. The wings have jagged edges, more so than the other comma species. The upperside is red-orange, with wide, dark borders. On the upperside of the hindwing, the dark border contains yellow spots, and the outer wing margin is edged in yellow. On the upperside of the forewing, note a large inner dot that is doubled across the vein. The underside is various shades of gray and brown, with the forewing tip lighter. A silver, boomerang-shaped mark is found on the underside of the hindwing, and greenish bands appear on the underside of both wings. In spring, the green bands may be difficult to see in an overwintered, worn specimen.

♂ T

COULD BE CONFUSED WITH The Comma, Question Mark, and Gray Comma all resemble the Green Comma; however, the Green Comma is very rare in Illinois and has jagged wings, a large dot that is doubled across a vein on the upperside of the forewing, and green bands and a silver mark on its underside.

HABITAT/LIFE HISTORY The Green Comma is a butterfly of cool, conifer forests of the north. It is more confined to woodlands than other comma species. While it will nectar at flowers and visit sap flows and rotting fruit, the adult prefers to sun along dirt roads and woodland trails. The female lays her eggs on several hosts, including birch and willow. There is only one generation per year, with the species overwintering as an adult. The adult flies from May through August.

WINGSPAN
1.75–2.5 in

STATUS The Green Comma has been collected in Illinois only at one site—Carroll County in July, 1963.[33] This area contains Illinois' version of a boreal forest.

♂ U

BUCKEYE
Junonia coenia (Hübner)

PREVALENCE
Widely
encountered
migrant

FLIGHT PERIOD

MAR	
APR	
MAY	
JUN	
JUL	
AUG	
SEP	
OCT	
NOV	

FIELD NOTES

A. Eyespots
surrounded by an
ivory-colored "6"
on forewing (T
& U)

B. Showy
eyespots (T)

Male

Female

DESCRIPTION The Buckeye has a wingspan of 1.5–2.75 inches and similar sexes. Its upperside ranges from dark to pale brown. The upperside of the forewing has two orange bars and an eyespot surrounded by ivory that roughly forms the number 6. The upperside of the hindwing has an orange border and two eyespots. The underside of the hindwing is shades of brown, with two small, yellow-rimmed dark spots; in late season specimens the hindwing will be a rose-brown color and the spots will not be visible. The Buckeye's wing colors are brighter in late season specimens.

COULD BE CONFUSED WITH The Buckeye is unique with its showy eyespots that dot its upperside.

HABITAT/LIFE HISTORY In Illinois, the Buckeye is associated with open, sunny areas—old fields, prairies, roadsides, and trails. The adult is fond of nectaring on a variety of flowers and basking. It usually flies only a foot or two above the ground. The male is very territorial and will chase other butterflies, grasshoppers, and anything else that is the same size. The female lays a single egg on a number of host plants. The butterfly overwinters either as a caterpillar or an adult. While the Buckeye may be seen in late spring, it is far more common in late summer and early fall. In Illinois, there are multiple generations.

STATUS The Buckeye is found statewide. As no life stages are able to withstand freezing temperatures, Illinois is recolonized each year from the south; this species migrates north with the spring and south in the fall. Some years only a few Buckeyes may be seen, while in other years, especially in the fall, nearly every butterfly appears to be a Buckeye.

♀ T

WINGSPAN
1.5–2.75 in

♀ U

♂ U
late
season

BALTIMORE
Euphydryas phaeton phaeton (Drury)

Female

PREVALENCE
Locally
encountered

FLIGHT PERIOD

MAR	
APR	
MAY	
JUN	
JUL	
AUG	
SEP	
OCT	
NOV	

FIELD NOTES

A. Orange-tipped
antennae

B. Two prominent
orange spots near
leading margin of
forewing (T)

C. Dark base
color with
prominent spots
(T & U)

Female

Male

DESCRIPTION The Baltimore is named after early American colonist George Calvert, the first Lord Baltimore, whose crest was orange and black. Illinois has two subspecies—the Baltimore and the Ozark Checkerspot. The Baltimore has a wingspan of 1.75–2.75 inches and similar sexes. The upper- and underside are dark and marked with orange and ivory spots. The upperside has an outer margin of orange spots, followed by ivory spots, then prominent orange spots. The underside has a margin of orange spots followed by a series of ivory and orange spots. The antennae are orange-tipped.

COULD BE CONFUSED WITH The Ozark Checkerspot is slightly larger and the orange spots on its upperside are reduced; otherwise the two species look almost identical (see page 364). The best way to tell the Baltimore and Ozark Checkerspot apart is by location; the Ozark Checkerspot is found on dry hillsides in the southern half of the state, whereas the Baltimore is found in wetlands from the northern half of Illinois.

HABITAT/LIFE HISTORY The Baltimore is a wetland species—wet meadows, fens, seeps, and marshes. The adult is seldom found far from turtlehead, the early instar caterpillar host plant. The female lays a cluster of eggs on the underside of turtlehead leaves. The early instar caterpillars feed communally; they form a silken web around the leaves they are currently feeding on, and extend the web to enclose additional leaves as needed. By late summer the caterpillars stop feeding, leave the host plant, and overwinter in the leafy debris in small groups silked together (Bowers 1978). When the temperatures warm in spring, each caterpillar wanders off to feed; it no longer just eats turtlehead, but has a wider host range. It soon pupates and emerges as an adult. One generation of adults appears from June through July.

STATUS The Baltimore occurs in the northern third of Illinois. While the species is restricted to vanishing wetland habitats, populations can be locally common.[34]

♂ T

♀ T

WINGSPAN
1.75–2.75 in

♂ U

OZARK CHECKERSPOT
Euphydryas phaeton ozarkae Masters

Female

PREVALENCE
Locally
encountered

FLIGHT PERIOD

MAR	
APR	
MAY	███
JUN	
JUL	
AUG	
SEP	
OCT	
NOV	

FIELD NOTES

A. Orange-tipped antennae

B. Reduced red-orange spots near leading margin of forewing (T)

C. Dark base color with prominent spots (T & U)

Female

DESCRIPTION The Ozark Checkerspot has a wing-span of 2.5–3.0 inches. The upperside is dark and has an outer margin of red-orange spots, followed by ivory spots; it has reduced red-orange spots near the leading margin of the forewing. The under-side is dark and has a margin of orange-red spots, followed by white spots, then orange-red and white spots. The antennae are orange-tipped.

COULD BE CONFUSED WITH While the Baltimore is slightly smaller and not as dark in color, the two spe-cies are almost identical (see page 364). The best way to tell them apart is by location; the Baltimore is found in wetland habitats in the northern half of Illinois, whereas the Ozark Checkerspot is found on dry hillsides in the southern half of the state.

HABITAT/LIFE HISTORY The Ozark Checkerspot inhabits barrens, dry hillsides, and open hardwood forests, often along rocky streams. The caterpillar host plants are false foxgloves; these plants are partial root parasites that require access to an oak root system. The female lays clusters of eggs on the underside of the caterpillar host plants' leaves. The early instar caterpillars feed communally; they form a silken web around the leaves they are cur-rently feeding on, and extend the web to enclose additional leaves as needed. By late summer the caterpillars stop feeding, leave the host plant, and overwinter in the leafy debris in small groups silked together (Bowers 1978). When the temperatures warm the following spring, each caterpillar wanders off to feed on other plants, pupates, and emerges as an adult. The Ozark Checkerspot has one gen-eration and is on the wing from mid-May through June; it usually flies two weeks earlier than the Baltimore.

STATUS The Ozark Checkerspot occurs in the southern third of Illinois, extending up the Missis-sippi River to the latitude of Keokuk, Iowa.

♂ T

♂ T

WINGSPAN
2.5–3.0 in

♂ U

SILVERY CHECKERSPOT
Chlosyne nycteis (E. Doubleday)

DESCRIPTION The Silvery Checkerspot has a wingspan of 1.5–2.0 inches and similar sexes. The upperside is orange, marked with bold black lines, patches, and spots.

PREVALENCE
Locally
encountered

FLIGHT PERIOD

MAR	
APR	
MAY	
JUN	
JUL	
AUG	
SEP	
OCT	
NOV	

FIELD NOTES
A. Some hindwing spots contain white centers (T)

B. Broken border of white crescents along hindwing margin (U)

C. Central row of brown-bordered, ivory cells on hindwing (U)

Courting pair

Female

The forewing tips are dark with little or no orange in them, and both wing margins have a dark border. A row of spots on the upperside of the hindwing usually has one or two of the black dots with white centers. The underside is shades of orange, ivory, and tan, with brown lines and black spots; it appears faded when compared to the upperside. The underside of the hindwing has a row of ivory, brown-bordered cells near its center and one or more large, white spots near its margin. When the Silvery Checkerspot has recently emerged, it is easy to see the underside markings, but as the butterfly ages (wears), its markings lose their contrast and the underside may look very plain.

COULD BE CONFUSED WITH The Gorgone Checkerspot is smaller; further, the row of black dots near its hindwing edge does not have any white in them, and its underside has a band of chevron-shaped spots. The Harris' Checkerspot is very rare in Illinois, and the underside of its hindwing is orange-red, with a bold, ivory-and-black pattern. The Pearl Crescent has white crescents along its hindwing margin, and no white-centered spots on the upperside of its hindwing (see page 360).

HABITAT/LIFE HISTORY The Silvery Checkerspot can be found in open areas—forest openings, streamsides, roadsides, meadows, and bottomlands. The adult, with its low, slow flight, nectars on a variety of plants. The female lays eggs in clusters on various daisies. The caterpillar moves as part of a group and overwinters when partially grown. The Silvery Checkerspot has two generations per year in Illinois, and has been observed from April to mid-September.

STATUS The Silvery Checkerspot occurs throughout Illinois, where it can be quite common. During late July 2011, the species seemed to be everywhere at Ballard Nature Center in Effingham County.

REMARK Jeffords and Post have just recently developed the "search image" for the Silvery Checkerspot, and reviewing past photos revealed that it was seen more often than originally thought.

♂ T

♀ T

WINGSPAN
1.5–2.0 in

♂ U

♀ U

GORGONE CHECKERSPOT
Chlosyne gorgone (Hübner)

Female

PREVALENCE
Locally
encountered

FLIGHT PERIOD

MAR	
APR	
MAY	
JUN	
JUL	
AUG	
SEP	
OCT	
NOV	

FIELD NOTES

A. Prominent row of white crescents on hindwing (T)

B. Strongly checkered fringe (T & U)

C. Zigzag pattern and angular, ivory band on hindwing (U)

Mating pair

DESCRIPTION The Gorgone Checkerspot has a wing-span of 1.25–1.75 inches and similar sexes. The upperside is orange with complex black markings; in fresh specimens, the edge of the wing is strongly checkered with a black and white fringe. The upperside of the hindwing has a row of black spots in from the margin and a row of white crescents in the dark wing margin. The underside of the hindwing has a zigzag pattern of brown and white bands, with a row of black spots near the wing margin and an angular, ivory band near the center of the wing.

COULD BE CONFUSED WITH In flight and from above, the Gorgone Checkerspot may be confused with any small, black-and-orange butterfly—especially the Pearl Crescent and Silvery Checkerspot (see page 360). However, the pattern on the underside of the Gorgone Checkerspot's hindwing—a zigzag pattern of brown and white—is unique. Futher, it is intermediate in size between the smaller Pearl Crescent and the larger Silvery Checkerspot.

HABITAT/LIFE HISTORY The Gorgone Checkerspot is found at dry, sunny sites—open areas, old fields, prairies, town gardens, and old railroad grades. The female lays her eggs in clusters on various species of sunflowers and asters. The species overwinters as a partially grown caterpillar. The Gorgone Checkerspot has multiple generations each year in Illinois and flies from early May to mid-September.

STATUS The Gorgone Checkerspot is a butterfly of the Great Plains; the Great Plains Butterfly is another of its common names. In Illinois, it is found north of Interstate 70. Work is underway to reintroduce this species to various Chicago remnant habitats. Populations of the Gorgone Checkerspot increased from the 1960s into the 1980s, especially in central Illinois. Since then numbers have markedly decreased. However, it can still be found in the sand and railroad prairies in the northern half of Illinois.

♂ T

♀ T

WINGSPAN
1.25–1.75 in

♂ U

♀ U

HARRIS' CHECKERSPOT
Chlosyne harrisii (Scudder)

Mike Reese

Female

PREVALENCE
Rare

FLIGHT PERIOD

MAR	
APR	
MAY	
JUN	■
JUL	
AUG	
SEP	
OCT	
NOV	

FIELD NOTES

A. Complete row of different-sized crescents (U)

B. Row of isolated, brown-bordered, ivory cells (U)

Mike Reese

A

B

Mike Reese

A

B

Female

DESCRIPTION The Harris' Checkerspot—named after Thaddeus Harris, a nineteenth century entomologist from Massachusetts—has a wingspan of 1.5–2.0 inches. Its upperside is orange with brownish-black markings, and while this coloration is similar to the other checkerspots, Harris' Checkerspot has more brown and appears darker. The underside is red-orange with the hindwing distinguished by a row of white crescents near the wing margin, and a large band made up of brown-bordered ivory cells in the middle of the wing.

COULD BE CONFUSED WITH In flight and from above, the Harris' Checkerspot may be confused with the Silvery or Gorgone Checkerspots (see page 360); however, the bold, red-orange, white, and ivory pattern on the underside of the Harris' Checkerspot's hindwing should dismiss any confusion.

HABITAT/LIFE HISTORY The Harris' Checkerspot is never far from its caterpillar host plant—flat-topped white aster. In Illinois, this plant is found in calcareous fens and bogs. The female lays her eggs in clusters under the host plant leaves. The caterpillar feeds on the leaves communally in a web. After the communal caterpillar group defoliates one plant, it moves *en masse* to another. The caterpillar overwinters at the base of the host plant, and thus is fire sensitive. The Harris' Checkerspot should be searched for in mid-June to mid-July.

STATUS Rare like its preferred habitat, the Harris' Checkerspot is at the southern edge of its range in Illinois. There are only two collection records for the state, one from Kane County in 1931, and one questionable record from Vermilion County in 1960.

♂ T

♀ T

WINGSPAN
1.5–2.0 in

♂ U

♀ U

PEARL CRESCENT
Phyciodes tharos (Drury)

DESCRIPTION The Pearl Crescent, with a wingspan of 1.25–1.75 inches, is the smallest and most common

PREVALENCE
Widely
encountered

FLIGHT PERIOD

MAR	
APR	
MAY	
JUN	
JUL	
AUG	
SEP	
OCT	
NOV	

FIELD NOTES

A. Orange mark
near forewing
margin (T)

B. White crescent
on outer margin
of hindwing (U)

Male

Female

crescent in Illinois. The species is quite variable in appearance, which can often create confusion—the female is slightly larger than the male, cold and warm weather forms exist, and geographical variation is common in both sexes.[35]

The upperside is a combination of black spots and mottling on an orange background. The black forewing margin is usually interrupted by an orange mark, and the black hindwing margin has a row of black spots just above it. The underside of the hindwing is various shades of tan and orange, with a white crescent on the outer margin; this crescent can be prominent (ivory) or difficult to detect. On cool weather forms, the underside of the hindwing has a darker brown and white marbling, while the warm weather form is a lighter yellow.

♂ T

♀ T

COULD BE CONFUSED WITH The Pearl Crescent lacks the zigzag pattern on the underside of the Gorgone Checkerspot's hindwing, and the white-centered spots on the upperside of the Silvery Checkerspot's hindwing (see page 360). It is more important to ask yourself, "Why is this not a Pearl Crescent?" as most checkerspots you will see in Illinois are likely to be the Pearl Crescent.

WINGSPAN
1.25–1.75 in

HABITAT/LIFE HISTORY The Pearl Crescent is a generalist that exploits a range of open habitats—prairies, old fields, gardens, road edges, and wood-lands—and may be found anywhere the caterpillar host plant, aster, grows. The adult, with its low, rapid flight, is an avid flower visitor, and will pump its wings slowly while sipping nectar. The female lays her eggs in clusters on the underside of aster leaves. There are multiple generations throughout the season, with the final one overwintering as a third instar caterpillar. The adult is found from late March through October.

♂ U

STATUS Irwin & Downey (1973) state, "One of our commonest butterflies, the diminutive pearl crescent abounds throughout the state from late spring through autumn." This is still true today. No matter where the authors look in the state for butterflies, the Pearl Crescent is usually on the day's list.

♀ U

TAWNY CRESCENT
Phyciodes batesii (Reakirt)

Male

A

Female

B

Male

PREVALENCE
Absent

FLIGHT PERIOD

MAR	
APR	
MAY	
JUN	
JUL	
AUG	
SEP	
OCT	
NOV	

FIELD NOTES

A. Reduced orange markings (T)

B. Straw yellow base color on hindwing (U)

DESCRIPTION The Tawny Crescent has a wingspan of 1.25–1.75 inches and similar sexes. Its upperside is dark brown and orange; the forewing is mostly dark with orange markings. The underside of the hindwing is straw-yellow with faint markings. The antennal knobs are black and white.

♂ T

COULD BE CONFUSED WITH The Pearl Crescent does not have as much black in the upperside of its forewing and the underside of its hindwing has a dark patch containing a crescent. The Tawny Crescent may not be part of the Illinois fauna.

HABITAT/LIFE HISTORY The Tawny Crescent is a northern species—Quebec, Ontario, and Northern New England, south to Nebraska and Wisconsin. It is found where its caterpillar host plant, wavy aster, grows—barrens and dry, gravel areas. Unfortunately, the wavy aster is only found in extreme southern Illinois. The female lays her eggs in clusters, and the caterpillar feeds with its siblings in a web during the first two instars. The caterpillar overwinters when half-grown. There is one generation per year, and the adult flies from May to July.

WINGSPAN
1.25–1.75 in

STATUS Only one questionable collection of the Tawny Crescent has been made in Illinois, and that was by Irwin in June, 1965, in La Salle County. Irwin states, "The locality is outside the usual range for *batesii*, being a little too far south." Various field guides may state that the species may be overlooked due to its similarity to the Pearl Crescent. In *Butterflies of Wisconsin*, Ebner states, "...a collector in Marinette County in 1955–56 attempted to discover this species in Wisconsin and collected over 5,000 crescents, of which only 3 were Tawny Crescents!" It is listed as a species of concern in both Michigan and Wisconsin.

♂ U

Goatweed Butterfly

SUBFAMILY CHARAXINAE
Leafwings

The subfamily Charaxinae is a New World tropics group of medium to large-sized butterflies. Illinois has two members—the Tropical Leafwing, a rare stray, and the Goatweed Butterfly, an uncommon resident and a yearly migrant. Leafwings are named because the underside of their wings resembles a dead leaf. The adult forewings are falcate (hooked) with a short tail projection on the hindwing. They are rapid, direct flyers, and often perch on tree limbs and trunks high in the canopy. This group has two seasonal forms—summer/wet season and winter/dry season. Adults rarely nectar; instead, they imbibe mineral-laden moisture at sap flows, rotting fruit, carrion, and moist roadsides. Like the Apaturinae (emperors), the males aggressively defend their territories, dashing out to challenge intruders, all the while searching for a mate. Leafwing caterpillars are solitary feeders, and the adults overwinter. In Illinois, leafwing adults may not survive severe winters.

SPECIES
- Tropical Leafwing
- Goatweed Butterfly

TROPICAL LEAFWING
Anaea aidea (Guérin-Méneville)

Male

PREVALENCE
Rare stray

FLIGHT PERIOD

MAR	
APR	
MAY	
JUN	
JUL	
AUG	
SEP	
OCT	
NOV	

FIELD NOTES

A. Rounded tail (T)

B. Pale orange cells (♀ T)

A
B
Female

A

DESCRIPTION The sexually dimorphic Tropical Leafwing has a wingspan of 2.5–3.1 inches. The upperside of both sexes is deep, orange-red. The male upperside has a very dark margin with two dark spots near the leading edge of the forewing. The female upperside has a more diverse pattern, with a series of lighter orange spots and an inner eyebrow of dark along the outside edge of the forewing and the leading margin of the hindwing. The underside of both sexes is mottled brown and resembles a dead leaf. Both sexes have a short, but prominent tail on the hindwing.

COULD BE CONFUSED WITH The Goatweed Butterfly is more orange and is the common species found in Illinois.

HABITAT/LIFE HISTORY The Tropical Leafwing is a butterfly of the American Tropics—ranging from Mexico to northwestern Costa Rica—and only occasionally strays into the U.S. The caterpillar host plants are *Croton* spp. (spurges), and although this plant genus occurs in Illinois (mostly in sandy or waste places), it is unlikely the Tropical Leafwing will breed here. The adult could be found anytime between April and October.

STATUS The Tropical Leafwing has only been documented once from Illinois (Jeffords 1978), in an abandoned railroad yard in Massac County in the early 1970s. We classify the species as a rare stray and it is certainly not a regular part of the Illinois butterfly fauna. The area where this species was found is now a subdivision.

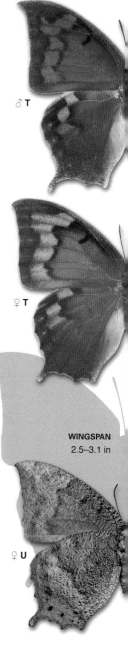

♂ T

♀ T

WINGSPAN
2.5–3.1 in

♀ U

GOATWEED BUTTERFLY
Anaea andria Scudder

Male

PREVALENCE
Locally
encountered

FLIGHT PERIOD

MAR	
APR	
MAY	
JUN	
JUL	
AUG	
SEP	
OCT	
NOV	

Male

FIELD NOTES

A. Falcate
forewing tip

B. Angular tail

C. Vivid orange
base color (♂ T)

D. Yellow band
(♀ T) [refer to ♀T
specimen on next
page]

Male

DESCRIPTION The sexually dimorphic Goatweed Butterfly has a wingspan of 2.5–3.0 inches. It has a sickle-shaped (falcate) forewing and a short hind-wing tail. The male upperside is vivid orange with dark margins. The female upperside is a subdued orange with brown mottling, a pale yellow-orange band, and a darker area toward the margin. The underside of both sexes is a gray-brown—the color of a dead leaf. When perched with its wings closed, the Goatweed Butterfly is a convincing leaf mimic.

COULD BE CONFUSED WITH The Question Mark is a duller orange, and has many dark spots on its upperside. Further, the underside of its hindwing has a curved, silver mark that the Goatweed Butterfly lacks.

HABITAT/LIFE HISTORY The Goatweed Butterfly is found in open woodland edges, scrub areas, waysides, and field edges. In southern Illinois, it is frequently encountered flying up and down woodland trails. The adult prefers to feed at sap flows, fruit, rotting wood, or on animal scat. The caterpillar feeds on *Croton* spp. (spurges). The Goatweed overwinters as an adult. In Illinois, there are two generations: the overwintering generation, that flies from August to May, and the summer generation, that flies from June to October.

STATUS The Goatweed Butterfly is primarily a resident of the southern Great Plains and the Mississippi River basin. Illinois is populated each year, either by the surviving overwintering generation, or by migrants from neighboring states. With the exception of the northwestern counties where the Goatweed has not been documented, the butterfly occurs throughout Illinois from late March into November. The larger populations occur in southern Illinois.

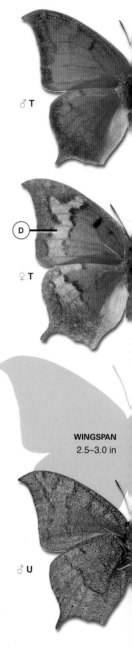

♂ T

Ⓓ

♀ T

WINGSPAN
2.5–3.0 in

♂ U

Gemmed Satyr

Common Wood Nymph

SUBFAMILY SATYRINAE
Satyrs

The subfamily Satyrinae contains the Satyrs; Illinois has nine species—the pearly-eyes, eyed browns, satyrs, and Common Wood Nymph. They may also be referred to as the "browns," a comment on their "drab and muted" wing color. While their upperside color may be "drab," their undersides are not without decorations—lines, ripples, eyespots, or gem-like markings occur. Unlike the other members of the Nymphalidae, which feed on dicots (plants with two seed leaves), Satyrinae caterpillars feed on monocots (plants with one seed leaf)—grasses, sedges, and cane. Adults rarely nectar at flowers; instead, they prefer sap, dung, and decaying matter. Adult males have scent patches (stigmata). Satyr flight is an unpredictable, slow, skipping flight with sudden drops. With the exception of the Common Wood Nymph, Illinois' species shun bright sun, as they are found in forest interiors or along sun-dappled trails.

SPECIES

- Southern Pearly-eye
- Northern Pearly-eye
- Creole Pearly-eye
- Eyed Brown
- Appalachian Eyed Brown
- Leeuw's Eyed Brown
- Gemmed Satyr
- Carolina Satyr
- Little Wood Satyr
- Common Wood Nymph

SOUTHERN PEARLY-EYE
Lethe portlandia (Fabricius)

PREVALENCE
Rare

FLIGHT PERIOD

MAR	
APR	
MAY	
JUN	
JUL	
AUG	
SEP	
OCT	
NOV	

FIELD NOTES

A. Orange antennae

B. Slightly curved row of four eyespots on forewing (U)

C. Noticeably straight, dark line on forewing (U)

D. Orange, iridescent cast (U)

Female

Female

DESCRIPTION The wingspan of the Southern Pearly-eye is about 2.5 inches, with the female larger than the male. This brown butterfly has eyespots on the upper- and underside of its wing margins. The upperside spots are black, while the underside spots are black with a white pupil and ringed with pale yellow. The underside of the forewing usually has a slightly curved row of these eyespots as well as a noticeably straight, dark line near the leading margin. The antennae are predominantly orange, especially the club. The underside of the wings has an orange, iridescent cast that is not apparent in the other two pearly-eyes.

COULD BE CONFUSED WITH The Northern and Creole Pearly-eyes are very similar (see page 366); however, both have predominantly black antennae with orange tips. Additionally, the dark line on the underside of the forewing is slightly curved on the Northern and wavy on the Creole.

HABITAT/LIFE HISTORY The Southern Pearly-eye is found in canebrakes. The caterpillar feeds only on giant cane, and is a dull, tan color (the color of a dead cane leaf) marked with brown lines. The Southern Pearly-eye is active throughout the day and will fly long after most butterflies have settled for the evening. Like most Satyrs, oozing tree sap, rotting fruit, carrion, and dung are favorite food sources for the adult. There are two generations—late May into June and late August into September. The species overwinters as a partially grown caterpillar.

STATUS The Southern Pearly-eye is only found in the immediate vicinity of canebrakes, where it is found in small, isolated populations. It is more scarce than the Creole Pearly-eye, and is the most difficult to find of our three pearly-eyes. The species occurs in far southern Illinois.[36]

♂ T

WINGSPAN
~2.5 in

♂ U

♀ U

NORTHERN PEARLY-EYE
Lethe anthedon (A. Clark)

PREVALENCE
Widely
encountered

FLIGHT PERIOD

MAR	
APR	
MAY	
JUN	
JUL	
AUG	
SEP	
OCT	
NOV	

FIELD NOTES

A. Antennal clubs
predominantly
black with
orange tips

B. Straight row
of four eyespots
on forewing (U)

C. Slightly
curved, dark line
on forewing (U)

Female

Male

DESCRIPTION The wingspan of the Northern Pearly-eye is about 2.5 inches, with the female slightly larger than the male. The sexes are similar in pattern. This brown butterfly has eyespots on the upper- and underside of its wing margins. The upperside spots are black, while the underside spots are black with a white pupil and ringed with yellow. The underside of the forewing usually has a straight row of these eyespots, as well as a slightly curved, dark line along the leading wing margin. The overall pattern on the upperside is sharper and crisper defined than in the other two pearly-eyes. The antennae are predominantly black with orange tips.

COULD BE CONFUSED WITH The Southern and Creole Pearly-eyes are both very similar (see page 366). However, the dark line on the underside of the forewing is straight in the Southern and wavy in the Creole. Additionally, the Southern has completely orange antennae.

HABITAT/LIFE HISTORY The Northern Pearly-eye is restricted to woodlands with large stands of grasses. In the southern half of Illinois, the caterpillar feeds on sea oats; further north, it feeds on other species of woodland grasses. The caterpillar is nearly identical to the Creole—bright green with almost no markings. The adult is active from early morning until late in the day. Like most Satyrs, oozing tree sap, carrion, rotting fruit, and dung are favorite food sources of the adult. The Northern Pearly-eye has two generations—one from late May into June and another in late August into September. The species overwinters as a partially grown caterpillar.

STATUS The Northern Pearly-eye is by far the most common of the three Illinois pearly-eye species. It is secure and likely occurs in every county in the state.

♂ T

WINGSPAN
~2.5 in

♂ U

♀ U

CREOLE PEARLY-EYE
Lethe creola (Skinner)

Male

Will Cook

Female

PREVALENCE
Rare

FLIGHT PERIOD

| MAR |
| APR |
| MAY |
| JUN |
| JUL |
| AUG |
| SEP |
| OCT |
| NOV |

FIELD NOTES

A. Antennal clubs predominantly black with orange tips

B. Sex scales (♂T) [refer to ♂T specimen on next page]

C. Row of five or more eyespots on forewing (U)

D. Noticeably waved, dark line on forewing (U)

DESCRIPTION The wingspan of the Creole Pearly-eye is about 2.5 inches, with the female larger than the male. It is a brown butterfly with eyespots on the upper- and underside of its wing margins. The sexes are similar in pattern; however, the male forewing is noticeably pointed and has raised sex scales (androconium) along the central veins on the upperside of the forewing. The upperside spots are black, while the underside spots are black with a white pupil and ringed with yellow or tan. The underside of the forewing usually has five (or more) of these eyespots, as well as a wavy, dark line along the leading wing margin. The antennal clubs are black with orange tips.

COULD BE CONFUSED WITH The Southern and Northern Pearly-eyes are both very similar (see page 366). However, the dark line on the underside of the forewing is straight in the Southern and slightly curved on the Northern. Additionally, the Southern has completely orange antennae.

HABITAT/LIFE HISTORY The Creole Pearly-eye is found in canebrakes and leads a secretive life hidden in the dense giant cane leaves. The bright green caterpillar has few or no markings and feeds only on giant cane. The adult is most active early and late in the day, flying long after most butterflies have settled. Even on cloudy days with a light rain, the adult is active. Oozing tree sap, carrion, rotting fruit, and dung are favorite food sources for the adult. The Creole Pearly-eye has two generations—late May into June and late August into September. The species overwinters as a partially grown caterpillar.

STATUS The Creole Pearly-eye is only found where giant cane is abundant, which limits its distribution to the lower counties of southern Illinois.[37] It can be locally common, but is generally considered rare; however, this could be due to an observer's lack of desire to venture into the swampy, mosquito-tick-and-chigger-infested canebrakes the Creole calls home.

B

♂ T

WINGSPAN
~2.5 in

♂ U

♀ U

EYED BROWN
Lethe eurydice (Linnaeus)

PREVALENCE
Locally
encountered

FLIGHT PERIOD

MAR	
APR	
MAY	
JUN	
JUL	
AUG	
SEP	
OCT	
NOV	

FIELD NOTES
A. Warm tan
base color (U)

B. Jagged line
across both
wings (U)

Female

Male

DESCRIPTION The wingspan of the Eyed Brown is 2.0–2.5 inches. The sexes are similar, but the female is larger and lighter in color. The upperside is brown (variable in shade) and the underside is a warm tan, often with a lighter area in the outer third of the forewing. Both the upper- and underside have black eyespots—usually four on the forewing and six on the hindwing—along the wing margins. On the upperside, these eyespots may have a small, whitish pupil; the pupil is more likely to appear on the 4th or 5th spot down. On the underside, these eyespots have a white center with a pale yellow ring. The underside also has three darker-colored lines running across the wings. The underside line nearest the eyespots is jagged, coming to a point at almost every wing vein; it is most prominent on the forewing.

COULD BE CONFUSED WITH The Appalachian and Leeuw's Eyed Browns are similar (see page 368); however, they have a slightly waved, not sharply jagged, underside line. Further, the Appalachian and Leeuw's Eyed Browns occur in more shaded habitats—along the edge of sedge meadows or in open flatwoods—not in open sedge meadows like the Eyed Brown.

HABITAT/LIFE HISTORY The Eyed Brown is found in sunny, moist sedge meadows and generally avoids shade. The caterpillar feeds on various sedges. The adult seldom strays from meadows, but can be drawn to rotting fruit. On occasion, the adult will visit flowers (e.g., swamp milkweed). The Eyed Brown has one long generation, with the adult present from June until August. The species overwinters as a partially grown caterpillar.

STATUS The Eyed Brown is fairly common north of Interstate 80. A few scattered populations exist to the south—the southernmost record is from Pike County, near Pittsfield, in 1966.[38] The species is secure in Illinois, but is habitat dependent.

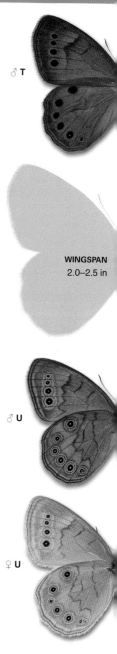

♂ T

WINGSPAN
2.0–2.5 in

♂ U

♀ U

APPALACHIAN EYED BROWN
Lethe appalachia appalachia R. Chermock

PREVALENCE
Locally
encountered

FLIGHT PERIOD

MAR	
APR	
MAY	
JUN	
JUL	
AUG	
SEP	
OCT	
NOV	

FIELD NOTES

A. Grocery-bag brown base color (U)

B. Wavy line across both wings (U)

Female

Female

DESCRIPTION The wingspan of the Appalachian Eyed Brown is 2.0–2.5 inches. The sexes are similar, with the female larger and paler. The upperside is olive-brown, with a slightly paler area around the forewing eyespots. The upperside eyespots are ill-defined. The underside is grocery-bag brown with a violet tint, at least when fresh, and has black eyespots with a white center that are encircled with whitish-yellow. There are usually three lines across the underside of the wings; the line closest to the eyespots is gently waved with no sharp points.

COULD BE CONFUSED WITH The Eyed Brown has a jagged line on its underside near the eyespots, and is found in open sedge meadows. Leeuw's Eyed Brown is lighter in color with more sharply defined markings; further, it is limited to the counties that border Lake Michigan in Illinois (see page 368).

HABITAT/LIFE HISTORY The Appalachian Eyed Brown is found in shrub swamps, flatwoods, and forested seep areas with patches of sedge. It haunts shaded woods and rarely comes into the open. The caterpillar host plants are sedges. The adult feeds mainly at moist areas and on tree sap. The Appalachian Eyed Brown has two generations, with the adult on the wing from early May through September, but mainly during June and August. The species overwinters as a partially grown caterpillar.

STATUS The Appalachian Eyed Brown occurs in scattered populations in the southern two-thirds of Illinois. This subspecies resides as far north as Iroquois County, where it is extremely localized. Bouseman and Sternburg (2001) placed this population under *L. a. leeuwi*; however, the specimens seen from there appear to be of the southern type *L. a. appalachia*. The Appalachian Eyed Brown is often overlooked. Just a few years ago there were no known populations in the state, but since then the species has been found in 7 or 8 counties—it no doubt occurs in other counties as well. It appears stable in Illinois.

♂ T

WINGSPAN
2.0–2.5 in

♂ U

♀ U

LEEUW'S EYED BROWN

Lethe appalachia leeuwi Gattrelle & Arbogast

PREVALENCE
Rare

FLIGHT PERIOD

MAR
APR
MAY
JUN
JUL
AUG
SEP
OCT
NOV

FIELD NOTES

A. Light beige base color (T)

B. Pale clay base color (U)

C. Wavy line across both wings (U)

Male

Female

DESCRIPTION The wingspan of Leeuw's Eyed Brown is about 2.0 inches. The sexes are similar, with the female larger and paler. The upperside is grayish brown, with sharper markings. The underside is the color of pale clay. There are usually three lines across the underside of the wings; the line closest to the eyespots is wavy.

COULD BE CONFUSED WITH The Eyed Brown and Leeuw's Eyed Brown are similar and could occur just a few feet away from each other, but seldom mingle. However, the Eyed Brown has a jagged line on its underside near the eyespots, and is found in open sedge meadows. The Appalachian Eyed Brown is darker in color with a more diffuse pattern; further, it is mostly found in the southern two-thirds of Illinois (see page 368).

HABITAT/LIFE HISTORY According to Irwin Leeuw, Leeuw's Eyed Brown prefers alder thickets, where it almost never ventures out. In the authors' experience, this is the shrubby transition zone—the band between open sedge meadows and forest. The caterpillar feeds on *Carex lacustris*, but may use other sedge species too. There is one generation, with the adult on the wing from late June through early August. The species likely overwinters as a partially grown caterpillar.

STATUS The Leeuw's Eyed Brown seems to be limited to the Chicago/Lake Michigan area.[39] In the past, this subspecies was fairly common, but usually only occurred in localized colonies. Habitat destruction is the subspecies' biggest threat, as it is found in a rather small region that has experienced intensive development. Northeast Illinois appears to be at the edge of the subspecies' range.

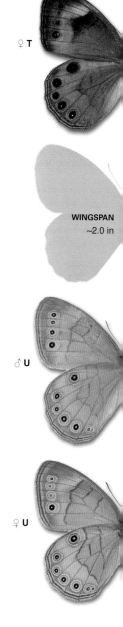

♀ T

WINGSPAN
~2.0 in

♂ U

♀ U

GEMMED SATYR
Cyllopsis gemma (Hübner)

PREVALENCE
Locally
encountered

FLIGHT PERIOD

MAR	
APR	
MAY	
JUN	
JUL	
AUG	
SEP	
OCT	
NOV	

FIELD NOTES
A. Metallic spots
(little gems) on
hindwing (U)

DESCRIPTION The Gemmed Satyr has a wingspan of about 1.5 inches and similar sexes. The upperside is brown with two small, dark spots on the outer margin of the hindwing. The underside is gray-brown to brown, with three darker, wavy lines (the outermost line is sometimes barely discernible) running across the wings. On the outer third of the hindwing is an ovoid, purplish-gray and cream-colored patch containing small, metallic blue and silver spots—these "little gems" are iridescent in sunlight. The springtime adult is usually darker and more subdued than later individuals, which are brighter and more sharply patterned.

COULD BE CONFUSED WITH The upperside of the Carolina Satyr is very similar, but its underside has eyespots running down the wings. The Little Wood Satyr is usually larger and has black eyespots on the upper- and underside of all wings.

HABITAT/LIFE HISTORY Look for the Gemmed Satyr in the shaded woodlands of southern Illinois. The caterpillar feeds on Bermuda grass. The adult is a sap, fermenting fruit, and carrion feeder. Its nervous, erratic flight is hard to follow, even with the metallic spots—"little gems" that glow when the dappled forest sunlight hits them. The butterfly seems to disappear as it enters shaded areas, only to reappear 50 feet away. Multiple generations occur in Illinois, and we have records for the Gemmed Satyr in every month from April through October. The species overwinters as a partially grown caterpillar.

STATUS The Gemmed Satyr is increasing in abundance in the southern fourth of Illinois.[40] While consistent records date back into the 1800s, the populations fluctuate. It would seem appropriate to classify this species as a sporadic, long-term colonizer, sometimes common and other times absent.

♂ T

♀ T

WINGSPAN
~1.5 in

♂ U

♀ U

CAROLINA SATYR
Hermeuptychia sosybius (Fabricius)

Bill Bouton

Female

PREVALENCE
Rare

FLIGHT PERIOD

MAR
APR
MAY
JUN
JUL
AUG
SEP
OCT
NOV

FIELD NOTES

A. Brown base color with no markings (T)

B. Row of eyespots on both wings (U)

Bill Bouton

Male

DESCRIPTION The Carolina Satyr has a wingspan of approximately 1.3 inches and similar sexes. The upperside is brown with no markings. The underside is gray-brown to brown, with three to four darker brown, wavy lines across the wings; a series of yellow-ringed eyespots occurs along the outer margins. Some of the eyespots have black centers with tiny, bluish highlights.

COULD BE CONFUSED WITH The Little Wood Satyr is usually larger and has black eyespots on the upper- and underside of both its wings. The Gemmed Satyr is very similar on the upperside; however, its underside lacks eyespots.

HABITAT/LIFE HISTORY The Carolina Satyr is a species of deep woods in far southern Illinois, usually found along streams. It often darts across an open area or path, only to quickly disappear into the shaded woods. The caterpillar feeds on a number of woodland grasses, both native and introduced, but Bermuda grass seems to be a favorite host. The Carolina Satyr has multiple generations, and flies during every month from April through October. The species overwinters as a partially grown caterpillar.

STATUS The Carolina Satyr can be locally abundant. Irwin and Downey (1973) stated: "We suspect *E. h. sosybius* occupies the same general range in Illinois as does *E. gemma*. It is probably not common and may be overlooked because of its resemblance to the abundant *E. cymela* on the wing." Until 1994, the only Illinois records of the Carolina Satyr were two specimens in the Carnegie Museum labeled "Illinois" and dated from the 1800s. Bouseman took one in Pope County in 1994, and Wiker collected specimens in the same county in 1995. Since 1999, there have been isolated population increases in southern Illinois.

♂ T

♀ T

WINGSPAN
~1.3 in

♂ U

♀ U

LITTLE WOOD SATYR
Megisto cymela (Cramer)

PREVALENCE
Widely
encountered

FLIGHT PERIOD

MAR	
APR	
MAY	
JUN	
JUL	
AUG	
SEP	
OCT	
NOV	

FIELD NOTES

A. Brown
base color with
eyespots (T)

B. Prominent
eyespots (U)

Female

Female

DESCRIPTION The Little Wood Satyr has a wingspan of 1.75 inches and similar sexes. The upperside is brown and has two yellow-ringed, black spots on each wing that contain a dash of blue scaling in the center. A double line follows the outer wing margins, and another line occurs farther in towards the black spots and crosses both wings. The upperside pattern is repeated on the underside; however, the underside is a lighter brown-to-tan color, and has an additional line between the thorax and midline of the wings. Several small, silvery spots are found above, below, and between the two black spots on the underside. Occasionally, one or two of these spots will have a hint of black in the center.

♂ T

COULD BE CONFUSED WITH The Carolina and Gemmed Satyrs are of similar size and color; however, the uppersides of these species lack black spots. The Gemmed Satyr also lacks black spots on its underside.

HABITAT/LIFE HISTORY The Little Wood Satyr inhabits woodlands around the state. The caterpillar feeds on various species of grasses, and perhaps some sedges. The adult frequently visits oozing tree sap, animal carcasses, dung, damp areas along streams, and fermenting fruit. Forest and field edges generally abound with the Little Wood Satyr in late May and June; the species begins to wane in July and is gone by August. It has a single generation that emerges over a long period of time each season. The species overwinters as a partially grown caterpillar.

WINGSPAN
1.75 in

STATUS The Little Wood Satyr is common in woodlands statewide; it is probably more abundant in the southern part of the state.

♂ U

COMMON WOOD NYMPH
Cercyonis pegala (Fabricius)

PREVALENCE
Locally
encountered

FLIGHT PERIOD

MAR	
APR	
MAY	
JUN	
JUL	
AUG	
SEP	
OCT	
NOV	

FIELD NOTES
A. Two large,
yellow-ringed
eyespots with
blue centers on
forewing (U)

Female

Mating pair

DESCRIPTION The wingspan of the Common Wood Nymph is 2.0–3.0 inches, with the female larger than the male. Eyespots occur on the upper- and underside of both wings and are typically black with a bluish pupil; however, these eyespots are quite variable and may be very prominent or nearly absent. The upperside is dark brown and has two eyespots on the outer third of the forewing that may be surrounded by a large, yellow patch; this yellow patch can be very bright, completely absent, or any gradation in between. While present in both sexes, the yellow patch is more often seen in the female. The upperside of the hindwing is brown and usually has a single spot low on the wing, near the bottom margin. The underside is brown with darker brown mottling, and the forewing generally has two large, yellow-ringed eyespots, often surrounded by a paler yellow patch (i.e., if there is a yellow patch on the upperside). The underside of the hindwing has between 3 and 8 (highly variable) small eyespots along the outer third of the wing.

COULD BE CONFUSED WITH The Common Wood Nymph should not be confused with anything else in Illinois.

HABITAT/LIFE HISTORY In the southern half of Illinois, the Common Wood Nymph frequents woodlands and wooded margins, seeking sap, carrion, and rotting fruit; it almost never nectars from flowers. In the northern half of Illinois, the species is generally smaller, darker, seldom has a yellow patch on the forewing, and lives in more open areas, especially prairies.[41] In this region, the adult is an avid flower visitor. The caterpillar feeds on various native grasses statewide. There seems to be one long emergence, with the adult on the wing across the state from late May through August. The species overwinters as a newly hatched caterpillar.

STATUS The Common Wood Nymph is found statewide—probably in all counties—and is local in suitable habitats.

♂ T

♀ T

WINGSPAN
2.0–3.0 in

♀ U

PART III

ADDITIONAL
INFORMATION

ABOVE Gorgone Checkerspots and Pearl Crescent interacting on butterfly-weed

RIGHT ABOVE Puddle club of Spicebush and Black Swallowtail

RIGHT BELOW Grouping of Great Spangled Fritillaries on colic root

COMMONLY CONFUSED ILLINOIS BUTTERFLIES

The above photo is an example of how difficult distinguishing similar species in the field can be; the two butterflies on the left are Gorgone Checkerspots, while the single individual on the right is a Pearl Crescent. In the following pages, we provide direct comparisons between species that we consider difficult to distinguish. The key to using these images effectively is to study the differences so you will be prepared when you encounter the species in the field. Think of the comparison pages as a multiple choice question (that has right and wrong choices), while identifying butterflies in the field is more of an open-ended essay question. The key for the observer is to find the correct access point (small orange and black butterflies should trigger either crescent or checkerspot, while a large black butterfly immediately says swallowtail) and then the comparison pages become most useful.

Swallowtail Mimicry Complex

Remember that these species are mimicking the Pipevine Swallowtail (*Battus philenor*). All are dark butterflies with blue hindwings (the shade of blue varies based on the species). Pipevine and Tiger Swallowtail specimens are shown two-thirds their normal size, while the Black Swallowtail, Spicebush Swallowtail, and Red-spotted Purple specimens are shown actual size.

Less defined color

Reflective, blue to bluish-green scales on outer two-thirds of hindwing

♂ **PIPEVINE SWALLOWTAIL**

Larger overall size

Faint black stripes

Sky blue scaling covers more of hindwing

TIGER SWALLOWTAIL (♀: DARK FORM)

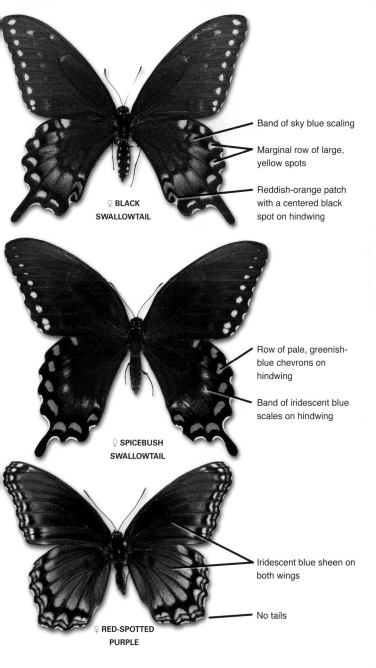

Band of sky blue scaling

Marginal row of large, yellow spots

Reddish-orange patch with a centered black spot on hindwing

♀ **BLACK SWALLOWTAIL**

Row of pale, greenish-blue chevrons on hindwing

Band of iridescent blue scales on hindwing

♀ **SPICEBUSH SWALLOWTAIL**

Iridescent blue sheen on both wings

No tails

♀ **RED-SPOTTED PURPLE**

Swallowtail Mimicry Complex

Remember that these species are mimicking the Pipevine Swallowtail (*Battus philenor*). All are dark butterflies with blue hindwings (the shade of blue varies based on the species). Pipevine and Tiger Swallowtail specimens are shown two-thirds their normal size, while the Black Swallowtail, Spicebush Swallowtail, and Red-spotted Purple specimens are shown actual size.

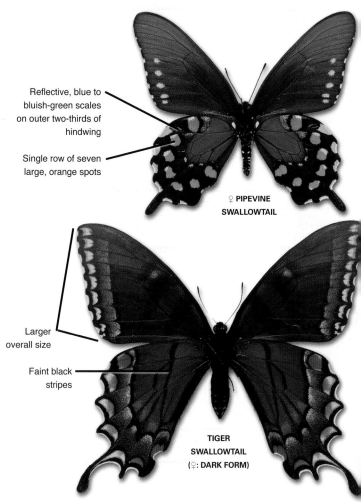

Reflective, blue to bluish-green scales on outer two-thirds of hindwing

Single row of seven large, orange spots

♀ PIPEVINE
SWALLOWTAIL

Larger overall size

Faint black stripes

TIGER
SWALLOWTAIL
(♀: DARK FORM)

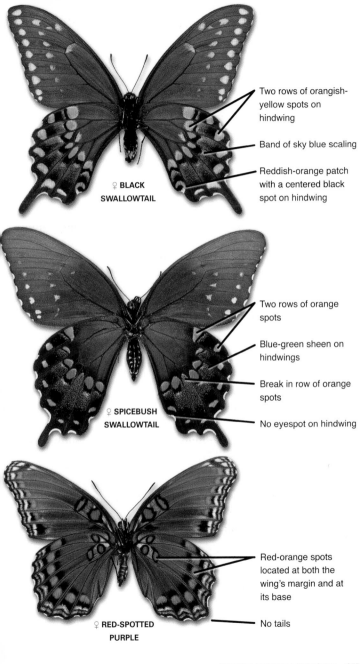

♀ **BLACK SWALLOWTAIL**

Two rows of orangish-yellow spots on hindwing

Band of sky blue scaling

Reddish-orange patch with a centered black spot on hindwing

♀ **SPICEBUSH SWALLOWTAIL**

Two rows of orange spots

Blue-green sheen on hindwings

Break in row of orange spots

No eyespot on hindwing

♀ **RED-SPOTTED PURPLE**

Red-orange spots located at both the wing's margin and at its base

No tails

Hairstreaks

For this group of hairstreaks, the defining features are on the underside as these species seldom sit with their wings open. Specimens are shown approximately 2× their normal size.

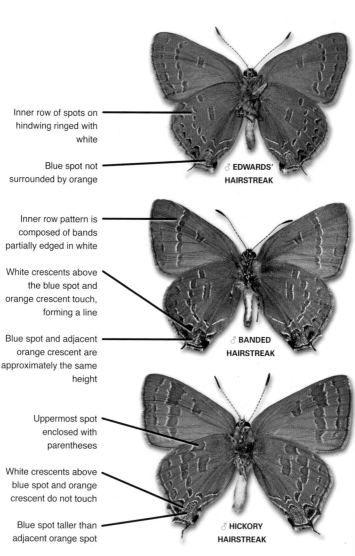

Inner row of spots on hindwing ringed with white

Blue spot not surrounded by orange

♂ **EDWARDS'**
HAIRSTREAK

Inner row pattern is composed of bands partially edged in white

White crescents above the blue spot and orange crescent touch, forming a line

Blue spot and adjacent orange crescent are approximately the same height

♂ **BANDED**
HAIRSTREAK

Uppermost spot enclosed with parentheses

White crescents above blue spot and orange crescent do not touch

Blue spot taller than adjacent orange spot

♂ **HICKORY**
HAIRSTREAK

♂ STRIPED HAIRSTREAK

Wide, broken, darker-brown bands edged in white

Large, blue spot capped with white, black, and orange

♀ NORTHERN HAIRSTREAK

Brown base color

Broken, black-and-white line across hindwing

NOTE: Very rare canopy species (seldom seen)

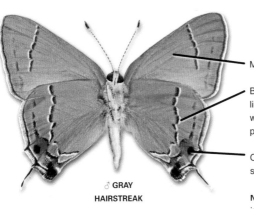

♂ GRAY HAIRSTREAK

Medium gray base color

Broken, tri-colored line across hindwing, with inner orange line prominent

Orange-capped black spot on hindwing

NOTE: Common butterfly in Illinois

Monarch and Viceroy

The most commonly confused butterflies in Illinois are the Monarch and Viceroy. With careful observation, two obvious differences can be detected.

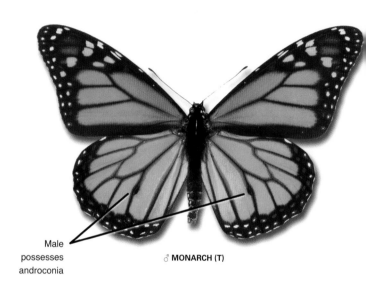

Male possesses androconia

♂ **MONARCH (T)**

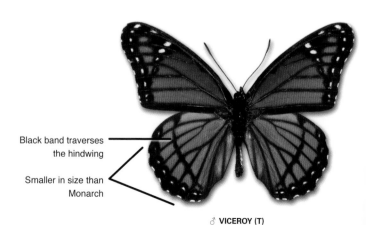

Black band traverses the hindwing

Smaller in size than Monarch

♂ **VICEROY (T)**

One is that the Monarch is always larger than the Viceroy. The second is that the Viceroy has a conspicuous, dark band crossing its hindwing (visible from top and underside). The two specimens presented here are shown actual size.

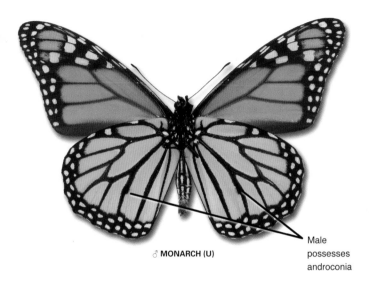

♂ **MONARCH (U)**

Male possesses androconia

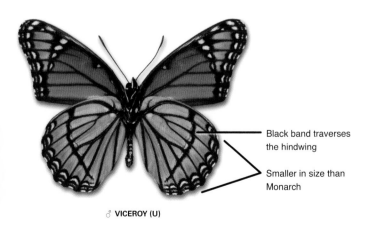

♂ **VICEROY (U)**

Black band traverses the hindwing

Smaller in size than Monarch

Fritillaries, Checkerspots, and Crescents

Small to medium-sized butterflies with variable orange, yellow, white/silver, and black markings. Specimens are shown actual size.

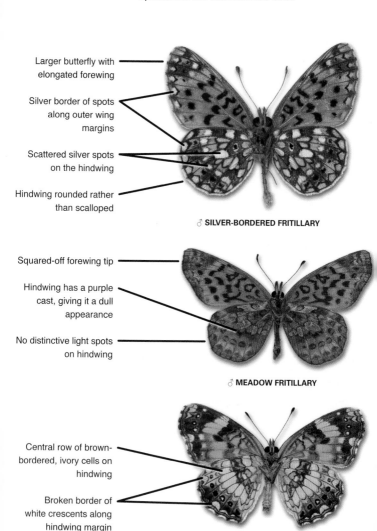

Larger butterfly with elongated forewing

Silver border of spots along outer wing margins

Scattered silver spots on the hindwing

Hindwing rounded rather than scalloped

♂ SILVER-BORDERED FRITILLARY

Squared-off forewing tip

Hindwing has a purple cast, giving it a dull appearance

No distinctive light spots on hindwing

♂ MEADOW FRITILLARY

Central row of brown-bordered, ivory cells on hindwing

Broken border of white crescents along hindwing margin

♂ SILVERY CHECKERSPOT

Strongly checkered fringe

Zigzag pattern and angular, ivory band on hindwing

♂ GORGONE CHECKERSPOT

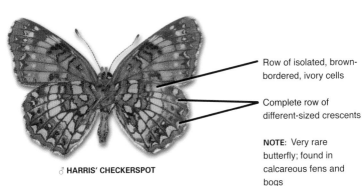

Row of isolated, brown-bordered, ivory cells

Complete row of different-sized crescents

NOTE: Very rare butterfly; found in calcareous fens and bogs

♂ HARRIS' CHECKERSPOT

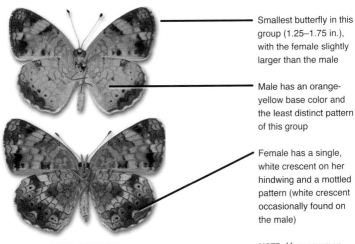

Smallest butterfly in this group (1.25–1.75 in.), with the female slightly larger than the male

Male has an orange-yellow base color and the least distinct pattern of this group

Female has a single, white crescent on her hindwing and a mottled pattern (white crescent occasionally found on the male)

PEARL CRESCENT
♂ and ♀, respectively

NOTE: Very common butterfly in Illinois

Greater Fritillaries

The Great Spangled Fritillary and Aphrodite Fritillary can be confused because they sometimes fly together in the same habitat. Specimens are shown actual size.

Wings darker near body

♂ **GREAT SPANGLED FRITILLARY (T)**

Small, distinctive black mark on forewing

Overall smaller size

♂ **APHRODITE FRITILLARY (T)**

♂ **GREAT SPANGLED FRITILLARY (U)**

Hindwing with wide, buff-colored band

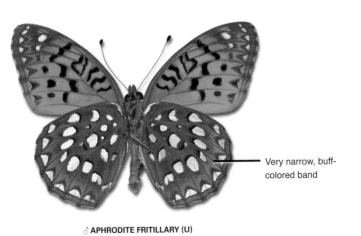

Very narrow, buff-colored band

♂ **APHRODITE FRITILLARY (U)**

Baltimore and Ozark Checkerspot

The Baltimore is found in wetlands in northern Illinois, whereas the Ozark Checkerspot is generally found in dry/open glades or woodland habitats in southern Illinois. The two specimens presented here are shown actual size.

Two prominent orange spots near leading margin of forewing

♂ BALTIMORE

Reduced red-orange spots near leading margin of forewing

♂ OZARK CHECKERSPOT

Two prominent orange spots near leading margin of forewing

♀ **BALTIMORE**

Reduced red-orange spots near leading margin of forewing

♀ **OZARK CHECKERSPOT**

Pearly-eyes

These pearly-eye species can occur together where woodlands overlap with cane thickets (in southern Illinois). Specimens are shown actual size.

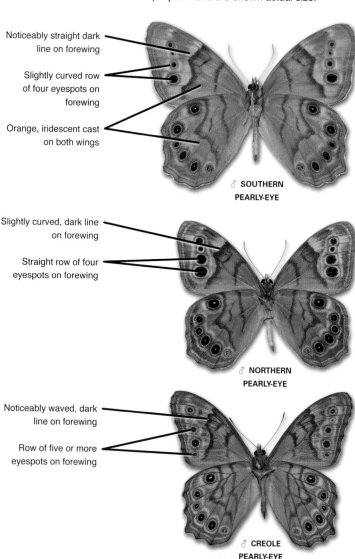

Noticeably straight dark line on forewing

Slightly curved row of four eyespots on forewing

Orange, iridescent cast on both wings

♂ SOUTHERN
PEARLY-EYE

Slightly curved, dark line on forewing

Straight row of four eyespots on forewing

♂ NORTHERN
PEARLY-EYE

Noticeably waved, dark line on forewing

Row of five or more eyespots on forewing

♂ CREOLE
PEARLY-EYE

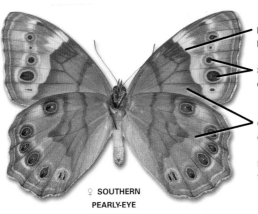

Noticeably straight, dark line on forewing

Somewhat curved row of eyespots on forewing

Orange, iridescent cast on both wings

NOTE: Restricted to cane thickets

♀ SOUTHERN PEARLY-EYE

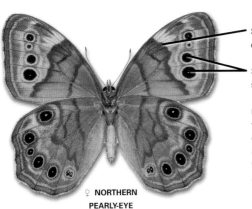

Slightly curved, dark line on forewing

Straight row of four spots on forewing

NOTE: Common woodland butterfly; does occur with Southern and Creole Pearly-eye when cane thickets are adjacent to woodlands

♀ NORTHERN PEARLY-EYE

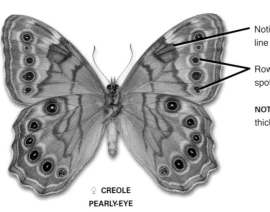

Noticeably waved, dark line on forewing

Row of five or more eyespots on forewing

NOTE: Restricted to cane thickets

♀ CREOLE PEARLY-EYE

Eyed Browns

Habitat preference and the physical features listed below are key in differentiating the eyed brown group. Specimens are shown actual size.

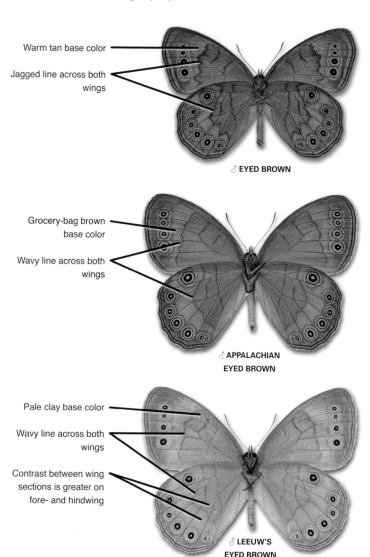

Warm tan base color

Jagged line across both wings

♂ EYED BROWN

Grocery-bag brown base color

Wavy line across both wings

♂ APPALACHIAN
EYED BROWN

Pale clay base color

Wavy line across both wings

Contrast between wing sections is greater on fore- and hindwing

♂ LEEUW'S
EYED BROWN

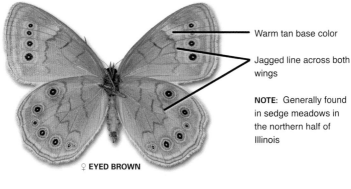

Warm tan base color

Jagged line across both wings

NOTE: Generally found in sedge meadows in the northern half of Illinois

♀ **EYED BROWN**

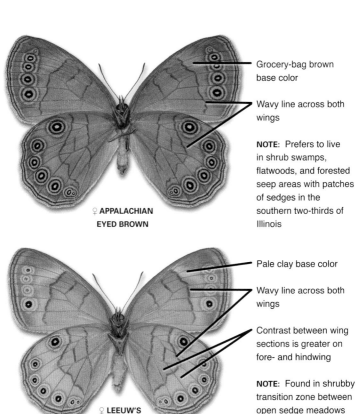

Grocery-bag brown base color

Wavy line across both wings

NOTE: Prefers to live in shrub swamps, flatwoods, and forested seep areas with patches of sedges in the southern two-thirds of Illinois

♀ **APPALACHIAN EYED BROWN**

Pale clay base color

Wavy line across both wings

Contrast between wing sections is greater on fore- and hindwing

NOTE: Found in shrubby transition zone between open sedge meadows and forests in Illinois' far northeast corner

♀ **LEEUW'S EYED BROWN**

SUPPLEMENTAL NOTES

1 SPRING AND SUMMER AZURES (PAGE 4)

The forewing of the Spring Azure male is covered with long, fork-shaped scales that are visible under magnification; the Summer Azure male lacks these scales. Many of the reported caterpillar hosts for the Spring Azure have been incorrectly attributed, due to taxonomic ambiguities. Any previous published data on this species may be suspect.

2 ATAVISTIC INDIVIDUALS (PAGE 75)

Pictured here is one of three specimens collected over a 25-year period in Randolph County, Illinois, by Todd Wiley. While the specimens appear to be a cross between a Viceroy and Red-spotted Purple, they are likely atavistic individuals. Atavism is an inherited trait that reappears in an individual after being absent. Atavistic traits usually represent an ancestral pattern.

3 JOAN'S SWALLOWTAIL (PAGE 105)

The Joan's Swallowtail (*Papilio joanae* Heitzman), a Missouri species, is virtually identical to the common Black Swallowtail. It has never been documented in Illinois, but may occur in the southwestern portion of the state, along the Mississippi River from Monroe to Alexander counties. A number of environmental factors are needed to identify this species—type of habitat (i.e., woodland), known caterpillar host plants (i.e., carrot family), and adult behavior. The Joan's Swallowtail is an extremely difficult butterfly to identify.

Richard Heitzman [personal communication with Wiker], stated: "...*joanae* is a woodland species. If you see what looks like a Black Swallowtail flying along or parallel with the road through a forested area, it is likely *polyxenes*. If, what appears to be a Black Swallowtail flies out of the woods, crosses the road, and disappears back into the woods, it's most likely *joanae*." The Joan's Swallowtail tends to avoid open areas, but a patrolling male will seek a female feeding in forest glade openings. The caterpillar feeds on members of the carrot family—yellow pimpernel, meadow parsnip, and golden alexander. In Missouri, the adult flies from mid-April to early June, and late July to early September. For

more information on this species see the original description by Heitzman (1973).

4 **PALAMEDES SWALLOWTAIL (PAGE 123)**
On August 22, 1999, Josh Nelson of Heyworth, Illinois, caught a butterfly in his neighbor's flower garden for his 4-H insect collection. He labeled it

ABOVE Female and male specimens, respectively, of Joan's Swallowtail

ILLINOIS, McLean County
S. Poland Street in Heyworth
1.5 Blocks N. of US Rt. 136
T22N-R2E. Section 34
August 22, 1999
Collected by Josh Nelson

ABOVE Palamedes Swallowtail—specimen collected by Josh Nelson in 1999

Giant Swallowtail. A few years later Wiker noticed this specimen in Josh's collection at the Illinois State Fair. After interviewing both Josh and his parents, it became apparent that this was the first known Illinois specimen of the Palamedes Swallowtail. The butterfly now resides in the Wiker collection. That same year (1999), local naturalist and writer Kathy Phelps of Saline County, Illinois, informed Wiker that she had observed what appeared to be a Giant Swallowtail at her flower garden in Pankeyville. However, she noticed "an underside that was Hershey Bar brown," and thought it might be something different. Unfortunately, when she tried to net it, the butterfly escaped and disappeared into the Shawnee Hills. With Kathy's description of the underside, Wiker concluded that it, too, was a Palamedes Swallowtail.

5 MEXICAN YELLOW (PAGE 129)
Multiple specimens have been seen and collected

in several years, but the peak year appears to be 1911. During that year, specimens were collected from DuPage and Champaign counties. Theodore Frison (1919) wrote, "On October 18 and 19, 1911, the writer took fourteen specimens of this species in Champaign, Illinois" and "Any number of specimens of this pierid might have been captured as they were flying in flocks as certain other butterflies do during migration."

6 DOGFACE (PAGE 139)
The *rosa* form was discovered and named by Jerome M'Neill of Moline, Illinois (1889) from three specimens he collected on September 16, 1887, "in a low-lying field, on the banks of the Mississippi, three miles east of Moline."

7 DOGFACE (PAGE 139)
A booklet by Gilbert Wright (1951), entitled *Common Illinois Insects*, included a plate on Common Illinois Butterflies that featured a male Dogface. The caption states that the species is "abundant in the southern part of the state." Wiker spent much of his youth in search of this "abundant" butterfly, without success, until his senior year of high school.

LEFT Mexican Yellow— specimen collected by T.L. Wiley in 1981

RIGHT Large Orange Sulphur—specimen collected by Todd Wiley in 1981

Sparta, Ill.
Randolph Co.
2 May 1981

T. L. Wiley
collector

8 ORANGE-BARRED SULPHUR (PAGE 143)

One of the three known specimens has only 1870 on its label, while the other two have August 10, 1937 and August 1952, respectively.

9 LARGE ORANGE SULPHUR (PAGE 145)

To our knowledge, the following are the only two Illinois records that exist: a specimen collected by Todd Wiley in Sparta, Randolph County on May 2, 1981 (it resides in the Southern Illinois University Insect collection) and a published observation made by Robert Sites on June 7, 1981, at Fountain Bluff in Jackson County. Both of these dates appear earlier than one would expect for a potential, late-summer migrant. There are a number of records from Missouri, particularly along the Missouri River, and several near the Mississippi River north of St. Louis.

10 MUSTARD WHITE (PAGE 151)

Due to changes in taxonomy (scientific classification), previous literature will refer to this butterfly as *Pieris napi* or *Pieris napi oleracea*. Statements by French (1878), Thomas (1880), Worthington (1880), and Middleton (1881) document that the

Mustard White occurred in the very northern portion of Illinois.

11 CHECKERED WHITE (PAGE 155)

Ironically, in 1878 the *Seventh Report of the State Entomologist* discussed control measures (hand or chicken picking*) for this occasional "pest" of cabbage. Entomologists referred to it as the "Southern Cabbage Butterfly." Unfortunately, due to competition from the introduced Cabbage Butterfly, the Checkered White is no longer found in the state in such numbers to warrant "pest" status.

*Chicken picking means allowing chickens to forage for insects in the garden.

12 GREAT SOUTHERN WHITE (PAGE 157)

On July 8, 1970, the Nance brothers—while baling hay for a farmer in Tower Hill, Shelby County—spotted an odd-looking, white butterfly. It was captured and the specimen remained with Dave Nance for nearly 40 years. While the Great Southern White has been collected a few times in western Missouri, the Nance brothers' specimen is the only known record of the species in Illinois.

LEFT Great Southern White—specimen collected by S. Nance in 1970 (now resides in the Wiker collection)

13 ATALA (PAGE 177)

Bouseman and Sternburg (2001) did not discuss the Atala because it was an accident, and will likely not cross the border of Illinois again. We believe, as did Irwin and Downey (1973), that it still deserves mention as an authentic record and is part of the Illinois species list, albeit only recorded once. George H. French, lepidopterist and professor at Southern Illinois University from 1878 until 1922, produced the first state list of Illinois butterflies in 1879, and wrote one of the first field guides for butterflies, *Butterflies of the Eastern United States*, in 1885. This work passed through four editions and was printed until 1914. In the Addenda section of the 1900 edition (and printings thereafter) French states, "In the catalogues this species is given Florida as a habitat. I believe, however, that it is more widely distributed, for I have found it once in Carbondale, Illinois." We, as did Irwin and Downey, conclude that French could not have confused this with anything else, and its presence may be explained by some unnatural method of transport. Irwin and Downey mention that at that time the Illinois Central Railroad had a direct line from Carbondale to South Florida. Perhaps a caterpillar crawled onto a railcar or onto freight and ended up in Illinois.

14 HICKORY HAIRSTREAK (PAGE 189)

After many years of searching collections and images, as well as performing many dissections of preserved specimens, Wiker has concluded that the Hickory Hairstreak is the most misidentified butterfly in Illinois. Many collections have specimens labeled Hickory Hairstreak that are, in fact, the Banded Hairstreak. Other collections have a Hickory or two hiding among a series of Banded Hairstreaks. The genitalia of all *Satyrium* species, both male and female, are very distinctive, and all species can be positively identified via dissection (Klots 1960, Klots and Clench 1952, Michener and Dos Passos 1942).

15 NORTHERN HAIRSTREAK (PAGE 193)

On May 28, 2010, Travis Mahan shot the species treatment photos for the Northern Hairstreak in Will County. These photos constituted the first record of this butterfly in northeastern Illinois. Mahan posted the photos on the Internet with a question whether the identification was correct. It was, and he had used the common name Northern Oak Hairstreak. Wiker responded to him with the following: "I would expect this butterfly to appear anywhere in Illinois, but it is not one you can ever plan to see. You just have to be lucky, as you were. Cherish it as it may never happen again." Jeffords and Post have also encountered the Northern Hairstreak, but in southern Illinois. Unfortunately, the specimen consisted of four wings quietly residing below a garden spider's (*Argiope*) web.

16 FROSTED ELFIN (PAGE 199)

The only known Illinois specimens of this butterfly are a male and female collected at Beach, in Lake County, on May 10, 1922, by Emil Liljeblad (Field Museum of Natural History). These specimens were apparently lost in a fire in 1970 at the University of Northern Iowa, while under study by John Downey. He had determined the two specimens to be the Hoary Elfin. Even though this area has been extensively collected over the years, the Frosted Elfin has not been seen again.

17 MARINE BLUE (PAGE 213)

While most Illinois records are of single specimen collections, in August, 1986, Todd Wiley of Sparta, Illinois, recorded a colony in a field next to his home. For a few weeks he saw several dozen individuals.

18 SUMMER AZURE (PAGE 219)

Despite written accounts to the contrary, Spring and Summer Azures emerge about the same time in Illinois. The Summer Azure can even appear first. No previous accounts of these species should be used without reexamination of the specimens. Research on the genus continues, and the group may, ultimately, be split into several additional species.

19 DUSKY AZURE (PAGE 221)

This butterfly has been suspected as being a different species since the 1800s. While it had been considered a melanic (dark) form of the Spring Azure, it was not until 1972 that Clench elevated it to species status under the name *Celastrina ebenina*. Through nomenclature research, an ear-

Lacon, Marshall Co., Illinois. Coll. by R. M. Barnes

lier race name had priority and the species name was changed to *C. nigra* in 1991. In Bouseman and Sternburg (2001), *Field Guide to Butterflies of Illinois*, it should be noted that the female pictured as *C. ebenina* on page 133 is actually a female *C. ladon*. The female is misidentified in many collections and numerous publications.

20 GREENISH BLUE (PAGE 223)

Another species that could be confused with the Silvery Blue is the Greenish Blue [*Plebejus saepiolus* (Boiseduval)], but it is a questionable rare stray. While a male specimen exists in the Illinois State Museum Collection labeled Lacon, Marshall Co., Illinois Coll. by R.M Barnes, 8-24-1930, it is something of a mystery as Marshall Co. is far removed from its normal range, and the collection date is outside of its normal flight period. This is possibly a mislabled specimen. The normal range for the Greenish Blue is from northwestern United States to southern Saskatchewan and Alberta. The species sometimes is found in northern Michigan and northern Wisconsin.

21 SILVERY BLUE (PAGE 223)

We lump all Illinois material under *Glaucopsyche lygdamus*. All known Illinois specimens fall under the subspecies *G. l. couperi*. Outside of the Chicago region, the only Silvery Blue record in Illinois was on May 6, 1979, by Dave Hess (Sedman and Hess, 1985) in Hancock County, along an abandoned railroad. Although it eluded capture and is a sight record, the individual was a Silvery Blue based on Hess' description. He states "it was considerably larger than the northern subspecies" and "it possessed large black spots underneath." This would place it in the southern subspecies *G. l. lygdamus*, or possibly one that is undescribed. The authors see no reason why the species should not occur in other areas of the state, as a number of records exist from Missouri, near St. Louis, and in Iowa, directly across from Hancock County. Searching the counties along the Mississippi River may reveal colonies of this seldom-encountered butterfly.

22 REAKIRT'S BLUE (PAGE 225)
During the late 1970s and into the early 1980s, a small population of Reakirt's Blue (observed by Wiker) existed along the railroad near Athens, Illinois. Adults were noted during August in several consecutive years. This butterfly has also been found, with some regularity, at Revis Hill Prairie in Mason County over the last 20 years.

23 KARNER BLUE (PAGE 227)
The history of the Karner Blue in Illinois is unclear. At the time of Irwin and Downey (1973), the only known specimens were from the Bolter collection labeled "N. Ill." (Illinois Natural History Survey) and date back to the 1800s. Dave Iftner (Pittsfield, Illinois) informed Wiker that he had seen Illinois Karner Blue specimens in the collection at the American Museum of Natural History in New York. Wiker has since seen those specimens and found they were collected in 1911, 1912, and 1948 from Elgin and Chicago. These records document a history of the butterfly in the state. Illinois is at the extreme edge of the Karner Blue's range, and it is unclear if the species was ever a long-term breeding resident or an occasional stray that could produce a temporary colony. The caterpillar host, lupine, is not a common plant in Illinois. The last Karner Blues seen in Illinois were discovered by Irwin Leeuw on August 17, 1992, in Lake County. The next day, Leeuw took Wiker and Bradd Sims (Illinois State Museum) to

the site and several were seen in a patch of lupine.

24 NORTHERN METALMARK (PAGE 231)

The Northern Metalmark [*Calephelis borealis* (Grote & Robinson)] is a denizen of eastern North America, with isolated populations found in Missouri. The species has yet to be recorded from Illinois. Its close relative, the Swamp Metalmark, is very similar, but has more pointed forewings and lacks the noticeable dark band on its upperside. The Swamp Metalmark's underside silvery marks are more square-shaped, while the Northern Metalmark's are crescent-shaped.

The caterpillar host of the Northern Metalmark, roundleaf ragwort, occurs in the southern half of Illinois, and is found mostly in the counties that border the peninsula formed by the Wabash, Ohio, and Mississippi rivers. The Northern Metalmark occurs in open, wooded habitat on high, dry ground with rock outcroppings. Missouri and Indiana populations exist on shale barrens and limestone soils. The adult flies in July. The species overwinters as a half-grown caterpillar and has nine instars.

Scudder (1889) writes,"…it [*C. borealis*] has since been taken in…, the township of Ohio, Ill. (Morrison), …The New York specimens were taken in July, the Illinois specimens May 7." At the time C. muticum was undescribed and the location is not within C. borealis's host plant range. It has been generally accepted that what Scudder was referring to was Swamp Metalmark (C. muticum) which was not recognized as a separate species until 1937.

25 SWAMP METALMARK (PAGE 231)

Irwin and Downey (1973) list several specimens from Elgin, Kane County, Illinois. The majority of specimens were collected by Maurice Bristol, and he either gave some of them to A. K. Wyatt, or brought Wyatt to the collection site. McAlpine (1937) in his original description of *C. muticum*, mentions "*C. muticum* from Chicago, Illinois… in the collection of Alexander K. Wyatt." Years later Irwin Leeuw was taken to this same locale by M. Bristol. Leeuw observed Swamp Metalmarks at the site until the late 1970s. In 1985, Mr. Leeuw introduced Wiker to the site, and although the Metalmark was not observed, the site contained appropriate habitat.

The area in which the above-mentioned specimens were collected was technically in Cook County, a few hundred yards from the Kane County line. Evers and Page (1977) list the Swamp Metalmark (and Harris' Checkerspot) from Trout Park in Elgin, Illinois (Kane County). We are not sure what these records were based on, but believe they are from the Cook County site. Also, see the text for Harris' Checkerspot (*Chlosyne harrisii*) for additional information (page 314).

26 GULF FRITILLARY (PAGE 247)

On August 8, 1999, Wiker observed a worn female laying eggs on passion-flower at his home in Athens (Menard County). Several were reared and adults emerged by September 3. Approximately the same time, Jean Graber of Golconda (Pope County) told Wiker of a colony on the levee along the Ohio River where she had observed several Gulf Fritillaries; the levee had been planted with passion-flower.

ABOVE The only Zebra specimen ever collected in Illinois

27 ZEBRA (PAGE 249)

Irwin and Downey (1973) listed this species under "Butterflies of Possible Occurrence in Illinois" and unknown to them, it had already been found. Tim Vogt found the first, and to our knowledge, the only Zebra ever collected in Illinois. The specimen is in the Illinois State Museum with the following collection data: Monroe Co., Illinois; 1 mile north of Waterloo (T2S-R10W, S13); 13 Aug. 1970; on petunia; Tim Vogt, Collector. This species has been noted by other authors to stray north to Kansas, Missouri, and Colorado.

28 DIANA (PAGE 257)

The most recent record for Illinois is 1960, from Vermilion County. Irwin and Downey (1973) state, "Apparently it was formerly of regular occurrence in the southern third of the state, but at present it must be extremely rare and local, or more probably extinct." They surmise that deforestation may be a factor in its absence from Illinois.

29 REGAL FRITILLARY (PAGE 263)

Due to the rarity of the Regal Fritillary, when one is actually seen flying over a blooming milkweed patch, the Monarch immediately comes to mind. Robert Pyle writes in *Mariposa Road*, "Something even larger flew a loop around me. Monarch, I thought, but the contrast was too great between the primaries and secondaries. Of course—regal fritillary!"

The western subspecies of the Regal Fritillary (*Speyeria idalia occidentalis*) was described in 2001 by Barry E. Williams, University of Illinois. He discovered consistent differences in the wing markings and genetic information separating them. A "Type Series" [the specimens designated by the person(s) creating the name] serves as the standard specimen(s) that show the defining characters for the species/subspecies. Type specimens have special labels and are of scientific importance. The type specimens for this subspecies were collected by Roderick R. Irwin, 1 mile S.E. of Crete, IL—one on 7 July and four on 23 August, 1965. The butterfly pictured here is from that same location and date, but is not included in the type series. Thus, this specimen is designated a topotype (collected from the same locality as the original types).

30 TEXAN CRESCENT (PAGE 281)

The Texan Crescent, *Anthanassa texana* (Edwards), is a species of the south and southwestern U.S. but may be a rare stray to Illinois. While Illinois is listed as part of the range in most literature, the

BELOW Topotype specimen of *Speyeria idalia occidentalis*, the western subspecies of the Regal Fritillary

1 mi. S.E. Crete, Ill.
VIII:24:65
R.R. Irwin leg.

RIGHT Texan Crescent specimen shown at approximately 1.5× its actual size

state's only record is a single sighting by C.L. Remington, on the campus of Principia College (Elsah), Jersey County, October 25, 1940. The species is distinctive in appearance and should not be confused with any other Illinois species. It is regularly found in western Missouri.

31 COMMA (PAGE 299)
Another name for this butterfly is the Hop Merchant. In areas where hops were grown, the farmers believed they could determine the hops market by the markings of the chrysalis dangling from the hops vine. If the chrysalis spikes were golden, the price of hops would rise, but if they were silver, the price would fall.

32 GRAY COMMA (PAGE 301)
In the 1871 *Report of the State Entomologist*, William LaBaron notes that he received a packet from a concerned citizen in Kankakee County who had sent Spinous Currant caterpillars (Gray Comma), and reported that these caterpillars were "doing considerable mischief by stippling the leaves from his currant bushes." This was the first state record of the Gray Comma feeding on currant, and the state entomologist concluded that if the insects become numerous, they would have to be destroyed in some way.

33 GREEN COMMA (PAGE 303)
Worthington listed the Green Comma in 1880 from Illinois, with no indication as to where it was found.

This species should be limited to northwestern Illinois. Don Laibly caught specimens in Carroll County during July 1963. When Wiker spoke with Laibly in January 2014, Laibly stated that he had found the species on a couple of occasions at [Mississippi] Palisades Sate Park. Unfortunately, the specimens no longer exist.

34 BALTIMORE (PAGE 307)

Post first saw this species on June 20, 2001, in the company of John Bouseman and James Sternburg, authors of *Field Guide to Butterflies of Illinois*, during a butterfly field class in Lee County. The Baltimore had been rumored to occur on the property's restored wetlands, but none of the class participants dared hope for a sighting. When Bouseman came back to the group with a wry smile on his face from a scouting trip, the class knew that a checkmark by *E. phaeton phaeton* was in their future. Not only did we see the species, we were able to watch and photograph a mating pair, resulting in Sternburg commenting to Bouseman, "This is a million-dollar opportunity: photographing mating Baltimores. I've never seen so many!"

35 PEARL CRESCENT (PAGE 317)

Research on the genus continues, and the group has been split into several species that may be found in northern Illinois habitats. Rearing and wing pattern comparisons will need to be done to document if any of the other potential crescents occur in Illinois. All presented here are treated as the Pearl Crescent.

36 SOUTHERN PEARLY-EYE (PAGE 329)

The species was first located by John Bouseman in Illinois during 1992, in Alexander County. We have since found it in Pope County, and it occurs in several other areas at the southern tip of the state. Farther south, it is considered more common than the Creole, but in Illinois, the Southern is the rarer species.

37 CREOLE PEARLY-EYE (PAGE 333)

Ernest Shull, in his 1987 book *The Butterflies of Indiana*, mentions Creole, "In the early 1930s, it was rare in the wooded area of our family farm in Girard, Illinois [NE Macoupin Co]." It appears that this record is based on misidentified material as northeastern Macoupin County is far from any known Creole populations or giant cane populations large enough to support it.

38 EYED BROWN (PAGE 335)
We have treated all Illinois *L. eurydice* as a single group. Published records referring to Illinois material in the subspecies *L. e. fumosa* do exist; however, neither Bouseman and Sternburg, Irwin and Downey, nor we have found any specimens that fall into that group. All Illinois material is *L. eurydice*.

39 LEEUW'S EYED BROWN (PAGE 339)
Although we are not proponents of splitting species into sub-specific groups, it seems appropriate here. Illinois is one of the few places where both subspecies occur. The butterfly was first noticed to be different by (and named after) Irwin Leeuw, a Chicago area resident who studied natural history and supplied material to many researchers. In July 1989, Irwin Leeuw took Wiker to sites in Illinois where he had found his namesake butterfly.

40 GEMMED SATYR (PAGE 341)
After much discussion with Rod Irwin, Wiker traveled extensively in the far southern counties during the 1980s seeking the species, but with no success. In 1992, Wiker and others found the Gemmed Satyr in Pope County; since then it has been found every year in steadily increasing numbers, pressing northward, with new records as far north as Marion and Coles counties.

41 COMMON WOOD NYMPH (PAGE 347)
In this field guide, we lump all Illinois populations under *C. pegala*. One could split them into at least three subspecies—*alope*, *nephele*, and *olympus* (the latter described from Chicago by Edwards, 1880—but no data or observations are consistent enough to allow comfortable use of any of these names. Many genetic questions about this species remain to be solved.

GLOSSARY

ABERRANT deviating from the normal type.

ANCESTRAL COLOR PATTERN a color pattern inherited from an earlier form or ancestor; the original color pattern not modified by various evolutionary factors, such as mimicry.

ANDROCONIAL SPOT scent scales on the wings that emit a pheromone to assist in courtship.

ANDROCONIUM (pl. ANDROCONIA) same as above.

APEX the part of the structure farthest away from the base; e.g., wing tip.

BARRENS open areas in a forest maintained by fire and soil characteristics (rocky).

BASK to orient with the broadest body or wing area perpendicular to the sun to raise body temperature.

BATESIAN MIMICRY a palatable species copies the pattern of an unpalatable species to obtain protection from predation (e.g., Spicebush Swallowtail females mimic the toxic Pipevine Swallowtail).

BOREAL northern; from or belonging to the north.

CANNIBALISM the tendency to feed on individuals of one's own species.

CANOPY the uppermost layer of foliage in a forest.

CHEVRON a V or an inverted V shape.

CHRYSALIS (PL. CHRYSALIDS) the pupal stage of a butterfly.

COMMUNAL resting, living, or feeding in groups.

CONTINUOUS GENERATIONS species that breed throughout the season and produce overlapping broods.

CREPUSCULAR active early or late in the day when light levels are low.

CRESCENT a figure with both convex and concave edges; e.g. crescent moon.

CRYPTIC (CRYPSIS) camouflaged by resembling some background feature.

DIAPAUSE a delay in development that is not caused by prevailing conditions; e.g., overwintering diapause triggered by a decrease in the photoperiod.

DICOT a plant with two seed leaves.

DIMORPHIC having two distinct forms.

EPHEMERALS organisms that exist only for a short period of time (e.g., spring ephemerals).

EVERT to turn inside-out, as in everting a gland (osmeterium).

EXTIRPATED removed (destroyed)

from a particular location.

EYE SPOTS   eyelike markings on butterfly wings or on caterpillars.

FALCATE   curved inward below the tip (apex) of the wing; hooked.

FOREWING CELLS   areas in the forewing that are completely enclosed by wing veins.

GLADE   an open area in the forest, usually with prairie-type vegetation.

GRAND KANKAKEE MARSH   an area of the upper Midwest that bordered the Kankakee River and once consisted of 500,000 to 600,000 acres of marsh land in Indiana.

GRAND PRAIRIE REGION   the area in east-central Illinois covered by the Wisconsin Glacier (18,000–10,000 BP). The landscape was over 90% tallgrass prairie.

GREGARIOUS   commonly existing in aggregations (e.g., caterpillars).

GROUND COLOR   the overall background color.

HAIR PENCIL   a brushlike structure contained in the abdomen in some male butterflies that can be everted for use in courtship.

HIBERNACULUM   a tent or sheath constructed from a leaf or other materials, where a caterpillar may hide or lie dormant.

HILL-TOPPING   behavior characterized by butterflies flying to the top of a hill or the highest point in the surrounding landscape.

HOARINESS   a grayish-white cast to the wings.

HONEYDEW   a watery fluid containing sugars that is excreted by aphids, scale insects, and mealy bugs.

INNER EDGE   the bottom part of butterfly wings that is closest to the body; also called inner margin.

INSTAR   the period between caterpillar molts.

INTERGRADE   an intermediate form, often between two subspecies.

LEADING MARGIN (EDGE)   the front part of a butterfly's wing; also called costal margin.

LISTED SPECIES   a species that appears on an area's threatened or endangered species list.

LOCALLY COMMON   existing in isolated populations, usually dependent on a particular habitat type that also exists only in isolated pockets on the landscape.

MELANIC   dark, or with a darkish cast.

MIMIC   a species that closely resembles another species from a different group.

MONOCOT   plants with only a single seed leaf, and with parallel leaf veins.

MOSAIC   an individual with the

characteristics of more than one sex or form.

MÜLLERIAN MIMICS individuals of several unpalatable species that exhibit a similar color pattern (e.g., the Viceroy and Monarch are Müllerian Mimics).

OSMETERIUM an eversible (see "evert" above), tubular gland on swallowtail caterpillars that has a distinctive odor. It is used for defense against predators and parasites.

OUTER EDGE the wing edge furthest from the body; also called outer margin.

OVERWINTER to survive the winter, usually in diapause or in a dormant state.

PALPS sensory structures, usually fingerlike and segmented, that are part of an insect's mouthparts.

POLYPHAGOUS feeding on a great variety of plants.

POLYTYPIC containing two or more taxonomic units within the immediate subordinate category (e.g., a genera with multiple species, or a species with multiple subspecies).

PUDDLE CLUB a group of butterflies (usually male) that gather at moist spots on the ground to imbibe moisture and nutrients.

SCENT PATCH see Androconial Spot.

SENESCING/SENESCED growing old, or aging; often refers to the wear and tear on a butterfly's wings.

STIGMA see Androconial spot.

TAXONOMY/TAXONOMIC the science of giving organisms names, or classification.

VAGRANT a stray butterfly that enters a territory it does not normally occupy.

WING CELLS areas in a butterfly wing that are enclosed by veins.

WING MARGIN the edge of the wing.

NOTE: *The Torre-Bueno Glossary of Entomology* was used as a source for this glossary.

SOURCES

Belth, J.E. 2013. Butterflies of Indiana. Indiana University Press. 344 pp.

Blatchley, W.S. 1891. A catalogue of the butterflies known to occur in Indiana. Annual Report of the Indiana State Geologist 17:365–408.

Bouseman, J.K., and J.G. Sternburg. 2001. Field guide to butterflies of Illinois. Illinois Natural History Survey Manual 9. xii+264 pp.

Bowers, M.D. 1978. Over-wintering behavior in *Euphydryas phaeton* (Nymphalidae). Journal of the Lepidopterists' Society 32(4): 282–288.

Brock, J.P., and K. Kaufman. 2003. Kaufmann field guide to the butterflies of North America. Houghton Miifflin Co. 392 pp.

Calhoun, J.V. 2003. The history and true identity of *Melitaea ismeria* (Boisduval & Le Conte): a remarkable tale of duplication, misinterpretation and presumption. Journal of the Lepidopterists' Society 57:204–219.

Calhoun, J.V. 2005. A signature worth a thousand words. News of the Lepidopterists' Society 47:114.

Calhoun, J.V. 2013. The Dodge family: an enduring tradition of entomology. Journal of the Lepidopterists' Society 67(3):206–220.

Carde, R.T., A.M. Shapiro, and H.K. Clench. 1970. Sibling species in the Eurydice group of *Lethe* (Lepidoptera: Satyridae). Psyche 77(1):70–103.

Cech, R., and G. Tudor. 2005. Butterflies of the East Coast an observer's guide. Princeton University Press, Princeton and Oxford. 345 pp.

Chermock, R.L. 1947. Notes on North American *Enodias* (Lepidoptera). Entomological News 58:29–35.

Conway, P.J. 1956. *Leptotes marina* and *Echinargus isola* (Lycaenidae) taken in Illinois. Lepidopterists' News 10:112.

Covell, C.V., Jr. 1999. The butterflies and moths (Lepidoptera) of Kentucky: an annotated checklist. Kentucky State Nature Preserves Commission Scientific and Technical Series 6:1–220.

Cowan, C.F. 1969. Histoire générale et iconographie des Lépidoptéres et des chenilles de l'Amérique septentrionale. Journal of the Society for Bibliography of Natural History 5:125–134.

Douglas, M.M., and J.M. Douglas. 2005. Butterflies of the Great Lakes region. University of Michigan Press. xii+345 pp.

Downey, J.C. 1966. Distribution of the Lycaenidae (Lepidoptera) in Illinois. Transactions of the Illinois State Academy of Science 59(2):163–168.

Ebner, J.A. 1970. The butterflies of Wisconsin. Issue 12 of Popular Science Handbook of Milwaukee Public Museum. 205 pp.

Edwards, W.H. 1868–1897. The butterflies of North America. Boston; Houghton, Mifflin & Co. Vol. 1; ii, 165+52 p., 50 pls. Vol. 2; i, 358 p., 51 pls. Vol. 3; viii, 432 pp., 51 pls.

Emmel, T.C., M.C. Minno, and B. A. Drummond. 1992. Florissant butterflies a guide to the fossil and present-day species of central Colorado. Stanford University Press, Stanford, California. 118 pp.

Evers, R.A. and L.M. Page. 1977. Some unusual natural areas in Illinois. Illinois Natural History Survey Biological Notes No. 100. 47 pp.

French, G.H. 1914. The butterflies of the eastern United States. 4th Edition, J.B. Lippincott Co., Philadelphia & London. 429 pp.

French, G.H. 1879. Analytical tables for the butterflies of Illinois. Pages 30–42 in Fifth annual report of the principal of the southern Illinois Normal University, with the accompanying reports of the several professors. Observer Print, Carbondale, Illinois.

French, G.H. 1878. Economic entomology of Illinois. Part II. Lepidoptera, or butterflies and moths, and their larva, or caterpillars. Pages 133–273 in Thomas, Cyrus, 1878.

Frison, T.H. 1919. The occurrence of Eurema mexicana Boisd. in Illinois (Lepid.) Entomological News 30:228–229.

Gatrelle, R.R., and R.T. Arbogast. 1974. A new subspecies of Lethe appalachia (Satyridae). Journal of the Lepidopterists' Society 28(4):359–363.

Grand Prairie Butterfly Club. Retrieved from http://castle.eiu.edu/~bflyclub/Grand_Prairie_Butterfly_Club/Home.html

Heitzman, J.R. 1973. A new species of Papilio from the eastern United States (Papilionidae). Journal of Research on the Lepidoptera 12(1):1–10

Heitzman, J.R., and J.E. Heitzman. 1987. Butterflies and moths of Missouri. Missouri Department of Conservaton, Jefferson City. viii + 385 pp.

Howe, H.H. 1975. The butterflies of North America. Doubleday & Company, Inc. 633 pp.

Holland, W.J. 1898. The butterfly book; a popular guide to a knowledge of the butterflies of North America. Doubleday & McClure Co. xx+382 pp.

Iftner, D.C., J.A. Shuey, and J.V. Calhoun. 1992. Butterflies and skippers of Ohio. Ohio Biological Survey Bulletin New Series 9(1):xii+212 pp.

Illinois Birders' Forum: Dragonflies, Butterflies & Moths. (n.d.). Retrieved from http://www.ilbirds.com/index.php?board=49.0

Irwin, R.R. 1970. Notes on *Lethe creola* (Satyridae), with designation of lectotype. Journal of the Lepidopterists' Society 24(2):143–151.

Irwin, R.R. 1972. A brief history of lepidopterology in Illinois. Transactions of the Illinois State Academy of Science 65(3/4):45–49.

Irwin, R.R., and J.C. Downey. 1973. Annotated checklist of the butterflies of Illinois. Illinois Natural History Survey Biological Notes 81:1–60.

Jeffords, M.R. 1977. A record of *Anaea aidea* (Nymphalidae) from southern Illinois. Journal of the Lepidopterists' Society 31:280.

Jeffords, M.R., J.G. Sternburg, and G.P. Waldbauer. 1979. Batesian mimicry: field demonstration of the survival value of Pipevine Swallowtail and Monarch color patterns. Evolution 33:275–286.

Jeffords, M.R., G.P. Waldbauer, and J.G. Sternburg. 1980. Determination of the time of day at which diurnal moths painted to resemble butterflies are attacked by birds. Evolution 34:1205–1211.

Klots, A.B. 1951. A field guide to the butterflies of North America, east of the Great Plains. Houghton Mifflin Company, Boston. xvi+349 pp., 40 pl.

Klots, A.B. 1960. Notes on *Strymon caryaevorus* McDunnough (Lepidoptera, Lycaenidae). Journal of the New York Entomological Society 68:190–198.

Klots, A.B., and H.K. Clench. 1952. A new species of *Strymon* Huebner from Georgia (Lepidoptera, Lycaenidae). American Museum Novitates 1600:1–19.

Lepidopterist's Society Season Summary. 1959–2013. Published annually in the News of the Lepidopterists' Society by the Lepidopterists' Society.

Losey, J.E., L.S. Rayor, and M.E. Carter. 1999. Transgenic pollen harms monarch larvae. Nature 399:214.

Lyons, S.J. 2004. A View from the Inland Northwest. Globe Pequot Press. 204 pp.

Masters, J.H. 1968. *Euphydryas phaeton* in the Ozarks (Lepidoptera: Nymphalidae). Entomological News 79:85–91.

McAlpine, W.S. 1937. A case of mistaken identity and discovery of a new metalmark

(*Calephelis*) from Michigan (Lepidoptera, Rhiodinidae [sic]). Brooklyn Enotomological Society Bulletin 32:43–50.

McAlpine, W.S. 1970. A revision of the butterfly genus *Calephelis* (Riodinidae). Journal of Research on the Lepidoptera 10(1):1–125.

Metzler, E.H., J.A. Shuey, L.A. Ferge, R.A. Henderson, and P.Z. Goldstein. 2005. Contributions to the understanding of tallgrass prairie-dependent butterflies and moths and their biogeography in the United States. Ohio Biological Survey Bulletin New Series 15(1): viii+143 pp.

Michener, C.D., and C.F. Dos Passos. 1942. Taxonomic observations on some North American *Strymon* with descriptions of new subspecies (Lepidoptera, Lycaenidae). American Museum Novitates 1210:1–7.

Middleton, N. 1881. Larvae of butterflies. Pages 73–98 *in* Thomas, C. Tenth Report of the State Entomologist on the noxious and beneficial insects of the state of Illinois. Illinois Entomologist's Report 10, Springfield.

Miller, J.Y. (ed.) 1992. The common names of North American butterflies. Smithsonian Institution Press, Washington and London. 177 pp.

M'Neill, J. 1889. *Colias cesonia*, Stoll. Canadian Entomologist 21:43–46.

Mohlenbrock, R.H. 2002. Vascular flora of Illinois 3rd edition. Southern Illinois University Press. 490 pp.

Mohlenbrock, R.H., and D.M. Ladd. 1978. Distribution of Illinois vascular plants. Southern Illinois University Press. 282 pp.

Nielsen, M.C. 1999. Michigan butterflies and skippers. Michigan State University Extension. 248 pp.

Oberhauser, K.S., M. Prysby, H.R. Mattila, D.E. Stanley-Horn, M.K. Sears, G.P. Dively, E. Olson, J.M. Pleasants, W.K.F. Lam, and R.L. Hellmich. 2001. Temporal and spatial overlap between monarch larvae and corn pollen. Proceedings of the National Academy of Sciences, USA 98:11913–11918.

Ogard, P., and S. Bright. 2010. Butterflies of Alabama: glimpses into their lives. University Alabama Press, Tuscaloosa. 486 pp.

Opler, P.A., and G.O. Krizek. 1984. Butterflies east of the Great Plains. Johns Hopkins University Press. 294 pp.

Opler, P.A., and V. Malikul. 1992. A field guide to eastern butterflies (Peterson Guide). Houghton Mifflin Co. 396 pp.

Pelham, J.P. 2008. (Revised 2012) A catalogue of the butterflies of the United States and Canada. Journal of Research on the Lepidoptera 40:658.

Pleasants, J.M., R.L. Hellmich, G.P. Dively, M.K. Sears, D.E. Stanley-Horn, H.R. Mattila, J.E. Foster, P.L. Clark, and G.D. Jones. 2001. Corn pollen deposition on milkweeds in or near cornfields. Proceedings of the National Academy of Sciencies, USA 98:11919–11924.

Prill, J.D. 1988. New Peoria records for *Agraulis vanillae nigrior* Michener (Lepidoptera: Nymphalidae) and *Erinnyis obscura* F. (Lepidoptera: Sphingidae). Transactions of the Illinois State Academy of Science 81(3/4):293–296.

Pyle, R.M. 1981. The Audubon Society field guide to North American Butterflies. A.A. Knopf, Inc. 917 pp.

Pyle, R.M. 2010. Mariposa Road the first butterfly big year. Houghton Mifflin Harcourt, Boston, New York. xvi+ 558 pp.

Remington, C.L. 1943. The Rhopalocera of Principia College. Transactions of the Illinois State Academy of Science 36(2):179–180.

Schlicht, D.W., J.C. Downey, and J.C. Nekola. 2007. The butterflies of Iowa. University of Iowa Press. xii+233 pp.

Schwegman, J.E., G.D. Fell, M. Hutchison, G. Paulson, W.M. Shepherd, and J. White. 1973. Comprehensive plan for the Illinois Nature Preserves System. Part II—The natural divisions of Illinois. Illinois Nature Preserves Commission, Springfield. 32 pp+maps.

Scott, J.A. 1986. The butterflies of North America, a natural history and field guide. Stanford University Press. 583 pp.

Scudder, S.H. 1889. The butterflies of the eastern United States and Canada, with special reference to New England. Published by the author, Cambridge. Vol. 1, p. i–xxiv, 1–766; vol.2, p. i–x, 767–1774; vol.3, p. i–vi, 1777–1958, pl.1–89, 3 maps.

Sears, M.K., R.L. Hellmich, D.E. Stanley-Horn, K.S. Oberhauser, J.M. Pleasants, H.R. Mattila, B.D. Siegfried, and G.P. Dively. 2001. Impact of Bt corn pollen on monarch butterfly populations: a risk assessment. Proceedings of the National Academy of Sciences, USA 98:11937–11942.

Sedman, Y., and D.F. Hess. 1985. The butterflies of west central Illinois. Western Illinois University Series in the Biological Sciences 11:1–117.

Shull, E.M. 1987. The butterflies of Indiana. Indiana Academy of Science, Bloomington and Indianapolis. viii+262 pp.

Sites, R.W., and J.E. McPherson. 1979. The first record in southern Illinois of *Polygonia progne* (Lepidoptera: Nymphalidae). Transactions of the Illinois State Academy of Science 72(2):93.

Sites, R.W. 1980. A new southern Illinois record of *Clossiana bellona* (Lepidoptera: Nymphalidae). Transactions of the Illinois State Academy of Science 73(1):39.

Sites, R.W., and J.E. McPherson. 1980. The first record in southern Illinois of *Celastrina ebenina* (Lepidoptera: Lycaenidae). Transactions of the Illinois State Academy of Science 73(1):86.

Sites, R.W., and J.E. McPherson. 1980. A key to the butterflies of Illinois (Lepidoptera: Papilionoidea). Great Lakes Entomologist 13(2):97–114.

Sites, R.W., and J.E. McPherson. 1981. A list of the butterflies (Lepidoptera: Papilionoidea) of the La Rue-Pine Hills Ecological Area. Great Lakes Entomologist 14(2):81–85.

Sites, R.W., and J.E. McPherson. 1981. The first records in Illinois of *Heliconius charitonius* (Lepidoptera: Heliconiidae) and *Phoebis agarithe* (Lepidoptera: Pieridae). Great Lakes Entomologist 14(4):205–206.

Snyder, A.J. 1896. Local list. Entomological News 7:99–103.

Snyder, A.J. 1900. The argynnids of North America. Occasional Memoirs of the Chicago. Entomological Society 1:27–38.

Stanley-Horn, D.E., G.P., Dively, R.L. Hellmich, H.R. Mattila, M.K. Sears, R. Rose, L.C.H. Jesse, J.F. Losey, J.J. Obrycki, and L. Lewis. 2001. Assessing the impact of Cry1Ab-expressing corn pollen on monarch butterfly larvae in field studies. Proceedings of the National Academy of Sciences, USA 98:11931–11936.

Sternburg, J.G., G.P. Waldbauer, and M.R. Jeffords. 1977. Batesian mimicry: selective advantage of color pattern. Science 195:681–683.

Strecker, H. 1878. Butterflies and moths of North American. Kessinger Publishing, LLC. 298 pp.

Swengel, A.B. 1997. Habitat associations of sympatric violet-feeding fritillaries (*Euptoieta*, *Speyeria*, *Boloria*) (Lepidoptera: Nymphalidae) in tallgrass prairie. Great Lakes Entomologist 30(1–2):1–18.

Swengel, A.B. 1998. Effects of management on butterfly abundance in tallgrass prairie and pine barrens. Biological Conservation 83(1):77–89.

Swengel, A.B. 2001. A literature review of insect responses to fire, compared to other conservation managements of open habitat. Biodiversity and Conservation 10(7):1141–1169.

Switzer, P.V., J.A. Switzer, and I.C. Switzer. 2003. New Illinois butterfly records for Clark, Coles, Cumberland, Douglas and Edgar counties. Transactions of the Illinois State Academy of Science. 96(3):235–241.

Thomas, C. 1878. Seventh report of the state entomologist on the noxious and benifical insects of the state of Illinois. Illinois Entomologist's Report 7, Springfield. 290 pp.

Thomas, C. 1880. Ninth report of the state entomologist on the noxious and benifical insects of the state of Illinois. Illinois Entomologist's Report 9, Springfield [2]+142+iii pp.

Thomas, C. 1881. Tenth report of the state entomologist on the noxioius and beneficial insects of the state of Illinois. Illinois Entomologist's Report 10, Springfield. 238+vi pp.

Torre-Bueno, J.R. de la, S.W. Nichols, G.S. Tulloch, and R.T. Schuh. 1989. The Torre-Bueno glossary of entomology. Rev. ed. New York, N.Y.: New York Entomological Society in cooperation with the American Museum of Natural History.

Wagner, D.L. 2005. Caterpillars of eastern North America a guide to identification and natural history. Princeton University Press, Princeton and Oxford. 512 pp.

Williams, B.L. 2001. Recognition of western populations of *Speyeria idalia* (Nymphalidae) as a new subspecies. Journal of the Lepidopterists' Society 55(4):144–149.

Wisconsin butterflies. Retrieved from http://wisconsinbutterflies.org/

Worthington, C.E. 1880. A list of diurnal Lepidoptera inhabiting the state of Illinois. Canadian Entomologist 12(3):46–50.

Wraight, C.L., A.R. Zangerl, M.J. Carroll, and M.R. Berenbaum. 2000. Absence of toxicity of *Bacillus thuringiensis* pollen ot black swallowtails under field conditions. Proceedings of the National Academy of Sciences, USA 97:7700–7703.

Wright, A.G. 1951. Common Illinois insects and why they are interesting. Illinois State Museum, Springfield. 32 pp.

[Wyatt, Alex K.] "Alexander Kwiat." 1905. Minutes of the entomological section, Chicago Academy of Sciences, January 19, 1905. Entomological News 16:124–128.

Zangerl, A.R., D. McKenna, C.L. Wraight, M. Carroll, P. Ficarello, R. Warner, and M.R. Berenbaum. 2001. Effects of exposure to even 176 *Bacillus thuringiensis* corn pollen on monarch and black swallowtail caterpillars under field conditions. Proceedings of the National Academy of Sciences, USA 98:11908–11912.

ILLINOIS BUTTERFLY CHECKLIST

FAMILY PAPILIONIDAE

☐ Pipevine Swallowtail — *Battus philenor* (Linnaeus)
☐ Zebra Swallowtail — *Eurytides marcellus* (Cramer)
☐ Joan's Swallowtail — *Papilio joanae* Heitzman
☐ Black Swallowtail — *Papilio polyxenes asterius* (Stoll)
☐ Giant Swallowtail — *Papilio cresphontes* Cramer
☐ Tiger Swallowtail — *Papilio glaucus* Linnaeus
☐ Spicebush Swallowtail — *Papilio troilus* Linnaeus
☐ Palamedes Swallowtail — *Papilio palamedes* Drury

FAMILY PIERIDAE

☐ Dainty Sulphur — *Nathalis iole* Boisduval
☐ Mexican Yellow — *Eurema mexicana* (Boisduval)
☐ Little Yellow — *Pyrisitia lisa* (Boisduval & Le Conte)
☐ Sleepy Orange — *Abaeis nicippe* (Cramer)
☐ Clouded Sulphur — *Colias philodice* Godart
☐ Alfalfa Butterfly — *Colias eurytheme* Boisduval
☐ Dogface — *Zerene cesonia* (Stoll)
☐ Cloudless Sulphur — *Phoebis senna* (Linnaeus)
☐ Orange-barred Sulphur — *Phoebis philea* (Linnaeus)
☐ Large Orange Sulphur — *Phoebis agarithe* (Boisduval)
☐ Falcate Orangetip — *Anthocharis midea* (Hübner)
☐ Olympia Marble — *Euchloe olympia* (W.H. Edwards)
☐ Mustard White — *Pieris oleracea* (T. Harris)
☐ Cabbage Butterfly — *Pieris rapae* (Linnaeus)
☐ Checkered White — *Pontia protodice* (Boisduval & Le Conte)
☐ Great Southern White — *Ascia monuste* (Linnaeus)

FAMILY LYCAENIDAE

SUBFAMILY MILETINAE
☐ Harvester — *Feniseca tarquinius* (Fabricius)

SUBFAMILY LYCAENINAE
☐ American Copper — *Lycaena phlaeas* (Linnaeus)
☐ Gray Copper — *Lycaena dione* (Scudder)
☐ Bronze Copper — *Lycaena hyllus* (Cramer)
☐ Purplish Copper — *Lycaena helloides* (Boisduval)

SUBFAMILY THECLINAE

☐ Atala — *Eumaeus atala* (Poey)
☐ Great Purple Hairstreak — *Atlides halesus* (Cramer)
☐ Acadian Hairstreak — *Satyrium acadica* (W.H. Edwards)
☐ Coral Hairstreak — *Satyrium titus* (Fabricius)
☐ Edwards' Hairstreak — *Satyrium edwardsii* (Grote & Robinson)
☐ Banded Hairstreak — *Satyrium calanus falacer* (Godart)
☐ Hickory Hairstreak — *Satyrium caryaevorus* (McDunnough)
☐ Striped Hairstreak — *Satyrium liparops strigosa* (T. Harris)
☐ Northern Hairstreak — *Satyrium favonius ontario* (W.H. Edwards)
☐ Olive Hairstreak — *Callophrys gryneus* (Hübner)
☐ Hoary Elfin — *Callophrys polios* (Cook & F. Watson)
☐ Frosted Elfin — *Callophrys irus* (Godart)
☐ Henry's Elfin — *Callophrys henrici* (Grote & Robinson)
☐ Eastern Pine Elfin — *Callophrys niphon* (Hübner)
☐ Gray Hairstreak — *Strymon melinus* Hübner
☐ White-M Hairstreak — *Parrhasius m-album* (Boisduval & Le Conte)
☐ Red-banded Hairstreak — *Calycopis cecrops* (Fabricius)

SUBFAMILY POLYOMMATINAE

☐ Marine Blue — *Leptotes marina* (Reakirt)
☐ Eastern Tailed Blue — *Cupido comyntas* (Godart)
☐ Spring Azure — *Celastrina ladon* (Cramer)
☐ Summer Azure — *Celastrina neglecta* (W.H. Edwards)
☐ Dusky Azure — *Celastrina nigra* (W. Forbes)
☐ Silvery Blue — *Glaucopsyche lygdamus* (E. Doubleday)
☐ Reakirt's Blue — *Echinargus isola* (Reakirt)
☐ Karner Blue — *Plebejus samuelis* (Nabokov)
☐ Greenish Blue — *Plebejus saepiolus* (Boisduval)

FAMILY RIODINIDAE

☐ Northern Metalmark — *Calephelis borealis* (Grote & Robinson)
☐ Swamp Metalmark — *Calephelis muticum* McAlpine

FAMILY NYMPHALIDAE

SUBFAMILY LIBYTHEINAE

☐ American Snout — *Libytheana carinenta bachmanii* (Cramer)

SUBFAMILY DANAINAE

☐ Monarch — *Danaus plexippus* (Linnaeus)
☐ Queen — *Danaus gilippus* (Cramer)

SUBFAMILIY HELICONIINAE

- ☐ Gulf Fritillary — *Agraulis vanillae* (Linnaeus)
- ☐ Zebra — *Heliconius charithonia* (Linnaeus)
- ☐ Variegated Fritillary — *Euptoieta claudia* (Cramer)
- ☐ Silver-bordered Fritillary — *Boloria selene* (Denis & Schiffermüller)
- ☐ Meadow Fritillary — *Boloria bellona* (Fabricius)
- ☐ Diana — *Speyeria diana* (Cramer)
- ☐ Great Spangled Fritillary — *Speyeria cybele* (Fabricius)
- ☐ Aphrodite Fritillary — *Speyeria aphrodite alcestis* (W.H. Edwards)
- ☐ Regal Fritillary — *Speyeria idalia occidentalis* B. Williams
- ☐ Atlantis Fritillary — *Speyeria atlantis* (W.H. Edwards)

SUBFAMILIY LIMENITIDINAE

- ☐ White Admiral — *Limenitis arthemis arthemis* (Drury)
- ☐ Red-spotted Purple — *Limenitis arthemis astyanax* (Fabricius)
- ☐ Viceroy — *Limenitis archippus* (Cramer)

SUBFAMILIY APATURINAE

- ☐ Hackberry Butterfly — *Asterocampa celtis* (Boisduval & Le Conte)
- ☐ Tawny Emperor — *Asterocampa clyton* (Boisduval & Le Conte)

SUBFAMILY NYMPHALINAE

- ☐ American Painted Lady — *Vanessa virginiensis* (Drury)
- ☐ Painted Lady — *Vanessa cardui* (Linnaeus)
- ☐ Red Admiral — *Vanessa atalanta* (Linnaeus)
- ☐ Milbert's Tortoiseshell — *Aglais milberti* (Godart)
- ☐ Compton Tortoiseshell — *Nymphalis l-album j-album* (Boisduval & Le Conte)
- ☐ California Tortoiseshell — *Nymphalis californica* (Boisduval)
- ☐ Mourning Cloak — *Nymphalis antiopa* (Linnaeus)
- ☐ Question Mark — *Polygonia interrogationis* (Fabricius)
- ☐ Comma — *Polygonia comma* (T. Harris)
- ☐ Gray Comma — *Polygonia progne* (Cramer)
- ☐ Green Comma — *Polygonia faunus* (W.H. Edwards)
- ☐ Buckeye — *Junonia coenia* (Hübner)
- ☐ Baltimore — *Euphydryas phaeton phaeton* (Drury)
- ☐ Ozark Checkerspot — *Euphydryas phaeton ozarkae* Masters
- ☐ Silvery Checkerspot — *Chlosyne nycteis* (E. Doubleday)
- ☐ Gorgone Checkerspot — *Chlosyne gorgone* (Hübner)
- ☐ Harris' Checkerspot — *Chlosyne harrisii* (Scudder)
- ☐ Texan Crescent — *Anthanassa texana* (W.H. Edwards)
- ☐ Pearl Crescent — *Phyciodes tharos* (Drury)
- ☐ Tawny Crescent — *Phyciodes batesii* (Reakirt)

SUBFAMILY CHARAXINAE

- ☐ Tropical Leafwing — *Anaea aidea* (Guérin-Méneville)
- ☐ Goatweed Butterfly — *Anaea andria* Scudder

SUBFAMILY SATYRINAE

- ☐ Southern Pearly-eye — *Lethe portlandia* (Fabricius)
- ☐ Northern Pearly-eye — *Lethe anthedon* (A. Clark)
- ☐ Creole Pearly-eye — *Lethe creola* (Skinner)
- ☐ Eyed Brown — *Lethe eurydice* (Linnaeus)
- ☐ Appalachian Eyed Brown — *Lethe appalachia appalachia* R. Chermock
- ☐ Leeuw's Eyed Brown — *Lethe appalachia leeuwi* Gattrelle & Arbogast
- ☐ Gemmed Satyr — *Cyllopsis gemma* (Hübner)
- ☐ Carolina Satyr — *Hermeuptychia sosybius* (Fabricius)
- ☐ Little Wood Satyr — *Megisto cymela* (Cramer)
- ☐ Common Wood Nymph — *Cercyonis pegala* (Fabricius)

INDEX

A

Abaeis nicippe, See Sleepy Orange

Acadian Hairstreak **180–181**, 183, 185

Aglais milberti, See Milbert's Tortoiseshell

Agraulis vanillae, See Gulf Fritillary

Alfalfa Butterfly 87, 97, 124, 125, 133, 135, **136–137**

American Copper 163, 164, **166–167**, 169, 171, 173

American Painted Lady 26, **282–283**, 285, 287

American Snout 233, 234, **236–237**

Anaea aidea, See Tropical Leafwing

Anaea andria, See Goatweed Butterfly

Anthanassa texana, See Texan Crescent

Anthocharis midea, See Falcate Orangetip

Apaturinae 275–279

Aphrodite Fritillary 245, 259, **260–261**, 263, 265, 362–363

Appalachian Eyed Brown 335, **336–337**, 339, 368–369

Ascia monuste, See Great Southern White

Asterocampa celtis, See Hackberry Butterfly

Asterocampa clyton, See Tawny Emperor

Atala **176–177**, 376

Atlantis Fritillary 245, 261, **264–265**

Atlides halesus, See Great Purple Hairstreak

B

Baltimore 44, **306–307**, 309, 364–365, 385

Banded Hairstreak 185, **186–187**, 189, 191, 356, 376

Battus philenor, See Pipevine Swallowtail

Black Swallowtail 75–77, 87, 98, **110–111**, 121, 350, 353, 355, 370

Boloria bellona, See Meadow Fritillary

Boloria selene, See Silver-bordered Fritillary

Bronze Copper 164, 167, 169, **170–171**, 173

Buckeye 48, 281, **304–305**

C

Cabbage Butterfly 60, 98, 125, 149, 151, **152–153**, 155, 157, 375

Calephelis borealis, See Northern Metalmark

Calephelis muticum, See Swamp Metalmark

California Tortoiseshell **292–293**

Callophrys gryneus, See Olive Hairstreak

Callophrys henrici, See Henry's Elfin

Callophrys irus, See Frosted Elfin

Callophrys niphon, See Eastern Pine Elfin

Callophrys polios, See Hoary Elfin

Calycopis cecrops, See Red-banded Hairstreak

Carolina Satyr 78, 341, **342–343**, 345

Celastrina ladon, See Spring Azure

Celastrina neglecta, See Summer Azure

Celastrina nigra, See Dusky Azure

Cercyonis pegala, See Common Wood Nymph

Charaxinae 321–325

Checkered White 47, 124, 125, 153, **154–155**, 157, 375

Chlosyne gorgone, See Gorgone Checkerspot

Chlosyne harrisii, See Harris' Checkerspot

Chlosyne nycteis, See Silvery Checkerspot

Clouded Sulphur 125, 131, 133,

ILLINOIS NATURAL HISTORY SURVEY MANUAL LIST

Illinois Natural History Survey Manuals, (includes field guides, field books, and field manuals), have been published at irregular intervals since 1936. These manuals are field guides that provide detailed descriptions and illustrations of a particular group of organisms (e.g., mammals, butterflies, reptiles and amphibians, freshwater mussels, etc). INHS Manuals should fit into a jacket or coat pocket when used in the field. They offer complete species descriptions, including natural history, distribution, and status. Nature lovers, ranging from professional scientists to school children, can make use of these books.

OUT OF PRINT:

Manual 1: Fieldbook of Illinois Wildflowers (1936)
Manual 2: Fieldbook of Illinois Land Snails (1939)
Manual 3: Fieldbook of Illinois Shrubs (1942)
Manual 4: Fieldbook of Illinois Mammals (1957)
Manual 9: Field Guide to the Butterflies of Illinois (2001)

IN PRINT:

Manual 5: Field Guide to Freshwater Mussels of the Midwest (1995)
Manual 6: Field Guide to Northeastern Longhorned Beetles (1996)
Manual 7: Waterfowl of Illinois: An Abbreviated Field Guide (1999)
Manual 8: Field Guide to Amphibians and Reptiles of Illinois (1999)
Manual 10: Field Guide to the Silk Moths of Illinois (2002)
Manual 11: Field Guide to the Skipper Butterflies of Illinois 2nd Ed. (2010)
Manual 12: Field Manual of Illinois Mammals (2008)
Manual 13: Field Guide to the Sphinx Moths of Illinois (2010)
Manual 14: Butterflies of Illinois: A Field Guide (2014)

FIELD NOTES

FIELD NOTES

FIELD NOTES

FIELD NOTES

FIELD NOTES

FIELD NOTES

FIELD NOTES

106

108   110   112   116   120   122

126   128   130   132   134   136

138   140   142   144   146   148

150   152   154   156   162   166

168   170   172   176   178   180

182   184   186   188   190   192

194   196   198   200   202   204

206   208   212   214   216   218

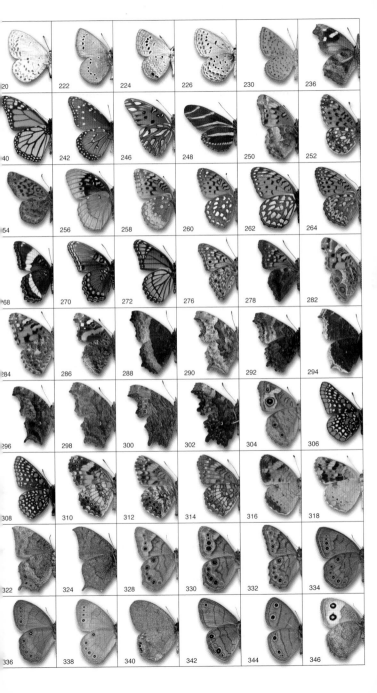